The Spoils of War

The Spoils of War

*Power, Profit and the
American War Machine*

Andrew Cockburn

VERSO

London • New York

First published by Verso 2021

1 3 5 7 9 10 8 6 4 2

Verso
UK: 6 Meard Street, London W1F 0EG
US: 20 Jay Street, Suite 1010, Brooklyn, NY 11201
versobooks.com

Verso is the imprint of New Left Books

ISBN-13: 978-1-83976-365-6
ISBN-13: 978-1-83976-367-0 (US EBK)
ISBN-13: 978-1-83976-366-3 (UK EBK)

British Library Cataloguing in Publication Data
A catalogue record for this book is available from the British Library

Library of Congress Cataloging-in-Publication Data
A catalog record for this book is available from the Library of Congress

Typeset in Sabon by Biblichor Ltd, Edinburgh
Printed and bound by CPI Group (UK) Ltd, Croydon, CR0 4YY

Contents

Part IV: Simple Billion-Dollar Money-Grubbing 209

Introduction

Innumerable wars originate, wrote Alexander Hamilton in Federalist No. 6, "entirely in private passions; in the attachments, enmities, interests, hopes, and fears of leading individuals in the communities of which they are members." As a principal illustration of this important truth, he cited the case of Pericles, lauded as the greatest statesmen of classical Athens, who "in compliance with the resentment of a prostitute, at the expense of much of the blood and treasure of his countrymen, attacked, vanquished, and destroyed the city of the Samnians" before igniting the disastrous Peloponnesian War in order to extricate himself from political problems back home.

It should come as no surprise that this version of Athenian history is not echoed by orthodox historians, despite credible sources buttressing Hamilton's pithy account. Instead, Pericles' attack on Samos is generally ascribed to more respectable motives, such as his concern for protecting a democratic regime in the neighboring city of Miletus, or the need to preserve Athenian "credibility" as a great power.

The compulsion to endow states and leaders with responsible, statesmanlike motives for their actions is far from being confined to ancient historians. In fact, it extends across the spectrum of contemporary foreign and defense policy analysis and commentary, from academic ivory towers housing international relations and national security studies departments, to think tanks, research institutes and, of course, media of every variety. Thus, in modern times, Woodrow Wilson's maneuverings that brought a hitherto reluctant

United States into World War I, or John F. Kennedy's readiness to risk global immolation rather than permit Soviet nuclear missiles in Cuba, are invariably attributed to the most personally disinterested of motives. But closer examination of the record indicates that Wilson was eager to join the fighting, driven by the need to distract popular attention from his failure to enact his progressive mandate, buttressed by his personal ambition to preside over a postwar settlement—"the noblest part," his friend and flatterer Colonel Edward House assured him, "that has ever come to a son of man." Kennedy's handling of the 1962 missile crisis might also appear to have been purely an exercise on behalf of the nation's welfare. But deeper scrutiny of the record suggests that Kennedy's prime consideration during the crisis was the domestic political impact of allowing Soviet missiles so close to the United States, especially in view of the imminent midterm congressional elections.

More recently, the expansion of NATO into Eastern Europe in the 1990s, despite firm promises to Moscow that there would be no such move, was supposedly prompted, as summarized by two former national security eminences for the Brookings Institute, by a desire to "promote peace and stability on the European continent through the integration of the new Central and Eastern European democracies into a wider Euro–Atlantic community, in which the United States would remain deeply engaged."

Actually, it wasn't. As I explain at greater length in "Game On," the driving force behind the expansion, which ensured Russian paranoia and consequent *in*stability in Eastern Europe for the foreseeable future, was the urgent necessity to open new markets for American arms companies, coupled with the prospect of political reward for President Bill Clinton among relevant voting blocs in the Midwest. Similar examples abound, most obviously, and dangerously, in the domain of nuclear forces, where "strategy" has indisputably been driven by competing needs of rival bureaucracies (most obviously, the US Air Force's adoption of a "counterforce" doctrine once the Navy's submarine-launched missile force rendered otiose its original function of deterrence) and arms corporations.

Outsiders generally find it hard to grasp an essential truth about the US military machine, which is that war-fighting efficiency has a low priority by comparison with considerations of personal and internal bureaucratic advantage. The Air Force, for example, as I explain in "Tunnel Vision," has long striven to get rid of a plane, the inexpensive A-10 "Warthog," that works supremely well in protecting ground troops. But such combat effectiveness is irrelevant to the service because its institutional prosperity is based on hugely expensive long range (and perennially ineffective) bombers which, as described in "Flying Blind," pose lethal dangers to friendly soldiers, not to mention civilians, on the ground. The US armed services are expending vast sums on developing "hypersonic" weapons of proven infeasibility (see "Like a Ball of Fire") on the spurious grounds that the Russians have established a lead in this field. Despite the fact that hundreds of thousands of veterans of the post–9/11 wars suffer from traumatic brain injury induced by bomb blast, the Army has insisted on furnishing soldiers with helmets from a favored contractor that *enhance* the effects of blast ("The Military-Industrial Virus"). The Navy's Seventh Fleet arranged its deployments around Southeast Asia at the behest of a contractor known as "Fat Leonard," who suborned the relevant commanders with the help of a squad of prostitutes.

Fat Leonard's inducements were not of course limited to carnal delights. The corrupt officers were also in receipt of quantities of cash (in return for directing flotillas to ports where he held profitable supply contracts), thus confirming the timeless maxim that "follow the money" is the surest means of uncovering the real motivations behind actions and events which might otherwise appear inexplicable. For example, half the US casualties in the first winter of the Korean War were due to frostbite, as I learned from a veteran of the conflict who related how, in the freezing frontline trenches, soldiers and marines lacked decent cold weather boots. Like some threadbare guerrilla army, G.I.s would therefore raid enemy trenches to steal the warm, padded boots provided by the communist high command to their own troops. "I could never figure out why I, a soldier of the richest country on earth, was having to steal boots from soldiers of the poorest country on earth," my friend recalled in describing these harrowing but necessary expeditions. The "richest country on earth" could of course afford appropriate footwear in limitless quantities. Nor was it skimping in overall military spending, which soared following the outbreak of war in Korea in 1950. To the casual observer, it might seem obvious that the fighting and spending were directly related. However, although the war served to justify the huge budget boost, much of the money was diverted far from the Korean peninsula, principally to build large numbers of B-47 strategic nuclear bombers as well as fighters designed to intercept enemy nuclear bombers, of which the Russians possessed very few and the Chinese and North Koreans none at all.

The reason for this disparity in the allocation of resources should be obvious: the aerospace industry, as aircraft manufacturers had sleekly renamed themselves, was infinitely more powerful and demanding than the bootmakers, and so that was where the money went. The pattern was repeated half a century later as American families went into debt to buy armored vests, socks, boots and night-vision goggles for sons and daughters in Iraq, even as some $50 billion was poured into esoteric devices to detect the insurgents' homemade $25 bombs. One such was "Compass Call," a $100 million Lockheed EC-130H aircraft equipped with ground-penetrating radar that could supposedly seek out the buried bombs. Unfortunately, an in-depth study of its effectiveness in Iraq by a military intelligence unit in Baghdad in April 2007 concluded, after analyzing hundreds of flights, that the system had "No Detectable Effect."

Raids on the public purse such as these are rendered easier by a widening gulf between the military services and the population at large. For decades, thanks to the draft, most Americans had either served in the military or knew someone who had, so were aware at some level that the services were beset with bumbling bureaucratic incompetence. But those days are long past, so the vast majority of the population is entirely ignorant of the military world, and relies for insight on a press that is all too often either ignorant or compromised by the need to maintain access to self-interested sources. This lack of awareness is exacerbated by an aversion to challenging military claims regarding technology, not least because such claims are broadcast and vigorously promoted by a well-endowed public relations apparatus. The June 2014 disaster in which a B-1 bomber, thanks to endemic technological shortcomings, killed six friendly servicemen (five Americans and one Afghan) provided an instructive example. As I describe in "Flying Blind," the Air Force responded rapidly to the tragedy by inviting a *New York Times* reporter for a joyride on a B-1, thereby generating a predictably uninformed but positive review for the lethal (especially to friendly troops and civilians) machine.

Even when a weapons program's deficiencies are too egregious to be ignored, media criticism seldom strays beyond timidity, such as decrying excessive "waste" in the program, without probing how and why huge costs have become routine. The significant truth that ballooning costs can be directly ascribed to ever more complex technology, as was exposed in detail as far back as the 1980s by the Pentagon analyst Franklin "Chuck" Spinney ("The Military-Industrial Virus"), is never addressed. Thus, for example, the high-volume alarm prompted by Russia's takeover of Ukraine in 2014 generated huge budgetary rewards for the Pentagon, but relatively puny forces in terms of fighting strength—initially a mere 700 troops in Poland, for example, to face putative Russian hordes poised to invade. Overall, despite remorseless growth in spending, the US military continues to shrink, fielding fewer ships, aircraft and ground combat units with every passing decade. Remarkably, more money apparently produces less defense. The reason for this paradox would appear to lie in the financial incentives to develop weapons of increasing complexity, especially electronics, which, since they cost more, yield greater profits for the manufacturer, thanks to "cost-plus" contracts. The built-in inflation ensures that the new systems can never be bought in the same quantities as their predecessors.

Uninterested in such prosaic realities, liberals bemoan the money spent on arms and lament the "militarism" manifest in

America's appetite for war, while avoiding the underlying driving force: the military services' eagerness for ever more money, shared with the corporations that feed off them, and the officers who will cash in with high-paid employment with these same corporations once they retire. In other words, the military are not generally interested in war, save as a means to budget enhancement. Thus, when Donald Trump was induced to order a minor surge in Afghanistan in 2018, a conclave of senior Marine generals agreed to go along with the plan on grounds, according to someone who was present at the relevant meeting, "that it won't make any difference in the war, but it will do us good at budget time." Colonel John Boyd, the former Air Force fighter pilot who famously conceived and expounded a comprehensive theory of human conflict, once pointed out that there was no contradiction between the military's professed mission and its seeming indifference to operational proficiency. "People say the Pentagon does not have a strategy," he said. "They are wrong. The Pentagon does have a strategy. It is: 'Don't interrupt the money flow, add to it.'"

Once this salient truth regarding our military strategy is understood and absorbed, it becomes simpler to make sense of US actions, notably in provoking a new cold war with Russia ("New Red Scare") as well as perennial toadying to the repellent Saudi regime—an ever-eager customer for US arms—even in the face of its evident complicity in the 9/11 attacks (see "Crime and Punishment") or its determined efforts at genocide in Yemen ("Acceptable Losses").

The true dynamics driving actions such as those described above are usually well understood internally, even if unnoticed or misunderstood by outsiders. Civilians may not comprehend what is at stake in the perennial inter-service battle for budget share, but every officer in the Pentagon surely does. Likewise, front-line soldiers and marines on the ground are well aware that they are condemned to rely for support on the dangerously inaccurate B-1 bomber because the Air Force is determined to protect its lucrative bomber mission at the expense of the effective A-10—a point generally lost on the press and public.

While people have no problem in understanding the real political dynamics affecting their own group, there appears to be a
barrier to understanding that the same dynamics might apply
elsewhere. For example, US Marines in Afghanistan's Helmand
Province long cherished the support of the powerful tribal leader
Sher Mohammed Akhundzada in battling the Taliban, whose
forces he would helpfully identify. But the enemy he designated
were all too often not Taliban, but supporters of his chief business
rival in the drug trade, another tribal leader who was meanwhile
enjoying a similarly fruitful alliance with the British forces
sharing the same headquarters as the Marine Corps ("Mobbed
Up"). Overall, this woeful ignorance pervaded the entire US-led
misadventure in Afghanistan, a saga of disastrous errors that is
comprehensible only if it is assumed that the basic object of
the entire effort was "to do us good at budget time," which, as the
trillion-plus dollar tab for the war attests, it certainly did.

Comprehending that it is private passions and interests that
customarily propel acts of state makes the consequences for their
victims appear even more disgusting. The CIA long ago struck
budgetary gold in covert warfare, leading it ultimately to forge a
profitable partnership with the terrorist group, Al Qaeda in various assorted nominations, that attacked America on 9/11 ("A
Special Relationship"). The agency's involvement in the Syrian
civil war, in de facto alliance with Al Qaeda spinoffs, is commonly
cited as the most expensive in its history. Equally gruesomely,
sanctions on Iraq throughout the 1990s, which killed hundreds of
thousands of children, were supposedly enforced to compel
Saddam Hussein to abandon his purported arsenal of weapons of
mass destruction. But, as was later confirmed to me by the chief
UN weapons inspector for much of the period, Rolf Ekéus, the
Clinton Administration knew very well, at least from the spring
of 1997, that Saddam had no WMDs, because he, Ekéus, had
secretly told them so and planned a conclusive report to the UN
detailing his findings. There would therefore have been no legal
basis for continuing the embargo ("A Very Perfect Instrument").
But Clinton was fearful that lifting sanctions would cost him

politically, since the Republicans would surely trumpet complaints that he had "let Saddam off the hook." Secretary of State Madeleine Albright therefore announced that sanctions would continue, WMDs or no, with the intended result that Saddam ceased cooperation with the UN inspectors, and uncountable more Iraqi children died.

Sometimes, the naked pursuit of self-interest is unabashed, as I report in recent episodes of Wall Street history ("Saving the Whale, Again," "Swap Meet," "The Malaysia Job") or in the account of how Ukraine has been reduced to an ongoing crime scene thanks to depredations described in "Undelivered Goods." But even when the real object of the exercise is camouflaged as "foreign policy" or "strategy," no observer should ever lose sight of the most important question: *cui bono?* Who benefits?

PART I
Warfare

1

Tunnel Vision

February 2014

An Afghan farm family were slaughtered as they brought their animals in for the night; one tragedy among millions. But the deaths of Shafiullah and his wife and children reveal much about America's way of war, to which reality is always an irritant.

Early on the evening of May 26, 2012, an instructive hourlong radio conversation attracted a growing audience among listeners in NATO forces across the Afghan theater of war. On one end of the conversation were the pilots of two US Air Force A-10 "Warthog" attack planes, who had been patrolling the eastern province of Paktia, not far from the Pakistani border. They were on call for any ground unit needing "close air support," a task for which the A-10 was expressly designed.

On the other end was a Joint Terminal Attack Controller (JTAC), a specialist whose job is to assign and direct air strikes. The JTAC was reporting Troops in Contact (TIC)—meaning that American soldiers were under fire. Although the entire, acronym-sprinkled transmission was on a secure "strike frequency," such communications customarily enjoy a wider audience, not only among the crews of other planes in the neighborhood but at various headquarters across the country and beyond. Such was the case with this particular mission, making it possible to piece together an account of the disaster that followed.

After reporting the TIC, the controller, who was inside a base headquarters somewhere in eastern Afghanistan, informed the pilots that the enemy force was a large one and read out a grid coordinate. Reaching the designated spot, however, the pilots reported "no joy"—i.e., no sign of action. They were directed to another grid, and then to a third, with the same result. At the fourth location, the flight leader reported the presence of a farm building. People and animals were visible, he said, but no one with a weapon, nor was there any sign of military activity.

The JTAC refused to accept this conclusion. According to one listener, he told the pilots that the ground commander, who was most likely sitting in the same room, "has determined that everybody down there is hostile." He then ordered them to prepare for a bombing or strafing run for the A-10, whose 30mm cannon is capable of firing 4,200 rounds per minute.

The pilots continued to insist that they could see nothing out of the ordinary, reporting "normal patterns of life." The JTAC had at least a rough means of confirming this situation: like many other aircraft, the A-10 carries a "targeting pod" under one wing, which in daylight transmits video images of the ground below, and infrared images at night. This video feed is displayed on the plane's instrument panel and is relayed to the JTAC's array of LCD screens in his operations center, and frequently to other intelligence centers around the globe.

The pilots, who could fly low and slow close to the target and study it through binoculars, had a much more detailed view. Circling above the mud-brick farm building, they affirmed it to be a "bad target." Suddenly, a new voice joined the conversation. A B-1 bomber, cruising high above the clouds, was checking in and reporting its position to the JTAC. Originally developed to deliver nuclear bombs to Moscow at supersonic speeds, the 150-ton plane with its four-man crew lacks the A-10's low-level maneuverability and detailed views from the cockpit. It relies instead on crude video displays coupled with instructions from the ground to hit its targets. Yet it is commonly employed for the same purpose as the A-10: close air support. Speaking on the common frequency, the B-1 pilot was offering to take on the mission. Meanwhile, the controller, sounding increasingly frustrated, continued to insist that the farm was a hostile target. Finally, his patience snapped, asking the A-10 flight leader if he was willing to prepare for an attack.

"No," replied the pilot. "No, we're not."

The controller addressed the same question to the B-1, which had been privy to the A-10's ongoing reports.

"Ready to copy," came the quick, affirmative reply.

Down below, the unwitting objects of all this potent dialogue, a farmer named Shafiullah and his family, were settling in for the night. They would not have understood what it meant when the whine of the A-10s was replaced by the deeper rumble of the huge bomber, which was meanwhile confirming that it had "weaponeered" a mixture of large and small satellite-guided bombs. As the A-10 pilots headed for home, they saw the darkening sky suddenly light up in their rearview mirrors as three huge explosions tore apart the farmhouse, killing Shafiullah, his wife and five of their seven children, the youngest only ten months old. Two other children were wounded but somehow managed to survive.

This obliteration of almost an entire family drew some attention in the media, though reporters had no idea of the real circumstances of the attack. NATO claimed that a ground patrol had come under heavy fire by more than twenty insurgents and had asked for close air support. "We are trying to determine whether the mission has any direct correlation to the claims of civilian casualties," a NATO spokesman told the *New York Times*. Shafiullah's relatives meanwhile took their complaints to the Afghan government, which duly investigated and concluded that the dead were neither Taliban nor Al Qaeda but civilians. According to Shafiullah's brother, Gul Khan, the Americans then admitted that the family had been killed by accident. Both the US ambassador and the military commander "shared their condolences and asked for forgiveness," he told me—but the promised compensation never arrived.

The death of the Shafiullah family might easily be one more addition to the sad roster of CIVCAS, as the military calls the civilian victims of our post–9/11 wars. It fits what has become a traditional pattern: a fatal strike elicits an official denial, followed by concession of responsibility (sometimes grudging and partial, and occasionally accompanied by an offer of compensation), followed by a pledge to mandate stricter procedures. But the events of this particular evening are worth further examination, for they tell us a lot about the way our military operates these days.

The A-10 pilots were able to make a detailed, independent judgment about the target because their aircraft was designed for that very purpose. Its bulletproof armor, along with other features such as reinforced fuel tanks, meant the plane could fly low without fear of enemy ground fire. On the other hand, no one was going to risk a lumbering, $300 million B-1 within easy range of rifles and machine guns, let alone thread it through narrow mountain valleys. (By contrast, the inflation-adjusted price tag for an A-10 is about $20 million.) Confined to high altitudes, and limited by its huge wingspan and turning radius, the B-1 is precluded from close observation of the ground below. Like our fleet of thin-skinned supersonic fighter jets—and like drone operators—it must rely largely on video.

The consequences are frequently bloody. In May 2009, bombs from a B-1 killed at least 140 men, women and children in Farah, Afghanistan, because the pilot, according to the Pentagon's own explanation, "had to break away from positive identification of its targets"—i.e., he couldn't see what he was bombing. Other mass CIVCAS incidents in the same conflict, such as those in Kunduz (ninety-one dead) and Herat (ninety-two dead), can be traced to the same fatal dependence on video-screen images rather than the human eye.

Video will often supply a false clarity to preconceived notions. One A-10 pilot described to me an afternoon he spent circling high over southern Afghanistan in May 2010, watching four people—tiny figures on his cockpit screen—clustering at the side of a road before they retreated across a field toward a house. Everything about their movements suggested a Taliban IED-laying team. Then the door to the house opened and a mother emerged to hustle her children in to supper.

"On the screen," he explained, "the only way to tell a child from an adult is when they are standing next to each other. Otherwise everyone looks the same."

"We call the screens *face magnets*," remarked another veteran, Lt. Col. Billy Smith, a former A-10 squadron commander who flew tours over Bosnia, Iraq and Afghanistan. "They tend to suck your face into the cockpit, so you don't pay attention to what's going on outside."

Smith recalled a 2003 night mission in pursuit of a Taliban contingent close to the Pakistani border: "We were looking for them under the weather in a deep, narrow valley, with steep mountains going up to 15,000 feet. Suddenly I saw a glow from a fire in a cave on the side of the mountain and called the ground commander." Smith was immediately cleared to attack the cave. Yet he still wasn't sure he had located the enemy. "So with my wingman covering me, I put my plane on its side and flew along the mountain so I was looking straight up through the top of my canopy into the cave. Didn't see anybody. Just to be sure, I turned around and flew back the opposite way, and this time I saw a whole family at the mouth of the cave, waving."

The characteristics that enable the A-10 to observe the battle ground with such precision, and safely to target enemy forces a stone's throw away from friendly troops, should ensure it a long life—at least until a superior replacement is developed. But the Air Force has other plans. Assuming the leadership gets its way, all A-10 units will be disbanded in 2015 and the aircraft itself will be junked. Close support will be assigned to the B-1 bomber fleet, along with various jet fighters, including the F-35, which has yet to undergo operational testing and is estimated to cost $200 million per plane.

This decision, which practically guarantees that more civilians as well as American soldiers will die, may seem bizarre and irrational, but in light of the core beliefs that give the Air Force its sense of identity, it makes absolute sense. Deep in the Air Force's psyche is the irksome memory of its early life as a mere branch of the Army, with less status and a smaller budget even than the artillery. Its subordinate role was widely recognized: in his 1931 sketch of the capital's social pecking order, the Washington columnist Drew Pearson described an official so lacking in status that he was routinely seated at dinner "beside the wives of the Second Assistant Postmaster General and the Commander of the Army Air Corps."

Consequently, the Army Air Corps (AAC) nurtured dreams and schemes of independence, on the presumption that strategic bombing could ensure victory without any need for armies or navies. This dogma they derived from the writings of an Italian artillery officer, Giulio Douhet, who argued that bombing the enemy heartland could, by itself, crush any foe. By the time World War II broke out, these crusaders had convinced themselves that the destruction of a limited set of targets supposedly vital to the German economy, such as electrical-generator factories, would bring victory within six months.

Politicians, including Franklin Roosevelt, took the bait. Drawing up war plans before Pearl Harbor, they budgeted for a huge bomber buildup. Then, thanks to a leak that makes the revelations of Edward Snowden appear trivial by comparison, the full details of this "Victory Plan" appeared on the front page of the isolationist *Chicago Tribune* just days before the Japanese attack. Suspicion fell on an Army general of alleged German sympathies. But the *Tribune*'s Washington bureau chief at the time, Walter Trohan, told me years ago it was the Air Corps commander, Gen. Henry "Hap" Arnold, who had passed along the information via a complicit senator. Arnold believed the plan was still too stingy in its allocation of resources to his service, and so aimed to discredit it at birth.

Attempts at daylight precision bombing of strategic targets in World War II proved ineffective. The bombers suffered heavy losses, and the enemy had to be defeated the old-fashioned way, with massive armies slogging across Europe or, in the case of Japan, the invasion of outlying islands together with strangulation by blockade. (These factors had already brought Japan to its knees by the time the atomic bombs were dropped in 1945.)

Air power did play a decisive role—but not in the way envisaged by Douhet's disciples, who considered fighter planes of secondary importance. One such fighter, the P-47, rugged and maneuverable at low altitudes, turned out to be ideally suited for attacking ground targets threatening friendly troops. This weapon proved so successful that during the Third Army's spectacular advance across France in the summer of 1944, Gen. George S. Patton depended almost entirely on close air support to protect his force's exposed right flank.

Meanwhile, back in the bowels of the newly built Pentagon, the AAC had put together a team to plan the most important campaign of all: winning independence from the Army and grabbing 30 percent of the defense budget. By design, none of these officers had any background in fighter planes—indeed, few had combat experience of any kind. With World War II in its last throes, they still believed that Douhet and his prewar adherents had been right all along: strategic bombing was the key to victory. Close air support, which essentially meant helping out ground operations, was definitely not on their agenda. They had much bigger things in mind, especially after they learned of proposals to create a postwar United Nations dedicated to preserving world peace.

Surely, argued the Air Corps staffers, this new authority would need a law-enforcement arm, an International Police Force—and the most obvious candidate to fulfill this role was the US strategic bomber fleet. As one 1943 planning document put it: "The essential nature of any Post War I.P.F. will be based on the application of Air Power, and such a force will essentially be an air force . . . [The I.P.F.] will eliminate subversive or dangerous focal points before they can develop to the point where they become a danger to the security of the world."

This dream of policing the globe in UN garb never panned out, but in 1947 the United States Air Force was finally born, complete with its own uniforms, budget, and exclusive control of all fixed-wing aircraft operating from land (the Navy managed to fight off attempts to take over its own planes). The Army feebly consented to this arrangement, having extracted a promise that the Air Force would always be there with close air support when needed.

Three years later, the Korean War broke out. The new service found itself in action as part of the overall US expeditionary force, but sent only unsuitable fighters to support beleaguered infantry units, many of which were consequently overrun. Meanwhile, heavy bombers soon succeeded in incinerating every city, town, and village in North Korea with little effect on the course of the war, which was once again decided by armies fighting it out on the ground.

Asked at the end of the Korean conflict what useful lessons had been learned, an Air Force general replied, "Nothing." A decade or so later, when the service was once again called on to provide ground support in Vietnam, it initially deployed jet fighters that flew too fast to keep targets in sight. The Air Force would ultimately make use of the A-1 Skyraider—which, though highly effective, was an unwelcome expedient, since it was not only old, dating back to 1945, but had been developed by the Navy.

The Navy, of course, was not the only rival on hand. By the late 1960s, the Army's burgeoning helicopter bureaucracy had conceived the notion of a fast, complex, heavily armed attack vehicle—which would lessen its dependence on the airmen. So ambitious was this project that the proposed machine, the AH-56 Cheyenne, promised to cost more than a jet fighter. This presented a serious threat to the Air Force budget: if the Cheyenne won a constituency in Congress and the industry, the close-air-support mission might be lost. Politically sensitive staff officers whispered in the ear of Gen. John P. McConnell that he was in danger of going down in history as the first Air Force chief of staff to lose a mission and the budget that went with it. Something had to be done.

The solution came from one of the "Whiz Kids," the brilliant group of analysts recruited by defense secretary Robert McNamara to challenge the hidebound orthodoxies of the military. Pierre Sprey was a mathematics prodigy who had been admitted to Yale when he was fourteen, then spent his summers during graduate school working at the Grumann Aircraft Engineering Corporation. Soon after arriving at the Pentagon in 1966, he had earned the enmity of the Air Force with a study demonstrating that its strategy for a war against the Soviets in Europe—deep-strike interdiction bombing—was essentially worthless. A rigorous empiricist, Sprey examined recent military history and concluded that close air support was the most useful contribution the Air Force could make to any conventional war.

McConnell's advisers reasoned that despite Sprey's otherwise repugnant views on air power, he might be just the man to help develop a close air support plane—something demonstrably better and cheaper than the dreaded Cheyenne helicopter. Accordingly, Sprey and a select group of Air Force staffers were detailed to draw up the requirements for such a plane. His research had already revealed, for example, that the majority of losses to antiaircraft fire were caused by fuel from punctured tanks leaking onto hot engines and igniting. So manufacturers bidding for the contract were required to separate these two components in their designs. "They howled about that," recalls Sprey, "since they were so used to wrapping the fuel tank around the engine."

Sprey's analysis led to other requirements: a tight turning radius at slow speeds, an ability to land on dirt strips, bulletproof armor enclosing the cockpit and a quick-firing 30mm cannon to devastate tanks, machine-gun nests and the like. Circulated to manufacturers, this checklist elicited a variety of designs, and ultimately the first-ever fly-off between two competing prototypes, from which the A-10, manufactured by the Fairchild Corporation, emerged victorious. Congress quickly approved a buy of 750 planes.

By 1977, when the A-10 first went into service, it had already fulfilled its primary mission. The Army threat had been beaten off, and the Cheyenne was canceled. Now, however, the Air Force had to live with the instrument of its victory, an aircraft that represented everything that it had fought so hard to escape. From early on, the A-10 was treated as the poor relation, unwelcome at the feast. During the Reagan years, a golden age for the military-industrial complex, the Air Force showered money on such cherished programs as the B-1 bomber and the F-15 and F-16 fighter jets. Meanwhile, the generals shut down the A-10 production line in 1984 (thirty-seven of the original 750 were still to be built) and firmly nipped in the bud any initiative to develop a replacement. In 1988, Gen. Robert Russ, head of Tactical Air Command, announced in the semi-official pages of *Air Force Magazine* that the A-10 had been far outclassed by such favorites as the F-16. "Slow ducks," Russ told his readers, "will be dead ducks."

Two years later, the United States deployed a huge force to Saudi Arabia in response to Saddam Hussein's invasion and occupation of Kuwait. No A-10s were included in the initial air deployment. Legend has it that Gen. Norman Schwarzkopf, commander-in-chief of the expedition, was well aware of the plane's potency against enemy armor, so he demanded of his air commander, Gen. Charles Horner: Where was the A-10?

"Oh," replied Horner, "the F-16s can do the job."

"Don't give me that Air Force political bullshit," snapped Schwarzkopf. "Bring me the A-10!"

It was a wise decision. While precision-guided bombs and missiles captured the imagination of the media and the public, thanks to the new CNN-funneled video footage they provided, these weapons turned out to be less useful at destroying targets—especially if the targets were moving. It was left to 144 grudgingly deployed A-10s to dispatch the bulk of the Iraqi armor, along with truck convoys, radar sites and other crucial targets. Some A-10s even flew off "hasty bases," rough strips secretly laid deep inside Iraq's western desert, the better to hunt for elusive Scud missile launchers. So useful did they prove that Horner, by all accounts an emotional character, was inspired at the war's end to send a signal back to Washington stating, "The A-10 saved my ass."

The general's heretical admission was very much off-message at a time when stealth bombers and precision-guided weapons were the military's pet projects. Horner recanted soon afterward, giving the F-16 most of the credit for the successful air war in Iraq. Throughout the 1990s, the Air Force began steadily retiring A-10s, consigning them to the "boneyard"—a vast parking lot of discarded planes at the Davis–Monthan Air Force Base outside Tucson, Arizona. By the end of the decade, the force was reduced to 390 aircraft, with increasingly confident predictions that the "old and slow" A-10 was finished.

Inconveniently for the official plan, however, the United States was soon at war again, first in Afghanistan, then in Iraq. As usual, the A-10 proved its worth, not least during Operation Anaconda, the badly planned 2002 assault on an Al Qaeda lair in Afghanistan. During the operation, US soldiers were pinned down by an unexpectedly large enemy force. Chaos ensued as warplanes of various descriptions crowded a confined airspace while 2,000-pound bombs dropped by B-52 bombers seven miles up rained down through their formations. "It was a case of accelerating dysfunction," one veteran recalls bitterly. "They were simply bombing GPS coordinates inside a ten-kilometer-square kill box." The situation was salvaged by an A-10 pilot, Lt. Col. Scott "Soup" Campbell, who set up an ad hoc air-traffic-control system while circling the mountainous battlefield, guiding the distant B-52s so that they didn't inadvertently bomb friendly troops.

Among the aircraft Campbell narrowly avoided colliding with that night was a Predator drone, streaming infrared pictures to US military installations around the globe, thereby unleashing a flood of contradictory orders from a hodgepodge of far-flung officers, all of whom believed that they had total "situational awareness" of the battle. Though Anaconda was widely considered a disaster, this particular aspect of the operation received only limited attention. The notion that information could be acquired and disseminated far more efficiently through video streams than by a pilot looking through his canopy was already taken for granted.

"If you want to know what the world looks like from a drone feed, walk around for a day with one eye closed and the other looking through a soda straw," an Air Force colonel with first-hand experience of the drone program remarked to me as we discussed the topic over a beer in the bar of an officers' club near Washington. "It gives you a pretty narrow view of the world." On another occasion, a weapons designer lamented that "people just don't realize that high-definition video isn't good enough to show the subtle stuff you've got to see to keep from hitting your own guys or killing civilians." He compared it to watching a Super Bowl telecast and attempting to pick out a spectator leaning on an AK-47 rather than a cane.

Experienced A-10 pilots make frequent use of the soda-straw analogy in describing the crucial, fragmentary visual snippets they pick up almost subconsciously when viewing a scene directly from the cockpit: the flare of a cigarette being lit, an interior car light flicking on when a door opens. Video images from their targeting pods are always available, of course, but these lack the gymnastic focusing power of both the human eye and the human brain.

"You can *find* people with the targeting pod," an A-10 pilot and veteran of Afghanistan told me. "But when it's zoomed in, I'm looking at a single house, not at anything else." Binoculars and a cockpit view deliver something else, commonly called the big picture. "I see these people standing around a house. Are they hiding? What are they hiding from? You can put all that together. If you're looking through the soda straw, you don't know everything else that's going on around them."

Even as drone warfare has lately dominated the headlines, the entire military-industrial complex, with the Air Force in the lead, was putting its weight behind a gigantic program officially calculated to cost $1.5 trillion: the F-35 fighter. The plane, built by Lockheed, is billed as "multi-mission"—capable of fulfilling the varying needs of the Navy, Marine Corps and Air Force. The Air Force version, we are told, will be designed for both the treasured "deep-strike interdiction" bombing and close air support.

Neither as hardened nor as maneuverable as the A-10, the plane does include multiple features designed to enhance the pilot's "informational awareness." There is, for example, a system that will allow an F-35 pilot to look "through" the floor of his aircraft, by means of a video feed projected onto his helmet visor. Unfortunately, because of the complexity of signal processing, these magical pictures will arrive one eighth of a second out of date. This means that a pilot targeting a weapon on the basis of what he sees while traveling at 400 miles an hour will miss by seventy-three feet, and that's assuming the picture is not unstable, which it usually is. (By contrast, an A-10 pilot firing his cannon "danger close" may be aiming within twenty feet of friendly troops.)

Despite these and copious other deficiencies, the F-35 has one attribute that outweighs all other considerations: its enormous cost and the consequent political influence that comes from supporting 133,000 jobs spread across forty-five states. As ballooning defense budgets give way to restrictions on Pentagon spending, the Air Force in particular has resolved to protect the F-35 at any cost to other programs. Not surprisingly, the A-10 is on the chopping block once more.

Other attempts at eliminating the plane have been beaten back before, most recently in 2012, when a plan to eliminate five squadrons was defeated by congressional opposition. This time, the Air Force is going in for the kill, insisting that "divestiture" of the A-10 would save a sorely needed $3.5 billion over five years. The first hint of this plan came from a confidential briefing slide detailing the service's budget request for 2015. Inadvertently disclosed by a senior Air Force general, the document revealed that the figure for the A-10 was a bald zero.

Further inquiry confirmed that the entire operation—pilots, planes, maintenance, training—would be dismantled and trashed. Legislators with A-10 bases in their districts, who might ordinarily attempt to save those jobs, were offered special inducements by the Air Force. Thus Michigan's Carl Levin, chairman of the Senate's Armed Services committee, has been guaranteed a squadron of aerial tanker planes that will provide substitute employment.

Other powerful legislators have been promised F-16 units—more, in fact, than the Air Force actually has available.

Despite such evasive maneuvers, the Air Force tactics generated a groundswell of opposition. Senator Kelly Ayotte of New Hampshire, herself married to an A-10 pilot, held up the confirmation of the incoming secretary of the Air Force, and followed this with legislation to keep the A-10 in service until an equivalent aircraft is fielded. At a seminar on close air support organized by a Washington public interest group and packed with combat veterans, including numerous present and former A-10 pilots, Pierre Sprey himself made a rare appearance. Long retired from the Pentagon, Sprey spoke of the bureaucratic betrayal of fighting men on the ground as a "festering sore." As I learned, Air Force officers had been warned away from the seminar with thinly veiled threats that such attendance would hurt their careers, and a camera recording the proceedings was pointedly turned away from the audience.

Listening to pilots and other combat veterans discuss their experiences at the seminar, it occurred to me that there was more at stake than a particular plane, or even whether we allow our soldiers and other nations' civilians to die in the name of budgetary politics. Most fundamentally, we're talking about a drive to eliminate a direct connection with outside reality—the sort of connection that prevents children from being mistakenly bombed as Taliban fighters. Instead, the military would rather focus on images relayed along electronic pathways, undeterred by the frequently catastrophic consequences.

The trend extends beyond the military, and beyond a president who relies on a soda-straw view of the world to draw up his weekly kill list. Much of the coverage of the Syrian conflict has been derived from heavily edited videos recorded and posted online by one or another warring faction, then rebroadcast by TV networks around the globe. There are still brave journalists covering the war directly, but declining budgets (and diminishing interest from both their employers and audiences) have made this sort of first-hand observation the exception.

In Paktia, on that May evening in 2012, it was Shafiullah and his family who paid the price for this disengagement. How will we learn about the next such target selected in error? It may not even be in the record. After all, every wartime US air mission generates a report for the files. When someone recently checked on the report for the Paktia incident, the involvement of the A-10s had been expunged. Sometimes reality is hard to bear.

The Air Force's campaign to dispense with the A-10, though briefly frustrated by determined opposition, has continued remorselessly, whittling down the force by starving it of spare parts.

2

Flying Blind

September 2014

Blowing away an Afghan family was an act with minimal consequence for the Air Force. Killing five American servicemen for basically the same reasons was more problematic, but only very slightly so.

President Obama's war against the Islamic State will represent, by a rough count, the eighth time the US air-power lobby has promised to crush a foe without setting boot or foot on the ground. Yet from World War II to Yemen, the record is clear: such promises have invariably been proven empty and worthless. Most recently, the drone campaign against the Yemeni jihadists has functioned mainly as an effective recruiting tool for the other side, now rapidly growing in strength (and pledging loyalty to the Islamic State).

Such realities, however, are of little concern to the lobby, which measures success in terms of budgets and contracts. Therefore, in assessing progress in the anti-IS crusade, observers should be aware that the choice of weapons and associated equipment being deployed will be dictated by Pentagon politics, not the requirements of the battlefield. Hence the appearance, in late August, of the $300 million B-1 bomber in the skies over Iraq.

Although its advertised function was to carry nuclear weapons to Moscow at supersonic speeds, the B-1 was developed principally to bolster Republican electoral fortunes in California, where it was built. Always a technical disappointment—with a full load of bombs, it cannot climb high enough to cross the Rockies—it has nonetheless been tenderly cherished by the Air Force brass. Like someone finding a job for a down-at-the-heels relative, the service has assigned the B-1 the task of attacking enemy troops and supporting friendly troops on the battlefield, a mission for which it is manifestly unsuited.

Close air support, as it is called, has always been considered a lowly and demeaning task by the Air Force, since it involved cooperation with ground troops. Thus the service is striving mightily to discard the A-10, a plane developed specifically for the job, while insisting that the lumbering bomber is a perfectly adequate substitute.

In contrast to the A-10, which can maneuver easily at low level, allowing pilots to see with their own eyes what they are shooting at, the B-1 flies high and relies instead on electronic images or map coordinates. Thanks to these and other limitations, B-1s have already left a trail of havoc in Afghanistan in the form of dead civilians and soldiers. As Obama prepares to sink more political capital into the Air Force's promises, he might also ponder the deaths of five American servicemen and one Afghan soldier in the Gaza Valley, a few miles northeast of Kandahar, on June 9 of this year.

The men were part of a team of US and Afghan soldiers assigned to "disrupt insurgent activity and improve security for local polling stations" in advance of the Afghan presidential runoff elections. Throughout the day, as they moved through the valley and searched farm compounds, they were intermittently sniped at without effect. By 7 p.m., the men moved to their helicopter pickup points. Twelve thousand feet above, a B-1 with a load of satellite-guided bombs was flying five-mile circles: if the team encountered any difficulty, it was ready to provide support.

At about ten minutes before eight, in the gathering dusk, one or two people began shooting at them. The Special Forces soldier assigned to coordinate air support, a so-called Joint Terminal

Attack Controller (JTAC), contacted the B-1 and reported the skirmish. Meanwhile, six members of the team climbed to a nearby ridgeline to outflank the enemy and began returning fire. Just over twenty minutes later, two 500-pound JDAM bombs launched from the B-1 landed in the midst of the little group. Five of the men were killed instantly, their bodies ripped apart by the blasts. The sixth died from his wounds shortly afterward.

This disaster occurred just as the fight in Congress over the plan to discard the A-10 was peaking, so the Air Force was bound to handle the mandatory investigation with the most delicate sensitivity. Just to make sure that the inquiry did not yield any unhelpful conclusions, it was assigned to a senior Air Force officer, Maj. Gen. Jeffrey L. Harrigian. His report, largely declassified and released on September 4, did not disappoint, neatly apportioning blame among all involved—the B-1 crew, the JTAC, and the ground-force commander—for displaying "poor situational awareness" and "improper target identification." With everyone blamed, the predictable consequence was that no one need take responsibility.

Yet a close examination of Harrigian's report reveals that these young men (the oldest was 28, the youngest 19) died because the Air Force insisted on entrusting their safety to a weapon system and crew that was unsuited for the task, yet cherished by the generals for their own peculiar ideological and political reasons. Most importantly: no one had bothered to inform the B-1 crew that their means for distinguishing friendly troops from enemies did not and could not work.

Special Forces soldiers customarily wear "firefly" strobes, which emit infrared light, on their helmets. These are designed to alert anyone using night-vision goggles (i.e., other US troops) that the wearer is a "friendly" without alerting the enemy. As night closed in on June 9, all the B-1 pilots could see of the firefight two and a half miles below were muzzle flashes. If those flashes were in close proximity to the blinking of a strobe, then they were friends. Otherwise, so far as the crew was concerned, they marked an enemy target.

The co-pilot did periodically peer through a pair of night-vision goggles. A B-1 cockpit is ill suited for their use, since the windows are especially thick—a legacy of the plane's genesis as a supersonic nuclear bomber—while the instrument panel emits a glare that clouds the goggles' vision. Like most other planes assigned to such missions, the B-1 also carried a "targeting pod" under its right wing, which transmitted an infrared image of the ground below onto a screen in the cockpit. But these pods, which use longer wavelengths of infrared light, cannot detect infrared strobes.

Amazingly, the Air Force had thought it unnecessary to inform B-1 crews of this salient fact. So, looking at the screen and seeing no strobe lights close to the muzzle flashes on the ridgeline, the crew prepared to bomb. The atmosphere in the cockpit was growing fraught. As the US war in Afghanistan winds down, there are decreasing opportunities for such crews to "go kinetic." (One of the pilots had not dropped a single bomb on his twenty-one previous missions.) The B-1 was also running low on fuel and would soon have to leave the scene, in which case the task would fall to another plane, an AC-130 gunship waiting nearby. Adding to the frustration was the fact that the radios on the $300 million bomber did not work very well due to poorly placed antennas, which meant that no less than twelve transmissions to and from the JTAC on the ground never got through.

Matters got worse when the B-1's weapons officer, who sits in a metal box with no view of the outside world whatsoever, attempted to load the target location information into the computer. The effort failed and the bombs did not drop. The pilot brought the plane around for a second pass, and again the system failed. The weapons officer now laboriously reprogrammed the computer to "bomb on target," which meant that he would manually aim the bombs by clicking the cursor on a video screen. This attempt failed as well. Finally, twenty-one minutes after the effort had begun, two bombs dropped, heading unerringly toward their unwitting victims.

Four minutes after the explosion, the JTAC on the ground called anxiously to the B-1. "That grid [target location] you passed me did not have any IR strobes at it, is that correct?"

"Affirm," replied one of the pilots.

"And your sensor can pick up IR strobes?"

"Affirm."

When other members of the team reached the ridgeline, they found one badly wounded man who murmured, "I can't breathe," and then died. The dismembered corpses of the others were littered over a wide area. All that could be located of one soldier, a 22-year-old corporal, was a small portion of a leg.

Apart from shipping the bodies home and commissioning an inquiry, the most immediate response from the Air Force was to take a *New York Times* reporter for a joyride on a B-1. Helene Cooper duly turned in an upbeat dispatch, noting that the "cockpit of a B-1 bomber in the middle of a fight—even a practice one—is a thing to behold." She described the "expansive" view from the pilot's seat as "nothing but sky." Civilians in targeted areas of Iraq and Syria, not to mention any US personnel assigned to guide the bombing, must wish the pilots, and the Washington officials who send them, had an equally expansive view of the ground.

As I subsequently discovered, General Harrigian had made strenuous efforts to pin the blame for the disaster entirely on the ground force commander, Capt. Derrick Anderson. The effort was narrowly foiled by Anderson's determined refusal to sign what amounted to a false confession of incompetence and responsibility for the death of his men. As it was, his career in the military was effectively doomed, and he accordingly resigned in 2016. Harrigian's career on the other hand took a predictably upward path, elevating him to four-star rank within five years and the command of all US Air Forces in Europe and Africa. Meanwhile, General Lloyd Austin, who as commander of CENTCOM, the operative command for Afghanistan, assigned Harrigian to oversee the so-called investigation, has gone to even greater reward, being appointed secretary of defense by President Biden in 2021.

3

How to Start a Nuclear War

August 2018

How easy is it to blow up the world? How and why do we spend trillions of dollars to make that possible?

Sitting in a US Air Force nuclear missile silo as a launch control officer in the early 1970s, Bruce Blair figured out how to start a nuclear war and kill a few hundred million people. His unit, stationed in the vast missile fields at Malmstrom Air Force Base, in Montana, oversaw one of four squadrons of Minuteman II ICBMs, each missile topped by a W56 thermonuclear warhead with an explosive force of 1.2 megatons—eighty times that of the bomb that destroyed Hiroshima. In theory, the missiles could be fired only by order of the president of the United States, and required mutual cooperation by the two men on duty in each of the launch control centers, of which there were five for each squadron.

In fact, as Blair recounted to me recently, the system could be bypassed with remarkable ease. Safeguards made it difficult, though not impossible, for a two-man crew (of either captains or lieutenants, some straight out of college) in a single launch control center to fire a missile. But, said Blair, "it took only a small conspiracy"—of two people in two *separate* control centers—to launch the entire squadron of fifty missiles, "sixty megatons targeted at the Soviet Union, China and North Korea." (The scheme would first necessitate the "disabling" of the conspirators' silo crewmates, unless, of course, they, too, were complicit in the operation.) Working in conjunction, the plotters could "jury-rig the system" to send a "vote" by turning keys in their separate launch centers. The three other launch centers might see what was happening, but they would not be able to override the two votes, and the missiles would begin their firing sequence. Even more alarmingly, Blair discovered that if one of the plotters was posted at the particular launch control center in overall command of the squadron, they could together format and transmit a "valid and authentic launch order" for general nuclear war that would immediately launch the entire US strategic nuclear missile force, including 1,000 Minuteman and fifty-four Titan missiles, without the possibility of recall. As he put it, "that would get everyone's attention, for sure." A more pacifically inclined conspiracy, on the other hand, could effectively disarm the strategic force by formatting and transmitting messages invalidating the presidential launch codes.

When he quit the Air Force in 1974, Blair, haunted by the power that had been within his grasp, resolved to do something about it. But when he started lobbying his former superiors, he was met with indifference and even active hostility. "I got in a fair scrap with the Air Force over it," he recalled. As Blair well knew, there was supposed to be a system already in place to prevent that type of unilateral launch. The civilian leadership in the Pentagon took comfort in this, not knowing that the Strategic Air Command, which then controlled the Air Force's nuclear weapons, had quietly neutralized it.

This reluctance to implement an obviously desirable precaution might seem extraordinary, but it is explicable in light of the dominant theme in the military's nuclear weapons culture: the strategy known as "launch under attack." Theoretically, the president has the option of waiting through an attack before deciding how to respond. But in practice, the system of command and control has been organized so as to leave a president facing reports of incoming missiles with little option but to launch. In the words of Lee

24

Butler, who commanded all US nuclear forces at the end of the Cold War, the system the military designed was "structured to drive the president invariably toward a decision to launch under attack" if he or she believes there is "incontrovertible proof that warheads actually are on the way." Ensuring that all missiles and bombers would be en route before any enemy missiles actually landed meant that most of the targets in the strategic nuclear war plan would be destroyed—thereby justifying the purchase and deployment of the massive force required to execute such a strike.

Among students of nuclear command and control, this practice of precluding all options but the desired one is known as "jamming" the president. Blair's irksome protests threatened to slow this process. When his pleas drew rejection from inside the system, he turned to Congress. Eventually the Air Force agreed to begin using "unlock codes"—codes transmitted at the time of the launch order by higher authority without which the crews could not fire—on the weapons in 1977. (Even then, the Navy held off safeguarding its submarine-launched nuclear missiles in this way for another twenty years.)

Following this small victory, Blair continued to probe the baroque architecture of nuclear command and control, and its extreme vulnerability to lethal mishap. In the early '80s, while working with a top-secret clearance for the Office of Technology Assessment, he prepared a detailed report on such shortcomings. The Pentagon promptly classified it as SIOP-ESI—a level higher than top secret. (SIOP stands for Single Integrated Operational Plan, the US plan for conducting a nuclear war. ESI stands for Extremely Sensitive Information.) Hidden away in the Pentagon, the report was withheld from both relevant senior civilian officials and the very congressional committees that had commissioned it in the first place.

From positions in Washington's national security think tanks, including the Brookings Institution, Blair used his expertise and scholarly approach to gain access to knowledgeable insiders at the highest ranks, even in Moscow. On visits to the Russian capital during the halcyon years between the Cold War's end and the renewal of tensions in the twenty-first century, he learned that the Soviet Union had actually developed a "dead hand" in ultimate control of their strategic nuclear arsenal. If sensors detected signs of an enemy nuclear attack, the USSR's entire missile force would immediately launch with a minimum of human intervention—in effect, the doomsday weapon that ends the world in *Dr. Strangelove*.

Needless to say, this was a tightly held arrangement, known only to a select few in Moscow. Similarly chilling secrets, Blair continued to learn, lurked in the bowels of the US system, often unknown to the civilian leadership that supposedly directed it. In 1998, for example, on a visit to the headquarters of Strategic Command (STRATCOM), the force controlling all US strategic nuclear weapons, at Offutt Air Force Base, near Omaha, Nebraska, he discovered that the STRATCOM targeting staff had unilaterally chosen to interpret a presidential order on nuclear targeting in such a way as to reinsert China into the SIOP, from which it had been removed in 1982, thereby provisionally consigning a billion Chinese to nuclear immolation. Shortly thereafter, he informed a senior White House official, whose reaction Blair recalled as "surprised" and "befuddled."

In 2006, Blair founded Global Zero, an organization dedicated to ridding the world of nuclear weapons, with an immediate goal of ending the policy of launch under attack. By that time, the Cold War that had generated the SIOP and all those nuclear weapons had long since come to an end. As a result, part of the nuclear war machine had been dismantled—warhead numbers were reduced, bombers taken off alert, weapons withdrawn from Europe. But at its heart, the system continued unchanged, officially ever alert and smooth running, poised to dispatch hundreds of precisely targeted weapons, but only on receipt of an order from the commander in chief.

The destructive power of the chief executive is sanctified at the very instant of inauguration. The nuclear codes required to authenticate a launch order (reformulated for each incoming president) are activated, and the incumbent begins an umbilical relationship with the military officer, always by his side, who carries the "football," a briefcase containing said codes. It's an image simultaneously ominous and reassuring, certifying that the system for initiating World War III is alert but secure and under control.

Even as commonly understood, the procedures leading up to a launch order are frightening. Early warning satellites, using heat-seeking sensors, followed a minute later by ground radars, detect enemy missiles rising above the curve of the earth. The information is analyzed at the North American Aerospace Defense Command (NORAD) in Colorado and relayed to the National Military Command Center in the basement of the Pentagon. The projected flight time of the missiles—thirty minutes from Russia— determines the schedule. Within eight minutes, the president is alerted. He then reviews his options with senior advisers such as the secretary of defense, at least those who can be reached in time. The momentous decision of how to respond must be made in as little as six minutes. Using the unique codes that identify him to the military commands that will carry out his instruction, he can then give the order, which is relayed in seconds via the war room and various alternate command centers to the missile silos, submarines and bombers on alert. The bombers can be turned around, but otherwise the order cannot be recalled.

Fortunately, throughout the decades of confrontation between the superpowers, neither US nor Soviet leaders were ever personally contacted with a nuclear alert, even amid the gravest crises. When Zbigniew Brzezinski, Carter's national security adviser, was awakened at three in the morning in 1979 by what turned out to be a false alarm regarding incoming Soviet missiles, the president learned what had happened only the following day.

Things are different today. The nuclear fuse has gotten shorter. Generally unrecorded by the outside world, there has been a "streamlining" of the system of command and control, as Blair put it in a somewhat opaque article in *Arms Control Today*. Though the shift, which dates to the George W. Bush era and was additionally confirmed to me by a former senior Pentagon official, may appear to outsiders as a merely bureaucratic rearrangement, it has deadly serious implications. Formerly, attack warnings were received and processed by NORAD, in its lair deep inside Cheyenne Mountain, and passed via the National Military Command Center to the White House. But intelligence of a possible attack now goes almost directly to the head of Strategic Command. From his headquarters, far from Washington at Offutt Air Force Base, Nebraska, this powerful officer, currently an Air Force general named John Hyten, reigns supreme over the entire US strategic nuclear arsenal. He now dominates the whole nuclear countdown process: alerting the president, briefing him on the threat, and guiding him through the various options for a retaliatory or, as is likely given the jamming, pre-emptive strike.*

At one level, the change reflects a skirmish in the perennial internecine battles for budget share within the military, in which STRATCOM has clearly triumphed at the expense of NORAD, which was relegated to a basement at Peterson Air Force Base in 2006. But it appears there was a more significant motive for the decision. The head of STRATCOM is invariably a four-star general or admiral commanding a global fiefdom of 184,000 people, in and out of uniform. As Hyten reminded a congressional committee this year, "US STRATCOM is globally dispersed from the depths of the ocean, on land, in the air, across cyber and into space, with a matching breadth of mission areas. The men and women of this command are responsible for strategic deterrence, nuclear operations, space operations, joint electromagnetic spectrum operations, global strike, missile defense, analysis and targeting."

In contrast, the director of the National Military Command Center is customarily a mere one-star officer, far down in the military pecking order. Furthermore, as befits an administrator,

---

* STRATCOM declined to comment on the process, citing its classification status, but a spokesperson for the Joint Chiefs of Staff noted that a review conducted in May suggested that STRATCOM should play an even larger role in the nuclear command and control system.

this officer is often absent from the command center, which is buried deep under the Pentagon. On 9/11, for example, the commander at the time was out of the building during the entirety of the attacks. The actual watch officers pulling eight-hour shifts in the center are colonels, even more lowly and therefore unpardonably reluctant to disturb or wake the commander in chief for what could be a false alarm. Four-stars, on the other hand, are the gods of the military hierarchy, accustomed to deference from all around them. Such panjandrums, especially those with the means to end human civilization, can be expected to have fewer inhibitions against disturbing presidential slumbers.

So it has proved. According to Blair's high-level sources, Bush and Obama received urgent calls from Omaha on "multiple occasions" during their time in office, and it would seem highly likely that Trump has had the same experience. This March, Col. Carolyn Bird, the battle watch commander in the STRATCOM Global Operations Center at Offutt, hinted at this privileged access in a CNN report, boasting, "There's nobody we can't get on the phone." Hyten himself dutifully attested to CNN that Trump "asked me very hard questions. He wants to know exactly how it would work," and sententiously acknowledged that "there is no more difficult decision than the employment of nuclear weapons." Hyten did not mention that in both actual alerts and exercises, according to Blair, it has sometimes proved impossible to locate and patch in officials such as the defense secretary, despite the fact that the system calls for them to be connected automatically. Thus, in a real or apparent crisis, the crucial and necessarily fraught conversation may be between two men: General Hyten and Donald Trump.

Furthermore, in addition to being shorter, the nuclear fuse may now be lit earlier. For decades, the typical scenario for a nuclear alert began with early-warning detection of Russian missiles piercing the clouds over Siberia and following a predictable trajectory. But these days the threats that necessitate those direct calls from Omaha to the White House are more diffuse and ambiguous. Ominous but unverified intelligence reports cite

Chinese and Russian progress in hypersonic weapons—missiles that launch toward space and then turn to race toward their targets at five times the speed of sound, allegedly rendering any form of defense impossible. Vladimir Putin has bragged publicly about Russia's development of intercontinental nuclear-powered cruise missiles and other innovations in his strategic arsenal. (He even personally fired four ballistic missiles in an exercise last October.) North Korean ICBMs, seemingly reliant on a stash of old Soviet rocket engines smuggled out of Ukraine, could supposedly threaten the West Coast of the United States. Iran has tested and deployed homegrown medium-range missiles, as have Pakistan and India.

This new world of multiple threats has sparked public alarm among the military leadership. General Hyten and other powerful officers, for instance, have spoken ominously of the Russian and Chinese hypersonic weapons, maneuvering in unpredictable fashion as they flash toward us at up to five miles a second. Blair has heard the same worries expressed by his sources, and not just about the hypersonics. "There are all kinds of missiles going off all the time now," he told me. "We're regularly picking up these launches and trying to figure out what the fuck's going on."

Presuming that the paths of these supposedly maneuverable weapons are unpredictable, an "imminent" threat no longer necessarily means that enemy missiles are already on the way. Today, the mere suspicion that something is about to happen could be enough for the general in Omaha to phone the presidential bedroom. Hypothetically, given the torrent of incoming and necessarily ambiguous information, intelligence reports that the command crew of a Chinese hypersonic missile squadron have canceled their dinner reservations could prompt such a call and a hurried, lethal decision. The jamming of the president, in other words, can begin earlier than ever.

While Bush and Obama were at the helm, their untrammeled power to launch excited little public concern, even though both men were prone to initiating conventional wars. Obama's commitment to "modernize" America's entire nuclear arsenal at a reported cost of at least $1.2 trillion generated no public outrage, or even much concern. According to Jon Wolfsthal, Obama's senior director for arms control and nonproliferation at the National Security Council, "There is no clear understanding of how much these weapons systems actually cost." When asked to produce a budget for the entire cost of our nuclear weapons forces, he told me, the Pentagon declined, on the grounds that it would be "too hard" to come up with that figure. But the arrival of Donald Trump, irascible, impulsive and ignorant, was a different matter, especially given his threats to destroy North Korea with fire and fury. For the first time in decades, nuclear weapons were becoming a matter of public interest and concern.

For the Pentagon, busy extracting more than a trillion dollars from taxpayers to buy and operate an entirely new force of nuclear weapons, Trump's irresponsible rants cannot have been a welcome development. As Maryland senator Ben Cardin remarked in a Foreign Relations Committee hearing last fall, "We don't normally get a lot of foreign policy questions at town hall meetings, but as of late, I've been getting more and more questions about, Can the president really order a nuclear attack without any controls?" The senators were seeking reassurance that Trump couldn't really incinerate the planet in a fit of pique, and to that end had summoned a former STRATCOM commander, C. Robert Kehler, as witness.

Kehler, a general who retired in 2013, was evidently anxious to put to rest any unwelcome notions the senators might entertain of overhauling the existing nuclear command system: "Changes or conflicting signals," he warned, "can have profound implications for deterrence, for extended deterrence, and for the confidence of the men and women in the nuclear forces." As the general chose to depict it, launching the nukes would be a somewhat laborious bureaucratic process, involving "assessment, review and consultation between the president and key civilian and military leaders" (including their lawyers), which would only then be "followed by transmission and implementation of any presidential decision by the forces themselves. All activities surrounding nuclear weapons are characterized by layers of safeguards, tests and reviews." Of course, as a recent commander, Kehler had to have known that in contemporary alerts and exercises it has sometimes proved impossible to get those key leaders (or their lawyers) on the line, let alone find time for "assessment, review and consultation."

But if the president determines that the United States is under the threat of an imminent attack, asked Ron Johnson of Wisconsin, "he has almost absolute authority" to launch, "correct?" Kehler gave a reluctant yes. But, persisted Johnson, what if the president (i.e., Trump) issued a completely unjustified strike order? What would Kehler have done? "I would have said I am not ready to proceed," answered the general. In other words, he would disobey the order.

Asked to comment on Kehler's statement at a security conference just a few days later, Hyten confirmed that he, too, was fully prepared to defy a direct order from his commander in chief. "The way the process works is this simple: I provide advice to the president. He'll tell me what to do, and if it's illegal, guess what's going to happen?"

"You say no," prompted the moderator.

"I'm going to say, Mr. President, it's illegal," continued Hyten, expressing confidence that the president, rather than brushing his objection aside and brusquely transmitting the order to launch, would obligingly respond, "'What would be legal?' And we'll come up with options of a mix of capabilities to respond to whatever the situation is."

Neither of the generals provided any example of what might actually constitute an illegal order (Kehler offered only some vague references to "military necessity" and "proportion"), still less any precedent for American military commanders defying civilian authority when ordered to launch an attack. In any event, though their comments may have served their purpose in calming public fears, they were entirely irrelevant. Unless the principal command center has been knocked out, once the president gives his order the STRATCOM commander has no role in actually executing the nuclear strike. He sees a presidential launch order at the same time as the other command centers that execute it.*

In the event that a commander did choose to defy the president, the former senior Pentagon official suggested, it could even lead to a situation where officers in the launch centers would be receiving contrary orders through different channels, leading to what he called "the biggest shitstorm in the world."

Despite the generals' reassurances and Kehler's plea to leave things alone, there are moves to curb the president's "absolute authority" to push the button. In September 2016, Ted Lieu, a Democratic congressman from California, introduced legislation, along with Senator Ed Markey of Massachusetts, to prevent the president from calling a first strike without congressional approval. Lieu, a former member of the Air Force judge advocate general well versed in the laws of war, could not see any legal justification for the president to unilaterally launch such an attack. The framers, he pointed out when we discussed the matter recently, gave Congress the power to declare war. "There's no way they would have let one person launch thousands of nuclear weapons that could kill millions of people in less than an hour and not have called that war. If you don't call that war, you run down the Constitution." He was unimpressed by the STRATCOM generals' pledge to defy an illegal launch order and hence felt the urgent need for legislation. "Do we really want to depend on military officers not following an order?"

Not only would Lieu's bill, which has attracted eighty-one cosponsors, preclude Trump from dropping a nuclear weapon on Syria "because he's angry at Assad" or some similarly impulsive initiative, it would also, he suggested, prevent launching in response to intelligence of a potential threat (it would not, however, prevent a US nuclear response in the event of incoming

---

* A STRATCOM spokesperson assured *Harper's Magazine* that any presidential order to employ nuclear weapons would be preceded by "a serious and deliberate discussion regarding all available options, to include diplomatic and conventional military actions, guided by the advice of the Cabinet, national security experts, and relevant military advisers."

missiles). As he reminded me, intelligence has a poor record on threat warnings. "We had intelligence that Iraq had weapons of mass destruction, and it turned out they didn't." He also cited the near-disaster of Brzezinski's late-night wake-up call.

In the past, it should be noted, reliance on intelligence warnings has brought us closer to disaster than we knew. In the '50s, Gen. Curtis LeMay, the father of the Strategic Air Command, secretly deployed his own fleet of electronic intelligence planes over the Soviet Union. As reported by Fred Kaplan in *The Wizards of Armageddon*, he told a visiting emissary from Washington, Robert Sprague, "If I see that the Russians are amassing their planes for an attack, I'm going to knock the shit out of them before they can take off."

"But General LeMay, that's not national policy," cried a horrified Sprague.

"I don't care," replied LeMay. "It's my policy. That's what I'm going to do."

In the event that faulty intelligence had actually led to a launch order during the Cold War, the civilian leadership would have been kept in the dark as to what was on the target list, just as they were unaware that LeMay planned to launch World War III on his own initiative. It is well known, for example, that since the early '60s the war plan has contained "counterforce" options allowing the president to strike military targets while "withholding" attacks on cities. Brilliant minds at the RAND Corporation and elsewhere labored to design such flexibility and have it adopted as policy. But in reality, the distinction was a fiction. War plans enjoined at the highest level were simply ignored by those charged with implementing them. As Franklin Miller, the director of strategic forces policy in the Office of the Secretary of Defense during the '80s, later explained, whatever the civilian leadership devised, the Joint Strategic Target Planning Staff at Offutt Air Force Base totally controlled the actual selection of targets and the weapons assigned to destroy them. If the civilians ever asked for specific information, the planners in Omaha coolly replied that they had "no need to know." So successfully did the

Offutt targeteers guard their turf that even the Joint Chiefs of Staff, the presiding military bureaucracy at the Pentagon, were denied access to their internal guide for assigning targets. Sheltered by secrecy, the planners were able to define "city" in their targeting guidance so narrowly, Miller later wrote, that had the president ordered a large-scale nuclear strike against military targets with the "urban withhold" option, "every Soviet city would have nonetheless been obliterated." The degree of overkill was extraordinary. One small target area, for example, five miles in diameter, was due to suffer up to thirteen thermonuclear explosions.

Things should be different today. Mild-mannered and professorial, Kehler and Hyten present a striking contrast to the bellicose, cigar-chewing LeMay, who promised to reduce the Soviet Union to a "smoking, radiating ruin at the end of two hours," or his successor as head of the Strategic Air Command, Gen. Thomas S. Power, whom even LeMay reportedly considered "not stable" and "a sadist." Modern communications ensure tighter command and control. The national nuclear weapons stockpile, which peaked at more than 30,000 in the late '60s, has now passed 6,000, of which some 1,800 are deployed on missiles and aircraft.

But the reduction in numbers obscures the staggering amount of destruction baked into today's war plans. Blair has published an authoritative estimate of America's global targets, identifying at least 900 such designated aim-points for US missiles and bombers in Russia, of which 250 are classed as "economic" and 200 as "leadership," most of them in cities. Moscow itself could be subject to a hundred nuclear explosions. Poverty-stricken North Korea supplies eighty targets, while Iran furnishes forty. "These are still just huge numbers of weapons," Blair said to me recently. "The targets are still in those three categories: weapons of mass destruction, which means nuclear; war-sustaining industry; and leadership, same as they always were." Much of the drawdown in warhead numbers, sanctified by arms control treaties, has been thanks to military confidence that both weapons and intelligence have become more accurate, meaning that fewer weapons need be assigned to any given target. Thus, whereas targeting plans once called for destroying every single bridge along a key Russian rail-road, current aim-points are far more select—destroying just one bridge to shut down the whole line. "They have gotten smart about where the real entrances are to command bunkers," says Blair. "You usually have a whole set of fake entrances, so you have to put down ten weapons on one major command post. Now we have intelligence on where the actual entrance is, so you only need one weapon for that."

Such confidence may be misplaced. The 1991 Gulf War was hailed at the time as a triumph of precision targeting and intelligence, as demonstrated by videos of missiles homing in unerringly on their targets. Yet a subsequent and exhaustive inquiry by the Government Accountability Office found that far from precision-guided-bomb maker Texas Instruments' claims of "one bomb, one target," it had required an average of four of the most accurate weapons, and sometimes ten, to destroy a given target. A Baghdad bunker destroyed in full confidence that it housed a high-level Iraqi command post had in fact sheltered more than 400 civilians, almost all women and children, almost all of whom were incinerated.

Even so, the Pentagon is working hard on developing the B61-12, a nuclear bomb that not only incorporates all the most desirable precision-guidance features but is also one of several "dial-a-yield" weapons in the US inventory, meaning that its explosive power can be adjusted as desired, in this case from as little as 0.3 kilotons (equivalent to 300 tons of TNT) all the way up to fifty kilotons. Such programs, as with the low-yield submarine-launched missile that is a key feature of the Trump Administration's Nuclear Posture Review, are supposedly aimed at "enhancing deterrence," justified as indicating to the Russians that if they use low-yield weapons, we can respond in kind. But these weapons appear to fulfill the function of conventional weapons in a conventional war, and therefore seem designed to fight, rather than deter, a nuclear war. The ongoing "modernization" (read "replacement") of the entire US nuclear arsenal that was set in motion by Obama included at least one low-yield bomb. Under

Trump, however, the drive to treat nuclear weapons as if they can be used in a conventional battle appears to have gained greater velocity. The most recent Nuclear Posture Review, after all, was co-written by Keith Payne, president of the National Institute for Public Policy, and best known for the dubious notion that "victory or defeat in a nuclear war is possible," as he wrote in 1980. He added that "such a war may have to be waged to that point; and, the clearer the vision of successful war termination, the more likely war can be waged intelligently at earlier stages." His directives on the means to win such a war (more weapons, better targeting) are coupled with pious assurances that they are in the interests of maintaining a "credible deterrent."

Concepts such as dial-a-yield are no less dangerous for being potentially undependable in practice. Thanks to its observance of the (unratified) Comprehensive Nuclear Test Ban Treaty, the United States has not detonated a nuclear bomb since 1992. New warheads, such as those planned by the Trump Administration, are tested by computer simulations that stop short of actually initiating a chain reaction. Phil Coyle, a former director of the Nevada Test Site in the days when the United States actually detonated nuclear weapons to test them, told me that new, experimental designs could sometimes fail to perform according to plan: "Sometimes, they wouldn't work. I can remember some series where it took five or six tries to finally get it right, so to speak. If you were expecting a particular yield, you might not get it," he said, explaining that a new design might on rare occasions produce a yield greater than expected, or less, or no yield at all. Coyle is adamant, however, that all weapons currently in the stockpile are a hundred percent reliable.

But such faith is necessarily based on "virtual" tests, and belief that such simulations adequately reflect the real world is not universally accepted. Referring to the specialists who perform such simulations, Thomas P. Christie, the former director of operational tests and evaluation at the Pentagon, told me: "I'm sure that community has done some great work so far as simulations are concerned, because they can't test. But, if you can't test, you can't verify. I'm very skeptical. All you have to do is get about five percent wrong and you've got a real problem." Such caveats are important, not because they make the case for renewed testing but because nuclear war plans tend to assume a degree of certainty in systems performance, a dangerous misapprehension when everything to do with nuclear war is uncertain.

The same uncertainty holds true of the human element. Blair's lifetime study of nuclear command and control has convinced him that in a real crisis the system would be "prone to collapse under very little pressure." This stark conclusion was confirmed on the only occasion when it was put to the test: the terrorist attacks on 9/11, when it failed utterly. According to a detailed exposé by William Arkin and Robert Windrem of NBC News, senior officials found they could not communicate with one another. The commander of NORAD (still a player at that time) moved US nuclear forces to a higher stage of nuclear alert and closed the blast doors at Cheyenne Mountain for the only time since the end of the Cold War. Putin, alarmed by these developments, wanted to call Bush to ask what was going on, but Air Force One, which was running out of fuel and looking for a secure place to land, could not receive phone calls. When the plane did land, at Barksdale Air Force Base in Louisiana, it was parked next to a runway littered with nuclear bombs— STRATCOM had been in the middle of a nuclear exercise when the hijackers hit the first tower and was now, while NORAD increased the level of nuclear alert, canceling the exercise and hurriedly unloading the active nukes from their bombers. Almost none of the senior officials in line to succeed the president followed their assigned procedures for evacuation to secure locations. One who did, Dennis Hastert, who as Speaker of the House was third in line for the presidency, took shelter in a secure bunker in Virginia, out of contact with the rest of the government. The education secretary, Rod Paige, sixteenth in line, who had gone with Bush to Florida, was left there when the president's party rushed to the plane. He eventually rented a car and drove back to Washington.

Even assuming every component of the system worked according to plan, the idea of initiating a nuclear exchange is obviously irrational in the extreme—a hundred nuclear explosions in and around Moscow? "Would it have made any difference if lots of weapons didn't go off, or (probably) a lot of missiles didn't get out of their silos?" Daniel Ellsberg emailed me in response to a query regarding the reliability of the weapons. "A first strike was insane from the start; and a damage-limiting second strike (which I acknowledge accepting, foolishly, for some years) not really less so."

Nevertheless, there has clearly been a rational motivation underlying all these elaborate preparations for nuclear war over the years: money. The counterforce option, spawned in the early '60s at the Air Force–funded RAND Corporation (the damage-limiting to which Ellsberg was referring), was enthusiastically endorsed by its patron because it parried a threat to Air Force budgets posed by the Navy's new submarine-launched missiles. Invulnerable to enemy attack, the subs clearly rendered the Air Force's land-based missiles and bombers superfluous to deterrence. But the sub-launched missiles were not sufficiently accurate, even in theory, to hit military targets on the other side of the world, whereas the land-based ICBMs supposedly were. When I asked Ellsberg, who worked at RAND for many years, whether he knew of any of its proposals that would have resulted in a cut to the Air Force budget, he said no. That little has changed in our own day is evidenced by the Obama–Trump modernization plan to annually produce eighty new plutonium pits—the core of a nuclear weapon—at a potential overall cost of $42 billion, even though the United States already has 14,000 perfectly usable pits in storage.

Critics of our current nuclear arrangements, while quick to advocate for arms reduction or call for a reduction in executive power, generally accept the fundamental premise of deterrence. Congressman Lieu, for example, despite his sensible suggestions for keeping the president's finger as far as possible from the button, is wholly in tune with the consensus. "For purposes of mutually assured destruction," he assured me, "if any country were to launch a nuclear first strike on us, all bets would be off." Given such assumptions, even among the well intentioned, there seems little chance that the nuclear war machine's massive apparatus will be dismantled anytime soon. When Kehler testified on the merits of deterrence and "extended deterrence" (threatening to use nukes in support of an ally) at the Senate hearing, no one disagreed.

But one individual who most certainly does disagree is a man who spent a large portion of his life in the heart of the US nuclear machine and rose to command it all. "I spent much of my military career serving the ends of . . . deterrence, as did millions of others," Lee Butler, who as a four-star general had headed the Strategic Air Command and its successor, STRATCOM, from 1991 to 1994, wrote in a 2015 memoir. "I fervently believed that in the end it was the nuclear forces that I and others commanded and operated that prevented World War III and created the conditions leading to the collapse of the Soviet empire." But he grew increasingly skeptical about the role of nuclear weapons in maintaining global peace.

> I came to a set of deeply unsettling judgments. That from the earliest days of the nuclear era, the risks and consequences of nuclear war have never been properly understood. That the stakes of nuclear war engage not just the survival of the antagonists, but the fate of mankind. That the prospect of shearing away entire societies has no politically, militarily or morally acceptable justification. And therefore, that the threat to use nuclear weapons is indefensible.

In retirement, Butler joined calls for the total abolition of nuclear weapons.

The fundamental fallacy regarding deterrence, he reasoned, lay in the assumption that we know how an enemy would react to a nuclear threat. As he put it in the memoir, "How is it that we subscribe to a strategy that requires near-perfect understanding of enemies from whom we are often deeply alienated and largely isolated?" Furthermore, he pointed out, the whole theory rested on each side having a credible capacity to retaliate to a nuclear first strike with its own devastating counterattack. But the forces required for such a counterstrike can easily be perceived by a suspicious enemy to be deliberately designed to carry out their own first strike. Since nuclear rivals can never concede such an advantage, "new technology is inspired, new nuclear weapons designs and delivery systems roll from production lines. The correlation of forces begins to shift, and the bar of deterrence ratchets higher."

Interviews with former Soviet military leaders immediately after the Cold War, conducted by the BDM Corporation on a Pentagon contract, confirm that Butler was entirely correct as to their reaction to US nuclear preparations in the name of deterrence. For years, the Soviets told the interviewers, they believed the United States was preparing for a first strike. They therefore prepared to launch a pre-emptive strike if and when they detected signs of such preparations. Ignorant of Soviet thinking, the United States failed to curb military activities that might have confirmed their suspicions and sparked such an attack.

None of this seems to have made much impression on the current crop of nuclear war planners, as Butler recently pointed out to me. "Over the past decade," he wrote in an email, "the Air Force has undertaken a concerted effort to resurrect the old deterrence arguments. In the process, they have dredged up all of the deplorable straw men to knock down the case for arms control/abolition." This effort, he lamented, has been largely successful: "Arms control is now relegated to the back burner with hardly a flicker of heat, while current agreements are violated helter-skelter.

"Sad, sad times for the nation and the world," he concluded bleakly, "as the bar of civilization is ratcheted back to the perilous era we just escaped by some combination of skill, luck and divine intervention."

~

Tragically, Bruce Blair died suddenly in July 2020. In his last published article he wrote:

> When set in motion, the US nuclear posture with its strategy, plans and emergency war operations, which enable a thousand nuclear weapons on launch-ready alert to attack thousands of opposing forces in a coordinated fashion, has a "mind" and momentum of its own.

4

The Military-Industrial Virus

May 2019

The US defense complex is best thought of not as an organiz-ation, but as a living, insatiable, creature, dedicated only to its own defense and power.

For a country that spends such vast sums on its national security apparatus—many times more than the enemies that supposedly threaten it—the United States has a strangely invisible military establishment. Military bases tend to be located far from major population centers. The Air Force's vast missile fields, for instance, are hidden away in the plains of the northern Midwest. It is rare to see service uniforms on the streets of major cities, even Washington. Donald Trump did dream of holding a "beautiful" military parade down Pennsylvania Avenue, complete with "a lot of planes going over and a lot of military might," but the Pentagon nixed the scheme by putting out word that the extravaganza would cost $92 million. The estimate was surely inflated—it was four times greater, in real dollars, than the price tag for the 1991 Gulf War victory parade—suggesting that the military prefers a lower profile.* It often takes an informed eye to appreciate signs

---

* Trump did finally get his parade, in 2019, churlishly cited by the *Washington Post* as one of the administration's "meagre accomplishments" that summer.

of defense dollars at work, such as the office parks abutting Route 28 south of Dulles Airport, heavily populated with innocuously titled military and intelligence firms.

Largely out of sight, our gargantuan military machine is also increasingly out of mind, especially when it comes to the ways in which it spends, and misspends, our money. Three decades ago, revelations that the military was paying $435 for a hammer and $640 for an aircraft toilet seat ignited widespread media coverage and public outrage. But when it emerged in 2018 that the Air Force was now paying $10,000 for a toilet-seat cover alone, the story generated little more than a few scattered news reports and some derisive commentary on blogs and social media. (This was despite a senior Air Force official's unblushing explanation that the ridiculous price was required to save the manufacturer from "losing revenue and profit.") The Air Force now claims to have the covers 3D-printed for $300 apiece, still an extravagant sum.

Representative Ro Khanna of California, a leading light of the Congressional Progressive Caucus who has spearheaded the fight to end US participation in the Saudi war of extermination in Yemen, told me recently that he sees this indifference as a sign of the times. "There's such cynicism about politics, such cynicism about institutions," he said, "that the shock value of scandals that in the past would be disqualifying has diminished." We were discussing another apparent defense rip-off, in which a company called TransDigm has been deploying a business model pioneered by the pharmaceutical industry. TransDigm seeks out unique suppliers of obscure but essential military components, such as a simple cable assembly, and buys the firm, quickly boosting the component's price (by 355 percent in the case of the assembly). Khanna was particularly depressed that the Defense Department's inspector general—whom he, along with Senator Elizabeth Warren of Massachusetts and Representative Tim Ryan of Ohio, had prompted to investigate the company—had concluded that TransDigm's way of doing business was, in his words, "awful, but legal." (Unsurprisingly, Wall Street loves the company; its stock price has doubled in the two years since Khanna first raised the issue.)

At a time when defense spending accounts for fifty-three cents out of every dollar appropriated by Congress, one might expect that the Pentagon would be under intense scrutiny by those who believe that the money is urgently needed elsewhere. Yet this is evidently not the case. Outrageous examples such as the toilet-seat cover or TransDigm come and go almost without comment, as does the ongoing trillion-dollar overhaul of the US nuclear arsenal, which surely poses as great an existential threat to the planet as climate change. True, Bernie Sanders, Elizabeth Warren and Tulsi Gabbard among the Democratic presidential contenders are campaigning for cuts in defense spending, but they all have spotty records when it comes to votes on military budget bills. The Progressive Caucus in the House of Representatives has indeed pressed for a freeze on the Pentagon's budget, along with "greater accountability and transparency in our Department of Defense," but the former effort has been stymied by opposition from centrist Democrats and the latter demand lacks specifics. Justice Democrats, a leftist PAC that has recently emerged as a potent force behind newly elected progressives such as Alexandria Ocasio-Cortez, Ayanna Pressley, Ilhan Omar and Rashida Tlaib, offers little detail on defense policy in its published platform beyond pledging to "End Unnecessary Wars and Nation Building."

When I asked Khanna what it means to be progressive on defense, he responded with similar language. "It means," he answered, "to understand that our recent unconstitutional wars have not made America safe. That our military is overstretched. That we are in too many battlefields overseas. That we need far greater restraint in the use of our military." For Khanna, the fault clearly lies with our aggressive foreign policy. "The reason the military budget is bloated," he continued, "is because we've got too large a presence and footprint overseas in a way that isn't making us safer." But why should a handful of comparatively small-scale operations "overstretch" a military with its largest budget since World War II? All indications are that the actual reason behind the military's bloated budget goes far beyond the ill-starred ventures of our twenty-first-century presidents, and has far more serious implications for both our defense and society.

In 1983, Franklin "Chuck" Spinney, a thirty-seven-year-old analyst in the Pentagon's Office of Program Analysis and Evaluation, testified to Congress that the cost of the ever-more complex weapons that the military insisted on buying always grew many times faster than the overall defense budget. In consequence, planes, ships and tanks were never replaced on a one-to-one basis, which in turn ensured that the armed forces got smaller and older. Planes, for instance, were kept in service for longer periods of time and were maintained in poor states of repair owing to their increasing complexity. As to be expected, the high command did not react favorably to these home truths. They allowed Spinney to keep his job but stopped assigning him anything of importance. He spent the rest of his career ensconced in a Pentagon office at the heart of the military-industrial machine, pondering and probing its institutional personality. Retiring in 2003, he maintained a steady output of pungent analyses of its workings. In a 2011 essay, "The Domestic Roots of Perpetual War," he discussed the pattern of "military belief systems and distorted financial incentives" that produced "a voracious appetite for money that is sustained by a self-serving flood of ideological propaganda." Delving deep into the historical details of Pentagon spending, Spinney illustrated his analyses in the form of intricate charts that not only tracked the actual dollar amounts expended but also showed how the projected budgets for various ambitious weapons-buying plans had never materialized, at least never to the degree necessary to buy the projected number of actual weapons—hence the shrinking forces.

Late in 2018, Spinney's longtime friend Pierre Sprey, a former Pentagon "whiz kid" revered for co-designing the highly successful A-10 and F-16 warplanes, and a trenchant critic of defense orthodoxy, suggested to Spinney that he add a novel tweak to his work by depicting budget changes from year to year in terms of percentages rather than dollar amounts. The analysis that Spinney produced at Sprey's suggestion revealed something intriguing:

although the US defense budget clearly increased and decreased over the sixty years following the end of the Korean War, the decreases never dipped below where the budget would have been if it had simply grown at 5 percent per year from 1954 on (with one minor exception in the 1960s). "Amazingly," emphasized Spinney, this behavior even held true for the large budget reductions that occurred after the end of the Vietnam War and, more significantly, after the end of the Cold War. It is as if there is a rising floor of resistance, below which the defense budget does not penetrate.

Only during Obama's second term did it first dip below this level with any degree of significance. Even more interestingly, every single time the growth rate had bumped against that floor, there had been an immediate and forceful reaction in the form of high-volume public outcry regarding a supposedly imminent military threat. Such bouts of threat inflation have invariably induced a prompt remedial increase in budget growth, regardless of whether the proclaimed threat actually existed. As Gen. Douglas MacArthur remarked, as far back as 1957: "Always there has been some terrible evil at home or some monstrous foreign power that was going to gobble us up if we did not blindly rally behind it by furnishing the exorbitant sums demanded. Yet, in retrospect, these disasters never seem to have happened, never seem to have been quite real."

In 1960, for example, as President Eisenhower was getting ready to denounce the dangerous power of what he would christen the military-industrial complex, the growth rate was pressing against the 5 percent floor. On cue, there appeared the fraudulent specter of a "missile gap" favoring the Soviets. The incoming Kennedy Administration duly opened the budgetary tap. A slow-down a few years later, as Kennedy tried to apply the brakes and free up money for domestic initiatives, was reversed under Johnson with the first major escalation in Vietnam. The end of that war again brought the rate down to 5 percent. True to form, there arose a chorus of alarms about the rising menace of Soviet military power: the CIA upwardly revised its estimates of enemy weapons prowess and spending; the Pentagon asserted that our nuclear forces faced a "window of vulnerability." The consequent spend-up accelerated sharply in the Reagan years, ultimately peaking at a record growth rate of 10 percent.

The end of the Cold War, which had underpinned the entire enterprise, might have been expected to bring a change. But no, the 5 percent limit held firm, and before too long the growth rate rose again as Clinton expanded NATO, thereby ensuring tense relations with Russia for the foreseeable future. The 9/11 attacks and the Bush–Obama wars pushed the year-on-year increases into overdrive until the rate dipped slightly below the 5 percent line in 2015. Donald Trump, for all his bombast about restoring the military, was at first apparently unwilling to undo this particular aspect of the Obama legacy—his initial budget plan for 2020 even featured an absolute decline in spending, from $717 billion to $700 billion. This aberration was brief, however. Following outcry from the military's representatives in Congress, Trump reversed course and dutifully boosted the projected amount to $750 billion, just shy of the historical status quo.

Now that the Democratic establishment, long wedded to the notion that Vladimir Putin somehow engineered the election of Donald Trump, have become as obsessively hawkish on the subject of Russia as any Republican, it seems likely that the line will soon climb north of 5 percent and stay there for years to come. Reports that the Russians, despite having a defense budget less than a tenth the size of ours, are somehow outpacing us in the development of weapons such as chimerical hypersonic missiles go largely unchallenged. Moscow's latest submarines, ships, tanks, cyberweapons and supposed mastery of "hybrid" warfare are regularly invoked to justify a level of spending that, even accounting for inflation, now runs almost double the Cold War average.

This entire process, whereby spending growth slows and is then seemingly automatically regenerated, raises an intriguing possibility: that our military-industrial complex has become, in Spinney's words, a "living organic system" with a built-in self-defense reflex that reacts forcefully whenever a threat to its food supply—our money—hits a particular trigger point. The implications are profound, suggesting that the MIC is embedded in our society to such a degree that it cannot be dislodged, and also that it could be said to be concerned, exclusively, with self-preservation and expansion, like a giant, malignant virus. This, of course, is contrary to the notion that our armed forces exist to protect us against foreign enemies and impose our will around the globe—and that corruption, mismanagement and costly foreign wars are anomalies that can be corrected with suitable reforms and changes in policy. But if we understand that the MIC exists purely to sustain itself and grow, it becomes easier to make sense of the corruption, mismanagement and war, and understand why, despite warnings over allegedly looming threats, we remain in reality so poorly defended.

That latter point may seem counterintuitive. Pentagon critics like Khanna tend to focus on the misuse of our military power, such as in the wars in Yemen or Afghanistan, and on the need to reallocate money away from defense to address pressing social needs. These are certainly valid approaches, but they overlook the fact that we've been left with a very poor fighting force for our money. The evidence for this is depressingly clear, starting with our bulging arsenal of weapons systems incapable of performing as advertised and bought at extraordinary cost. Some examples, such as the F-35 Lightning II fighter planes bought by the Air Force, Navy and Marines, have achieved a certain muted notoriety and served as the occasional butt of jokes made by comedians on cable TV. Yet there is little public appreciation of the extent of the disaster. The F-35 first saw combat last year, seventeen years after the program began. The Marines sent just six of them on their first deployment to the Middle East, and over several months only managed to fly, on average, one combat sortie per plane every three days. According to the Pentagon's former chief testing official, had there been opposition, these "fighters" could not have survived without protection from other planes. The most expensive weapons program in history at a projected lifetime cost of

$1.5 trillion, the F-35 initially carried a radar whose frequent freezing required the pilot to regularly switch it on and off. While the radar problem was eventually corrected, the Air Force version of the plane still features an unacceptably inaccurate gun that remains to be fixed, though the Air Force claims to be working on it.

The Navy is in possibly worse shape. Mines, to take one striking example, are a potent naval weapon and ubiquitous among our potential enemies. Fear of mines caused the United States to cancel a major amphibious landing during the Korean War, and concerns over possible Iraqi mines prevented a planned seaborne assault on Kuwait during the 1991 Gulf War. A single mine (and Iran has thousands of them) in the Strait of Hormuz, through which a third of the world's oil transported by sea passes every day, would throw markets into total chaos. Yet the Navy currently possesses a mere eleven minesweepers, dilapidated vessels long past retirement age, with just four available for the entirety of the Middle East. Fifteen of the new and failure-ridden class of Littoral Combat Ships, known to crews as "little crappy ships," will supposedly be dedicated to mine-hunting and minesweeping, but none of their specialized equipment—designed to detect and disable mines, including underwater drones—has been found to work. A July 2018 report from the Defense Department's inspector general found that the Navy deployed the relevant systems "prior to demonstrating that the systems were effective." Asked to comment, the Navy nevertheless claimed that everything works or, as in the case of the underwater drone, insisted they are "on track" to produce something that does.

Thus the lion's share of our defenses against mines must be borne by a small, decaying fleet of huge MH-53E helicopters that search and destroy mines by towing large sensor-laden sleds through the ocean. The MH-53E, and its variant for the Marines, the CH-53E, are lethal machines—lethal, that is, to those who operate them. According to the journalists behind the documentary *Who Killed Lt. Van Dorn?*, the helicopters have crashed 59 times and killed 132 crew and contractors since their introduction in the 1980s, making them the most dangerous aircraft in the US military.

The Navy's shortcomings have been most vividly highlighted by a plethora of scandals in the Seventh Fleet, which operates in the western Pacific. In recent years, Leonard Glenn Francis, a contractor known as "Fat Leonard" who serviced the fleet's port visits around Asia and held over $200 million in contracts, was found to have been bribing a wide range of officers, among them senior admirals, with lavish entertainment—including drunken parties that lasted days and featured a group of prostitutes known as the "Thai SEAL team"—as well as cash, to secure overpriced contracts. It also emerged that fleet movements had at times been dictated not by the Navy's strategic requirements but by officers repaying Francis's hospitality by directing ships to ports where he stood to make the most money. Though whistle-blowers had been sounding the alarm for years, their complaints were routinely suppressed by officers on Francis's payroll. When the Navy finally got around to investigating his activities, in 2010, no fewer than sixty admirals fell under suspicion. To date, sixteen officers, serving and retired, have been found guilty of bribery, fraud and related crimes, while a further twelve are awaiting trial. Another 550 active-duty and retired military personnel were investigated, although the statute of limitations precluded prosecution in some cases.

Meanwhile, the fleet itself has been progressively deteriorating, as became tragically evident when two destroyers, the USS *Fitzgerald* and the USS *John S. McCain,* collided with merchant vessels in Asian waters in 2017, leaving a total of seventeen sailors dead. The disasters were found to be the direct consequence of incompetent commanders and ill-trained, overworked, shorthanded crews struggling to operate broken-down equipment they did not know how to repair. The failures in leadership, investigations revealed, extended all the way to the top of the chain of command.

The Army and Marines present a hardly less depressing picture. For decades, the Army has been engaged in an expensive struggle to supply troops with reliable radios. One recent portable model, which the Institute for Defense Analyses found would cost $72,000 each, is called the Manpack. Not only is the Manpack twice as heavy as the model it replaces, with a shorter range, but it has displayed a tendency to overheat and severely burn the unfortunate infantrymen carrying it. The helmets worn by soldiers and Marines in Iraq and Afghanistan have also been shown to be faulty. As the authors of the recent book *Shattered Minds* have demonstrated, their design can actually *amplify* the effects of an explosion on one's brain. Furthermore, many of the helmets have been found to be dangerously vulnerable to bullets and shrapnel, thanks to a corrupt contractor skimping on the necessary bulletproof material. As is common with those who speak up about official malpractice, the whistle-blowers who exposed this particular fraud were viciously harassed by their superiors and driven out of their jobs.

Scholarly commentators and pundits generally shrink from ascribing base pecuniary motives to the military-industrial complex. Thus, one recent academic study of the reasons behind declining force numbers finds the answer in "an American cultural disposition favoring technology," suggesting that our military leadership is driven to pour funds into technologically complex weapons systems, thereby skimping on troops' basic needs, by some innate cultural imperative. The reality would seem to be somewhat simpler: the MIC has a compulsion to demand and receive more of our money every year. Contrary to common belief, this imperative does not mean that the budget is propelled by foreign wars. Rather, the wars are a consequence of the quest for bigger budgets. Recently, the Pentagon even proposed a war budget that won't be spent on a war. The proposed 2020 budget includes $165 billion for "Overseas Contingency Operations" (OCO), a special category invented in 2009 to support ongoing wars, rather as if a police department demanded extra money for catching criminals. In previous years, large chunks of this money have been quietly diverted to more urgent Pentagon priorities, such as funding new weapons programs. But now the diversion has become official—the budget request acknowledges that $98 billion of the OCO money is for routine "base requirements," rather than fighting abroad.

In other words, it's all about the Benjamins. Understanding this fundamental fact makes it easier to understand the decisions underlying our defense policy. Why, for example, was the Seventh Fleet sent to sea on unnecessary deployments with shorthanded crews and broken equipment? The answer, according to an investigation by *ProPublica*, was that senior officials in Washington, led by Ray Mabus, secretary of the Navy throughout the Obama presidency, and the chief of naval operations, Adm. Jonathan Greenert, were determined to funnel as much money as possible into building more ships, a decision that proved quite profitable for politically influential shipyards. Why do we maintain a vulnerable land-based missile force as well as an invulnerable submarine-based one? Because eliminating the Air Force's ICBMs would entail a severe blow to the Air Force budget and defense contractors' balance sheets.

We're left with a fighting force that needs to rely on loved ones for vital needs such as armor and night-vision goggles, while we throw hundreds of millions of dollars at exotic contraptions such as the Compass Call NOVA, a completely dysfunctional aircraft tasked with detecting IEDs. The pattern such boondoggles follow is predictable: the services insist that new weapons are needed to replace our rapidly obsolescing fleets. Inevitably, unforeseeable and rapid enemy advances require new and more "capable" weapons, costing 50 to 100 percent more than their predecessors. The presumption that more capable weapons must cost more generally goes unquestioned, despite the fact that prices for more advanced personal computers and other civilian technologies have moved in the opposite direction. Once budgets for an optimistically priced new weapon are approved by the Pentagon leadership and Congress, a program schedule is devised so that no single failure to meet a deadline or pass a test can threaten the flow of funding. In addition, the contract, inevitably of crushing complexity, is designed to ensure the contractor gets paid to cover any and all technical and management failures, which generally guarantees another doubling or tripling of the cost beyond the originally inflated estimate.

This process is little understood by the outside world, which is why taxpayers are prepared to accept a $143 million price tag on an F-22 fighter (that's just the Lockheed sticker; the real price per plane was over $400 million) as somehow justified by its awesome technological capabilities. The late A. Ernest Fitzgerald, who was fired from his job as a senior Air Force cost-management official on the direct orders of President Nixon for divulging excessive spending on an Air Force program, used to point out that $640 toilet seats and $435 hammers (he was the first to bring these to public attention) were merely emblematic of the whole system, and that items such as a $400 million fighter were no more reasonably priced than the toilet seat.

The beauty of the system lies in its self-reinforcing nature. Huge cost overruns on these contracts not only secure a handsome profit for the contractor but also guarantee that the number of weapons acquired always falls short of the number originally requested. For example, the Air Force first planned to buy 750 F-22s at a projected cost of $139 million apiece, but rising costs compelled the defense secretary at the time, Robert Gates, to cancel the program in 2009, capping the fleet at 187. With reduced numbers, weapons systems are kept in service longer: the Air Force's planes average twenty-eight years in service, and some still in use were built well over half a century ago. The F-35, for example, costs almost six times more than the F-16 it is replacing, while the Navy's Zumwalt-class destroyer ($7.5 billion each) costs four times more than the Arleigh Burke destroyers it was supposed to replace. (The Zumwalt's overruns were so enormous that although the original plan called for thirty-two ships, production was cut to just three.) On occasion, the system reaches the ultimate point of absurdity when gigantic sums are expended with no discernible results. Such was the case with Future Combat Systems, a grandiose Army program to field ground forces of manned vehicles, robots and assorted weaponry, all linked via electronic networks, and with Boeing as the prime contractor. Twenty billion dollars later, the enterprise was shuttered, an extensive exercise in futility.

Enormous outlays for marginal or even nonexistent returns attract little attention, let alone objection, among our politicians. Congress routinely waves through the Pentagon's budgets with overwhelming bipartisan majorities. Part of the reason for this must lie in the belief that defense spending is a bracing stimulant for the economy and for the home districts of members of Congress. This point was spelled out with commendable clarity in a March *New York Times* op-ed by Peter Navarro, director of the White House Office of Trade and Manufacturing Policy. The occasion was Trump's impending visit to the Lima, Ohio, plant that manufactures the US Army's Abrams tank. Touting Donald Trump's role in expanding tank production (though the Army already has a huge surplus of tanks in storage), Navarro laid out the economic benefits for both Lima and Ohio, claiming the plant would employ more than 1,000 people there and thousands more across the nation. "Consider," he wrote, "the ripple effects of the Lima plant. In Ohio alone, 198 of its suppliers are spread out across the state's sixteen congressional districts." Few elected representatives could miss the point, including the state's liberal Democratic senator, Sherrod Brown, who had worked alongside Republican lawmakers to boost funding for the project. Major contractors have turned the distribution of defense contracts across as many congressional districts as possible into a high art. Contracts and subcontracts for Lockheed's F-35, for example, are spread across 307 congressional districts in forty-five states, thus ensuring the fealty of a commensurate number of congresspeople as well as ninety senators.

The jobs argument holds sway even when an embrace of defense spending would seem to violate alleged political principles. For example, the F-35 is due to be stationed in Vermont at Burlington International Airport, home of the Vermont Air National Guard. Because the F-35 is at least four times noisier than the F-16s it will replace, large swaths of the surrounding low-cost neighborhood, by the Air Force's own criteria, will be rendered unfit for residential use, trapping some 7,000 people in homes that will only be sellable at rock-bottom prices. Nevertheless, the F-35 proposal enjoys political support from the state's otherwise liberal elected leadership, notably Senator Bernie Sanders, who has justified his support on the grounds that, while he is opposed to the F-35, he supports its being stationed in Vermont from the perspective of job creation.

Yet deeper scrutiny indicates that defense contracts are not particularly efficient job generators after all. Robert Pollin and Heidi Garrett-Peltier of the Political Economy Research Institute at the University of Massachusetts Amherst have calculated the number of jobs spawned by an investment of $1 billion in various industries, ranging from defense to health care, renewable energy and education. Education came in first by a wide margin, producing 26,700 jobs, followed by health care at 17,200. Defense, generating 11,200 jobs, ranked last. "All economic activity creates some employment," Pollin told me. "That isn't at issue. The relevant question is *how much* employment in the US gets created for a given level of spending in one area of the economy as opposed to others." The fact is that defense spending generates fewer jobs than green energy, education and other critical industries.

Studies such as these are rare. Research on the impact of defense spending on the US economy as a whole is rarer still, even though weapons account for about 10 percent of all US factory output. A generation ago, Seymour Melman, a professor of industrial engineering at Columbia, devoted much of his career to analyzing this very subject. He concluded that defense spending's impact on the broader economy was wholly harmful, a consequence of the bad habits injected into the bloodstream of American manufacturing management by a defense culture indifferent to cost control and productivity. The US machine-tool industry, for example, had powered postwar US manufacturing dominance thanks to its cost-effective productivity that in turn allowed high wage rates for workers. But, Melman wrote, as more and more of its output shifted to defense contracts, the industry's relationship with the Pentagon became an invitation to discard the old tradition of cost minimizing. It was an invitation to avoid all the hard work . . . that is needed to offset cost increases. For now it was possible to cater to a new client, for whom cost and price increase was acceptable—even desirable.

In consequence, as Melman detailed, the US machine-tool industry gradually ceased to compete effectively with nations such as Germany and Japan, where cost control still reigned supreme.

Of course, some sections of postwar US manufacturing indebted to defense dollars still led the world, most notably civilian aircraft as represented by the Boeing Company. The airliners that rolled out of its Seattle plant were well designed, safe and profitable. Boeing had a huge defense component as well, but senior management enforced an unwritten rule that managers from the defense side should never be transferred to the civilian arm, lest they infect it with their culture of cost overruns, schedule slippage and risky or unfeasible technical initiatives.

That began to change in 1997, when Boeing merged with McDonnell Douglas, a defense company. In management terms, the merger was in effect a McDonnell takeover, with its executives—most importantly CEO Harry Stonecipher—assuming command of the combined company, bringing their cultural heritage with them. The effects were readily apparent in the first major Boeing airliner initiative under the merged regime, the 787 Dreamliner. Among other features familiar to any student of the defense industry, the program relied heavily on outsourcing subcontracts to foreign countries as a means of locking in foreign buyers. Shipping parts around the world obviously costs time and money. So does the use of novel and potentially risky technologies: in this case, it involved a plastic airframe and all-electronic controls powered by an extremely large and dangerously flammable battery. All this had foreseeable effects on the plane's development schedule, and, true to form for a defense program, it entered service three years late. This technology also had a typical impact on cost, which exceeded an initial development estimate of $5 billion by at least $12 billion—an impressive overrun, even by defense standards. Predictably, the battery did catch fire, resulting in a costly three-month grounding of the Dreamliner fleet while a fix was devised. The plane has yet to show a profit for the corporation, but expects to do so eventually.

The two recent crashes of the Boeing 737 Max, which together killed 346 people, were further indications that running civilian programs along defense-industry lines may not have been the best course for Boeing. The 737 had been a tried and true money-spinner with an impressive safety record since 1967. Several years ago, however, under the auspices of CEO Dennis Muilenburg, previous overseer of the Future Combat Systems fiasco, and Patrick Shanahan (currently the acting secretary of defense), who had headed up Boeing's Missile Defense Systems and the Dreamliner program before becoming general manager of Boeing's commercial airplane programs, the airliner was modified in a rushed program to compete with the Airbus A320. These modifications, principally larger engines that altered the plane's aerodynamic characteristics, rendered it potentially unstable. Without informing customers or pilots, Boeing installed an automated software Band-Aid that fixed the stability problem, at least when the relevant sensors were working. But the sensors were liable to fail, with disastrous consequences. Such mishaps are not uncommon in defense programs, one such instance being Boeing's V-22 Osprey troop-carrying aircraft (supervised for a period by Shanahan), in which a design flaw, long denied, led to multiple crashes that killed thirty-nine soldiers and Marines. But the impact of such disasters on contractors' bottom lines tends to be minimal, or even positive, since they may be paid to correct the problem. In the commercial market, the punishment in terms of lost sales and lawsuits are likely to be more severe.

In the immediate aftermath of the Cold War, before tensions with Russia were reignited, the BDM Corporation, a major defense consulting group, received a Pentagon contract to interview former members of the Soviet defense complex, very senior officials either in the military or in weapons-production enterprises. Among the interesting revelations that emerged (which included confirmation that US intelligence assessments of Soviet defense policy had been almost entirely wrong throughout the Cold War) was an authoritative account of how disastrous the power of the military-industrial complex had been for Soviet defense and the economy. BDM learned that "the defense-industrial sector used its clout to deliver more weapons than the armed services asked for and to build new weapons systems that the operational military did not want." A huge portion of Soviet industrial capacity was devoted just to missile production. "This vast industrial base," according to one former high-ranking bureaucrat, "destroyed the national economy and pauperized the people." Calls for cuts in this unnecessary production were dismissed by the Kremlin leadership on grounds of "what would happen to the workers." The unbearable burden of the Soviet military-industrial complex was undoubtedly a prime cause of the ultimate collapse of the Soviet state—the virus had consumed its host.

The BDM contract had been issued in the belief that it would confirm a cherished Pentagon thesis that the sheer magnitude of US spending, particularly the huge boost initiated in the Reagan years, had brought down the Soviets by forcing them to try to compete—a welcome endorsement for mammoth defense budgets. But the ongoing BDM project, even before the researchers finished their work, made it clear this was not what had happened; the Soviet burden was entirely self-generated for internal reasons, such as maintaining employment. When Pentagon officials realized that BDM's research was leading toward this highly unwelcome conclusion, the contract was abruptly terminated. The system knows how to defend itself.

The unwelcome news that the Russians had bankrupted themselves unilaterally, rather than responding to the American buildup, should have put paid to the notion of a superpower "arms race." But it is far too useful to discard, for Russian profiteers as well as their American counterparts.

5

Like a Ball of Fire

May 2020

Threats don't have to be real to shake the money tree.

At the end of last year the Russian military announced that it had deployed a revolutionary weapon, designed to give Russia a decisive advantage in the strategic nuclear arms race. Avangard, as the new system is called, is a 'hypersonic glide' missile. Unlike traditional Intercontinental Ballistic Missiles, which follow a fixed and predictable trajectory, arcing up as high as 1,200 miles into space and re-entering the atmosphere at around 15,000 miles an hour before plunging down to their target, the Avangard glider is launched by an ICBM booster on a much lower trajectory to skirt the edge of the atmosphere, between 25 and 60 miles up. It then separates and shoots through the upper atmosphere at about 7,000 miles per hour while maneuvering on an unpredictable course toward its distant target. That's the hope, at least.

Vladimir Putin revealed Russia's development of Avangard in his annual address to the Russian Federal Assembly in March 2018. He boasted that it was "absolutely invulnerable to any air or missile defense system"—"It flies to its target like a meteorite, like a ball of fire"—and treated the audience to a short video animation depicting the weapon zigzagging around the globe before striking Florida. When he had warned NATO leaders about the advent of such strategic systems years earlier, he said, "nobody wanted to listen to us . . . Listen to us now." Putin's bellicose claim, two weeks before the presidential election in which he was running for a fourth term, and the more recent official announcement that Avangard had now entered service, drew alarmed and unquestioning attention in the West. "Russia Deploys Hypersonic Weapon, Potentially Renewing Arms Race," the *New York Times* blared. "The new Russian weapon system flies at superfast speeds and can evade traditional missile defense systems. The United States is trying to catch up."

Across the military-industrial complex, the money trees shook, showering dollars on eager recipients. A complacent Congress poured money into programs to develop all-new missile defenses against the new threat, as well as programs to build offensive hypersonic weapons to close the "technology gap." The sums allocated for defensive initiatives alone exceeded $10 billion in the 2020 Pentagon budget, including $108 million in seed money for a "Hypersonic and Ballistic Tracking Space Sensor"—an as-yet undesigned array of low-orbit satellites that would detect and track Russia's weapons. Last September, Marillyn Hewson, the CEO of Lockheed Martin, the world's largest arms manufacturer, hefted a golden shovel to break ground in Courtland, Alabama, on new facilities to develop, test and produce a variety of hypersonic weapons. By then Lockheed already had more than $3.5 billion of hypersonic contracts in hand. Excitement was running high. "You can't walk more than ten feet in the Pentagon without hearing the word 'hypersonics'," one official remarked to an industry-sponsored conference. Michael Griffin, undersecretary of defense for research and engineering, a hypersonics enthusiast, has spoken of the need for "maybe thousands" of hypersonic weapons. "This takes us back to the Cold War," he announced cheerfully, "where at one point we had 30,000 nuclear warheads and missiles to launch them."

Ivan Selin, a senior Pentagon official, would inform newly arrived subordinates in the 1960s Pentagon that they would be programming "weapons that don't work to meet threats that don't exist." Such irreverence regarding high-tech modern weaponry is rare; the norm is uncritical acceptance of reality as the arms industry and its uniformed customers choose to define it. This credulity persists partly because of the secrecy rules deployed to cloak the realities of shoddy performance and unfulfilled promises. More important, complex weapons programs, however problematic, benefit from a widespread and unquestioning faith—not least among journalists—in the power of technology to challenge the laws of physics. One example: for several decades the US Air Force has spent billions of dollars on efforts to produce an airborne laser weapon. But laser beams powerful enough to destroy a target require enormous amounts of energy, which means a power source far bigger than any that can be carried on an aircraft. These efforts have inevitably come to nothing, but the funds continue to flow smoothly, accompanied by breathless headlines such as the *Washington Post*'s recent declaration that "the Pentagon's newest weapons look like something out of *Star Wars*." Throughout the Cold War, similarly, work continued on a program to develop a nuclear-powered bomber—"Atom Plane on Way to Drawing Board; First Phase Ended" the *New York Times* announced in 1951—despite the plain fact that the weight of the lead shielding required to protect crews from lethal radiation made such a plane impossible.

In the 1960s, when Selin was issuing his mordant warning, the US had a hugely expensive arsenal of 1,000 intercontinental Minuteman missiles, originally justified by the threat of a "missile gap" in the Soviets' favor, despite classified intelligence reports which made it clear that no such gap existed. At least 40 percent of the Minutemen were equipped with faulty guidance systems; the Air Force generals were aware of the problem but preferred to ignore it. For many years afterwards, US intelligence agencies continued to insist that the Soviets were able to match the US and its allies militarily and even economically. This was the justification given for commensurate defense spending by the US. Half a century later, we know that the Soviet Union was even then rotting from within, with a sclerotic leadership presiding over armed forces enfeebled by drunkenness and poor training. When the end finally came, troops in the elite divisions stationed in East Germany, so long a specter haunting NATO, were revealed as an undernourished, demoralized rabble eager to sell their uniforms to get money for food.

Today, once again, Russia is the presiding threat. Its "aggressive actions," according to the closing communiqué of December's NATO summit in London, "constitute a threat to Euro–Atlantic security." Congress has voted for $738 billion in military spending for 2020: $38 billion more than Trump initially asked for and the highest-ever peacetime military budget. The other NATO members, under US pressure, have pledged to maintain their own military spending at 2 percent of GDP. This despite the fact that Russia's overall military expenditure is comparatively tiny: in dollar terms somewhere between $45 billion and $68 billion (depending on the ruble–dollar conversion rate), and in decline since 2016. What's more, it seems that much of the money goes missing: in 2011 *Novaya Gazeta* reported that the Ministry of Defense was Russia's most corrupt government department, ahead of strong competition from the ministries of transport, economic development, education and health. (So much of the defense budget was being stolen or spent on bribes that at one point the armed forces had to buy Israeli drones.) But it is clearly not in Putin's political interest to advertise military weakness. As his economy suffers from sanctions and the low price of oil, he has been determined to show his domestic constituency that Russia is still a military superpower: hence his advertisement of the supposedly invincible hypersonic "meteorite," along with other thermonuclear innovations, in his March 2018 speech, including an intercontinental underwater drone and a nuclear-powered cruise missile.

It's worth taking a closer look at Putin's claim, and the credulous response to it in the media and in the Western military-industrial complex. Far from being a cutting-edge twenty-first-century innovation, the Avangard was conceived as long ago as 1987, though at the time the program was known as Albatross. According to Pavel Podvig, an expert on Russian nuclear weapons, Albatross was intended to counter Reagan's missile defense program, which supposedly threatened the ability of Soviet ICBMs to strike the US. Podvig also shows that Albatross was to some extent a make-work project, designed to provide business for the relevant defense contractor, NPO Mashino-stroyeniya, with its 10,000 employees in Rostov. (At almost the same time, Andrei Sakharov was busy persuading Gorbachev that America's "Star Wars" program could never pose a significant threat to Soviet missiles.) The Albatross program survived the fall of the Soviet Union, though only just: mothballed in the 1990s, it was revived and renamed Avangard under Putin, who gave the go-ahead after attending a launch in 2004—even though that test was reportedly a failure. In subsequent years there were further unsuccessful tests, and in 2014 the program was nearly canceled when the designers reported that they couldn't make the system maneuver—the essential selling point for any hypersonic weapon.

Hypersonic endeavors in the US have an even longer history, having originated in the imaginations of German scientists during the Second World War. Walter Dornberger, a favorite of Hitler who oversaw the V2 rocket program and its extensive slave labor workforce, emigrated to the US after the war and soon found employment in the arms industry. In the 1950s he presented the US Air Force with a proposal for a "boost-glide" weapon, first conceived by his former colleagues in Germany. His initiative led to Dyna-Soar, a manned aircraft that would be boosted to the edge of space by a powerful rocket and then glide at high speed around the planet, dropping nuclear bombs at designated spots along the way. Dyna-Soar was canceled in 1963 by the then defense secretary, Robert McNamara, having never left the drawing board, having already absorbed almost a billion dollars—a lot of money in those days. But the dream never died, lingering on in obscure budgetary allocations over ensuing decades, none of them yielding anything of practical use. Despite the bombast on both sides of what we have to call the New Cold War, current efforts will almost certainly be no more successful than their predecessors—except in improving arms corporations' balance sheets—for reasons that bear some scrutiny.

Conceptually, hypersonic vehicles come in two basic variants. They can be powered by onboard "scramjet" engines throughout the period of flight; or they can be boosted by an attached rocket to the height and speed required before gliding while maneuvering to avoid missile defenses. Although scramjet cruise received a great deal of Pentagon funding in the early part of this century, little has been heard of it recently, possibly because officials recognize that the problems with the technology may be insurmountable. In a scramjet engine, air passes through the engine at supersonic speed and is ignited by the fuel to generate thrust. But the slightest perturbation in the airflow—as during maneuvers—leads to shockwave disruption in the smooth supersonic flow of air. This leads to a sharp increase in pressure, and in extremis to the explosive breakup of the engine, which was the apparent reason for the almost instant failure of two out of the three tests of DARPA's experimental X-51 "Waverider" prototypes (DARPA is the Pentagon's Defense Advanced Research Projects Agency). True to form, the UK Ministry of Defence is still investing heavily in this problematic technology.

As a result, essentially all attention and funding in the US has shifted to "boost glide," the conceptual basis for Avangard. But this approach poses its own problems. While gliding, these missiles travel through, rather than above, the atmosphere so as to benefit from wing-lift, just like any aircraft. The control surfaces on the wings enable them to change direction—up, down and sideways. Here is the difficulty. As Pierre Sprey, a Pentagon analyst who played a major role in designing the highly successful F-16 and A-10 warplanes, explained to me, the friction or drag that comes with flying through the atmosphere at extremely high supersonic speeds causes the missile to heat up to near white heat, and to slow down in a hurry. That's why space capsules and ballistic missile warheads have blunt-shaped noses with heat shields. The heat energy from their high-speed re-entry into the atmosphere gets dumped into melting and burning off the heat shield. This protects the passengers or payload inside. But to get any range, a hypersonic glider can't afford the high drag of that blunt, heat-dumping shape.

If the in-the-atmosphere glider is to achieve a tenable range, it must have a longer, far more slender body-wing shape to minimize drag—"real pointy-nosed, just like the old Concorde airliner." Without a blunt heat shield, the missile is forced to absorb much more of the heat internally. What's more, at the moment it detaches from its booster rocket, it is of necessity pointing down (otherwise it would shoot into space), so it must pull up the nose to create the wing-lift needed to level out. But the lift for this pull-up maneuver greatly multiplies drag, causing the glider to slow precipitously. To enjoy the advertised advantages of unpredictable defense-evading trajectories, further maneuvers on the way to the target are necessary, and each maneuver exacts yet another penalty in speed and range. It's true that both Russian and American developers have claimed successful tests over long distances, though not many. "I very much doubt those test birds would have reached the advertised range had they maneuvered unpredictably," Sprey told me. "More likely, they were forced to fly a straight, predictable path. In which case hypersonics offer no advantage whatsoever over traditional ballistic missiles."

There are other problems intrinsic to hypersonics that render them unviable as effective weapons. Achieving adequate range mandates an ultra-slender and ultra-low-weight design, which inevitably means that hypersonic missiles can carry very little in the way of explosive payload. Small weapons payloads need very accurate guidance systems, since they have to hit a target dead-on to destroy it. All projected designs rely for navigation on GPS, which is eminently jammable, and only works for fixed, well-mapped targets. For mobile targets such as aircraft carriers and other ships, or truck-mounted ICBMs and air defense missiles, some sort of sensor (such as radar) is needed to guide the missile to the target at the end of its journey. But a radar and its antenna would have to be very small and light to avoid compromising drag and range, and small antennas have an inadequate range of detection and are poor at distinguishing land or sea targets against cluttered backgrounds. Infrared and electro-optical seekers are defeated by weather, smoke, camouflage and decoys. The speed-induced heating of the missile to 1,000°C or higher creates further problems for navigation and electronics. At that temperature steel glows nearly white hot and titanium becomes soft as plastic. There may be no GPS antenna that can survive such conditions. Functioning radar dishes and lenses for infrared and optical sensors may not be possible either. The cooling needed to protect internal-guidance computers and explosive payloads against speeds of Mach 5 (3,000 mph) and higher may prove to be unachievable given the tight weight and space constraints of a hypersonic missile.

Putin has presumably never heard of Ivan Selin, but in promoting his hypersonic arsenal he is surely confirming the truth of Selin's axiom, since the threat that it is supposed to meet does not, in fact, exist. Putin's justification for his hypersonic initiatives has been based, as he said in 2018, on America's "constant, uncontrolled growth of the number of antiballistic missiles, improving their quality and creating new missile launching areas." By this he meant that American Star Wars–type missile defenses have become capable and extensive enough to prevent traditional Russian nuclear missiles from reaching their targets, to the point where a US leader could conceivably choose to launch an attack on Russia without fear of reprisal. Such confidence in US military-technical prowess is hard to understand unless Putin takes every boast emanating from the Pentagon at face value, or at least finds it politically desirable to pretend to do so. At least $200 billion has been showered on missile defense since Reagan unveiled the Star Wars program in 1983, and yet as Tom Christie, the Pentagon's director of Operational Test and Evaluation under George W. Bush, puts it, "Here we are, almost forty years on, and what have we got to show for it?" Very little, it seems. As he told me recently, "We've tested against very rudimentary threats, and even then [the defense systems] haven't worked with any degree of confidence." An apparently insoluble problem is that no defensive system is able to distinguish reliably between incoming warheads and decoys, such as balloon reflectors that mimic missiles on radar and can be deployed by the hundred at little cost. "There's a very simple technical reason there's essentially no chance—and, I mean, really essentially, no chance—that these missile defenses will work," Ted Postol of MIT, a long-term critic of Star Wars, told me.

> And that is because they must function in the near vacuum of space. And in the near vacuum of space, a balloon and a warhead will travel together essentially forever. So, if you deploy balloons, for example, or any object that has the same appearance from tens of kilometers range or hundreds of kilometers range, remember the sensors have to see things at very long range. It's going to look like a warhead. It's very, very, easy . . . it's trivially easy to build credible decoys. It takes no effort at all, and so, this is fundamental to the whole problem.

Thanks to this awkward fact, the balloon decoys in what Postol likes to call our "choreographed" tests are made larger than the target warheads so that they can easily be distinguished—not something that would happen in an actual attack scenario. Even so, tests fail half the time.

Given these ineradicable technical limitations, of which even the most remotely well-informed Russian security official must be aware, Putin's mission to destabilize American missile defense initiatives seems to make no sense. Why embark on the great expense of building new high-tech weapons when the old ones—Russia's existing force of ICBMs—do the job perfectly well? One possible answer is that Putin understands that the American system presents no danger, but worries that the US leadership may be deluded enough to believe the nonsense promoted by the military and associated industry—such as the Pentagon's claim in 2010 that "the United States is currently protected against the threat of limited ICBM attack"—and will proceed accordingly. But it's more likely that Putin is interested in dispensing billions of rubles to his supporters in the defense industry while simultaneously reassuring the citizenry that Russia is still a superpower. If the US takes it seriously as a superpower competitor then it is one. Meanwhile, the US is lavishing large amounts of money on anti-hypersonic programs. Given the gross deficiencies of both hypersonics and current missile defense systems, this indicates that the US and Russia have both taken Selin's axiom a step further: they mean to deploy a weapon that doesn't work against a threat that doesn't exist that was in turn developed to counter an equally nonexistent threat.

The notion that the Cold War was a nuclear arms race with each side developing systems to counter the other's increasingly deadly initiatives is generally taken as a given. Today, hypersonic weapons are depicted as products of a similar competitive impulse. But a closer look at the history of the Cold War and its post-Soviet resurgence reveals a very different process is at work, in which the arms lobby on each side has self-interestedly sought capital and bureaucratic advantage while enlisting its counterpart on the other side as a justification for its own ambition. In other words, they enjoy a mutually profitable partnership. In the 1970s the Soviets fielded multiple different designs of ICBMs—a surfeit of activity adduced by the US arms lobby as clear evidence of Soviet malignance. In reality, as revealed in the post-1991 thaw, the Soviet generals regarded the redundant ICBMs as jobs programs: as with Albatross/Avangard, they were a budget-draining exercise with no actual military relevance.

Old Pentagon hands tell of the time, many years ago, when a fraught negotiation with Congress over the US Navy budget was speedily resolved in the admirals' favor thanks to the sudden appearance of a Soviet submarine just outside San Francisco Bay. Queried about the timeliness of this providential intervention, a Navy spokesman responded, "We just got lucky, I guess." The ease with which the chimerical menace of hypersonic weapons has been launched into the budgetary stratosphere by the arms lobby suggests that their luck will hold for a long time yet.

~

As of early 2021, the Pentagon had at least seventy hypersonic weapons development programs up and running, or at least spending, and at an ever-accelerating rate. Competition between the services for the money was growing increasingly bitter, with a senior Air Force general openly denouncing army hypersonic plans as "stupid." All tests of proposed systems, however unchallenging, had failed.

PART II
New Cold War

6

Game On

January 2015

The murky story of how we got NATO up, running and buying weapons again, or why Romanian hospitals had to go without running water.

On Monday, March 3, 2014, Representative Mike Rogers, Republican of Michigan and chairman of the House Intelligence Committee, hosted a fund-raising breakfast on Washington's K Street, heart of the lobbying industry. As befitted an overseer of the nation's $70 billion intelligence budget, Rogers attracted a healthy crowd to the breakfast meet, almost all of whom were lobbyists for defense contractors. For a Republican hawk, the timing was auspicious. Five days before, Russian troops had seized control of Crimea, and Rogers had lost no time in denouncing the Obama Administration's weak response to the crisis. "Putin is playing chess and I think we are playing marbles, and I don't think it's even close," he declared on Fox News the day before the fund-raiser. Curious as to how the military-industrial complex was reacting to alarming events abroad, I asked a lobbyist friend who had attended about the mood at the meeting. "I'd call it borderline euphoric," he replied.

Just a few months earlier, the outlook for the defense complex had looked dark indeed. The war in Afghanistan was winding down. American voters were regularly informing pollsters that they wanted the United States to "mind its own business internationally." The dreaded "sequester" of 2013, which threatened to cut half a trillion dollars from the long-term defense budget, had been temporarily deflected by artful negotiation, but without further negotiations the defense cuts were likely to resume with savage force in fiscal 2016. There was ugly talk of mothballing one of the Navy's nuclear-powered carriers, slashing the Army to a mere 420,000 troops, retiring drone programs, cutting headquarters staffs and more.

Times had been dark before, sometimes rendered darker in the retelling. Although defense budgets had actually increased in the post-Vietnam 1970s, for example, veterans of the era still shared horror stories about the "hollow" military in the years that followed the final withdrawal from Saigon. That cloud had lifted soon enough, thanks to sustained efforts—via the medium of suitably adjusted intelligence assessments—to portray the Soviet Union as the Red Menace, armed and ready to conquer the Free World. On the other hand, the end of the Cold War and the collapse of the Soviet Union had posed a truly existential threat. The gift that had kept on giving, reliably generating bomber gaps, missile gaps, civil defense gaps and whatever else was needed at the mere threat of a budget cut, disappeared almost overnight. The Warsaw Pact, the USSR's answer to NATO, vanished into the ashcan of history. Thoughtful commentators ruminated about a post–Cold War partnership between Russia and the United States. American bases in Germany emptied out as Army divisions and Air Force squadrons came home and were disbanded. In a 1990 speech, Senator Sam Nunn of Georgia, revered in those days as a cerebral disperser of military largesse, raised the specter of further cuts, warning that there was a "threat blank" in the defense budget and that the Pentagon's strategic assessments were "rooted in the past."

An enemy had to be found.

For the defense industry, this was a matter of urgency. By the early 1990s, research and procurement contracts had fallen to about half what they'd been in the previous decade. Part of the industry's response was to circle the wagons, reorganize and prepare for better days. In 1993, William Perry, installed as deputy defense secretary in the Clinton Administration, summoned a group of industry titans to an event that came to be known as the Last Supper. At this meeting he informed them that ongoing budget cuts mandated drastic consolidation and that some of them would shortly be out of business.

Perry's warning sparked a feeding frenzy of mergers and take-overs, lubricated by generous subsidies at taxpayer expense in the form of Pentagon reimbursements for "restructuring costs." Thus Northrop bought Grumman, Raytheon bought E-Systems, Boeing bought Rockwell's defense division, and the Lockheed Corporation bought the jet-fighter division of General Dynamics. In 1995 came the biggest and most consequential deal of all, in which Martin-Marietta merged with Lockheed.

The resultant Lockheed-Martin Corporation, the largest arms company on earth, was run by former Martin-Marietta CEO Norman R. Augustine, by far the most cunning and prescient executive in the business. Wired deeply into Washington, Augustine had helped Perry craft the restructuring subsidies for companies like his own—essentially, a multibillion-dollar tranche of corporate welfare. In a 1994 interview, he shrewdly predicted that US defense spending would recover in 1997 (he was off by only a year). In the meantime, he would scour the world for new markets.

In this task, Augustine could be assured of his government's support, since he was a member of the little-known Defense Policy Advisory Committee on Trade, chartered to provide guidance to the secretary of defense on arms-export policies. One especially promising market was among the former members of the defunct Warsaw Pact. Were they to join NATO, they would be natural customers for products such as the F-16 fighter that Lockheed had inherited from General Dynamics.

There was one minor impediment: the Bush Administration had already promised Moscow that NATO would not move east, a pledge that was part of the settlement ending the Cold War.

Between 1989 and 1991, the United States and the Soviet Union had amicably agreed to cut strategic nuclear forces by roughly a third and to withdraw almost all tactical nuclear weapons from Europe. Meanwhile, the Soviets had good reason to believe that if they pulled their forces out of Eastern Europe, NATO would not fill the military vacuum left by the Red Army. Secretary of State James Baker had unequivocally spelled out Washington's end of that bargain in a private conversation with Mikhail Gorbachev in February 1990, pledging that NATO forces would not move "one inch to the east," provided the Soviets agreed to NATO membership for a unified Germany.

The Russians certainly thought they had a deal. Sergey Ivanov, later one of Vladimir Putin's defense ministers, was in 1991 a KGB officer operating in Europe. "We were told . . . that NATO would not expand its military structures in the direction of the Soviet Union," he later recalled. When things turned out otherwise, Gorbachev remarked angrily that "one cannot depend on American politicians." Some years later, in 2007, in a furious speech to Western leaders, Putin asked: "What happened to the assurances our Western partners made after the dissolution of the Warsaw Pact? Where are those declarations today? No one even remembers them."

Even at the beginning, not everyone in the administration was intent on honoring this promise. Robert Gates noted in his memoirs that Dick Cheney, then the defense secretary, took a more opportunistic tack: "When the Soviet Union was collapsing in late 1991, Dick wanted to see the dismantlement not only of the Soviet Union and the Russian empire but of Russia itself, so it could never again be a threat to the rest of the world." Still, as the red flag over the Kremlin came down for the last time on Christmas Day, President George H. W. Bush spoke graciously of "a victory for democracy and freedom" and commended departing Soviet leader Gorbachev.

But domestic politics inevitably dictate foreign policy, and Bush was soon running for re-election. The collapse of the country's longtime enemy was therefore recast as a military victory, a vindication of past imperial adventures. "By the grace of God, America won the Cold War," Bush told a cheering Congress in his 1992 State of the Union address, "and I think of those who won it, in places like Korea and Vietnam. And some of them didn't come back. Back then they were heroes, but this year they were victors."

This sort of talk was more to the taste of Cold Warriors who had suddenly found themselves without a cause. The original neocons, though reliably devoted to the cause of Israel, had a related agenda that they pursued with equal diligence. Fervent anti-Communists, they had joined forces with the military-industrial complex in the 1970s under the guidance of Paul Nitze, principal author in 1950 of the Cold War playbook—National Security Council Report 68—and for decades an ardent proponent of lavish Pentagon budgets. As his former son-in-law and aide, W. Scott Thompson, explained to me, Nitze carefully fostered this potent union of the Israel and defense lobbies by sponsoring the Committee on the Present Danger, an influential group that in the 1970s crusaded against détente and defense cutbacks, and for unstinting aid to Israel. The initiative was so successful that by 1982 the head of the Anti-Defamation League was equating criticism of defense spending with anti-Semitism.

By the 1990s, the neocon torch had passed to a new generation that thumped the same tub, even though the Red Menace had vanished into history. "Having defeated the evil empire, the United States enjoys strategic and ideological predominance," wrote William Kristol and Robert Kagan in 1996. "The first objective of US foreign policy should be to preserve and enhance that predominance." Achieving this happy aim, calculated these two sons of neocon founding fathers, required an extra $60 billion–$80 billion a year for the defense budget, not to mention a missile defense system, which could be had for upward of $10 billion. Among other priorities, they agreed, it was important that "NATO remains strong, active, cohesive and under decisive American leadership."

As it happened, NATO was indeed active, under Bill Clinton's leadership, and moving decisively to expand eastward, whatever prior Republican understandings there might have been with the Russians. The drive was mounted on several fronts. Already plushly installed in Warsaw and other Eastern European capitals were emissaries of the defense contractors. "Lockheed began looking at Poland right after the Wall came down," Dick Pawloski, for years a Lockheed salesman active in Eastern Europe, told me. "There were contractors flooding through all those countries."

Meanwhile, a coterie of foreign policy intellectuals on the payroll of the RAND Corporation, a think tank historically reliant on military contracts, had begun advancing the artful argument that expanding NATO eastward was actually a way of securing peace in Europe, and was in no way directed against Russia. Chief among these pundits was the late Ron Asmus, who subsequently recalled a RAND workshop held in Warsaw, just months after the Wall fell, at which he and Dan Fried, a foreign service officer deemed by colleagues to be "hard line" toward the Russians, and Eric Edelman, later a national security adviser to Vice President Cheney, discussed the possibility of stationing American forces on Polish soil.

Eminent authorities weighed in with the reasonable objection that this would not go down well with the Russians, a view later succinctly summarized by George F. Kennan, the venerated architect of the "containment" strategy:

> Expanding NATO would be the most fateful error of American policy in the post–cold war era. Such a decision may be expected to inflame the nationalistic, anti-Western and militaristic tendencies in Russian opinion; to have an adverse effect on the development of Russian democracy; to restore the atmosphere of the cold war to East–West relations, and to impel Russian foreign policy in directions decidedly not to our liking.

In retrospect, Kennan seems as prescient as Norm Augustine, but it didn't make any difference at the time. When he wrote that warning, in 1997, NATO expansion was already well under way, and with the aid of a powerful supporter in the White House. "This mythology that it was all neocons in the Bush Administration, it's nonsense," says a former senior official on both the Clinton and Bush National Security Council staffs who requested anonymity. "It was Clinton, with the help of a lot of Republicans."

This official credits the persuasive powers of Lech Wałęsa and Václav Havel at a 1994 summit meeting with Clinton's conversion to the cause of NATO expansion. Others point to a more urgent motivation. "It was widely understood in the White House that [influential foreign policy adviser Zbigniew] Brzezinski told Clinton he would lose the Polish vote in the '96 election if he didn't let Poland into NATO," a former Clinton White House official, who requested anonymity, assured me.

To an ear as finely tuned to electoral minutiae as the forty-second president's, such a warning would have been incentive enough, since Polish Americans constituted a significant voting bloc in the Midwest. It was no coincidence then that Clinton chose Detroit for his announcement, two weeks before the 1996 election, that NATO would admit the first of its new members by 1999 (meaning Poland, the Czech Republic and Hungary). He also made it clear that NATO would not stop there. "It must reach out to all the new democracies in Central Europe," he continued, "the Baltics and the new independent states of the former Soviet Union." None of this, Clinton stressed, should alarm the Russians: "NATO will promote greater stability in Europe, and Russia will be among the beneficiaries." Not everyone saw things that way; in Moscow there was talk of meeting NATO expansion "with rockets."

Chas Freeman, the assistant secretary of defense for international security affairs from 1993 to 1994, recalls that the policy was driven by "triumphalist Cold Warriors" whose attitude was, "The Russians are down, let's give them another kick." Freeman had floated an alternate approach, Partnership for Peace, that would avoid antagonizing Moscow, but, as he recalls, it "got overrun in '96 by the overwhelming temptation to enlist the Polish vote in Milwaukee."

In April 1997, Augustine took a tour of his prospective Polish, Czech and Hungarian customers, stopping by Romania and Slovenia as well, and affirmed that there was great potential for selling F-16s. Clinton had spoken of NATO being as big a boon for Eastern Europe as the Marshall Plan had been for Western Europe after the Second World War, and many of the impover-ished ex-Communist countries, some with small and ramshackle militaries, were eager to get on the bandwagon. "Augustine would look them in the eye," recalls Pawloski, the former Lockheed salesman, "and say, 'You may have only a small air force of twenty planes, but these planes will have to play with the first team.' Meaning that they'd be flying with the US Air Force and they would need F-16s to keep up." Actually, Augustine had rather more going for him than this simple sales pitch, including a lavish dinner for Hungarian politicians he threw at the Budapest opera house.

Meanwhile, back in Washington, a new and formidable lobby-ing group had come on the scene: the US Committee to Expand NATO. Its cofounder and president, Bruce P. Jackson, was a former Army intelligence officer and Reagan-era Pentagon official who had dedicated himself to the pursuit of a "Europe whole, free and at peace." His efforts on the committee were unpaid. Fortunately, he had kept his day job—working for Augustine as vice president for strategy and planning at the Lockheed Martin Corporation.

Jackson's committee stretched ideologically from Paul Wolfowitz and Richard Perle (known as the neocon "Prince of Darkness") to Greg Craig, director of Bill Clinton's impeachment defense and later Barack Obama's White House counsel. Others on the roster included Ron Asmus, Richard Holbrooke and Stephen Hadley, who subsequently became George W. Bush's national security adviser.

When I reached Jackson recently at his residence outside Bordeaux, he reiterated what he had always said at the time: his efforts to expand NATO were undertaken independently of his employer. He suggested that they had even imperiled his job. "I would not say that senior executives *supported* my specific projects," Jackson said. "They thought I should be free to do what I wanted politically, provided I did not associate [Lockheed] with my personal causes. In short, they did nothing to stop me, and suggested to other employees to leave me alone so long as I did not drag LMC into politics or foreign policy. I finally left because I enjoyed my nonprofit work more than my day job."

In this atmosphere of disinterested public service, Jackson and his friends devoted their evenings to cultivating support for congressional approval of Polish, Czech and Hungarian membership in NATO, followed by further expansion. The setting for these efforts was a large Washington mansion not far from the British Embassy and the vice-presidential residence: the home of Julie Finley, a significant figure in Republican Party politics at that time who had, as she told me, "a deep interest in national security." A friend of hers, Nina Straight, describes Finley as someone who "knows how to be powerful and knows how to be useful." As Finley relates, she noted in late 1996 that NATO expansion was facing opposition in Washington. "So I called Bruce Jackson and Stephen Hadley and Greg Craig and said, 'Holy smokes, we have to get moving!'"

"We always met at Julie Finley's house, which had an endless wine cellar," reminisced Jackson happily. "Educating the Senate about NATO was our chief mission. We'd have four or five senators over every night, and we'd drink Julie's wine while people like [Polish dissident] Adam Michnik told stories of their encounters with the secret police."

Meanwhile, other European countries were experiencing a less congenial form of lobbying. Romania, for example, was among those hoping to join the alliance and enjoy the supposed fruits of this latter-day Marshall Plan. But the country was in ruins, with an economy that had barely recovered from the levels induced by the demented economic policies of Nicolae Ceauşescu, the tyrannical ruler who had been overthrown and executed in 1989. A 1997 World Bank report noted that "the majority of the poor live in traditional houses made of mud and straw, do not have access to piped water and have no sewage facilities." Such dire conditions made little impression on visiting arms salesmen. Representatives of Bell Helicopter Textron, manufacturer of the Cobra attack helicopter, persuaded the Romanian government in 1996 to agree to a $1.4 billion deal for ninety-six Super Cobra helicopters, to be manufactured locally and rechristened the Dracula.

This presented Daniel Daianu, a respected economist appointed Romania's finance minister in December 1997, with a problem. His country didn't have the money. "There were huge payments, billions, coming due in '98 and '99, in external debt payments," he told me. "That was why I was so against the deal." In response, the United States applied leverage. Picking his words carefully, Daianu explained that Americans in Washington and Bucharest "intimated to me with clarity that this was the way to get easier access into NATO"—in the first round, along with Poland and the others.

Daianu was learning some interesting things about the way Washington works. He found himself the object of "gentle pressure" from "American businesspeople and people who were a sort of conduit between the American administration of the time and the companies involved in this deal." As he stuck to his principles, the pressure from such people "intimated" that "this is the way to take care of your retirement, and your children's."

At the same time, there was pressure back *in* Washington, some of it not so gentle. Romania was heavily dependent on an IMF loan guarantee, which gave the fund considerable leverage over the country's budget. As it happened, Karin Lissakers, the US executive director on the IMF's board during the Clinton Administration, knew a lot about the sales practices of arms corporations—she had worked during the 1970s for Senator Frank Church's Subcommittee on Multinational Corporations. The subcommittee had delved into the unwholesome sales techniques of US arms corporations abroad, uncovering many egregious cases of bribery. So, when a Textron representative came calling to demand that the fund remove the block it had effectively imposed on the Romanian deal, she was not impressed.

Her visitor, Richard Burt, had been a *New York Times* reporter specializing in national security issues before moving over to the State Department, where he ultimately served as ambassador to West Germany. After leaving government service in 1991, he found steady employment as a high-powered consultant. Among his clients was the Textron Corporation (he sat on the firm's international advisory council), and he had a separate connection to Bell Helicopter, from which a company he chaired, IEP Advisors, had collected $160,000 between 1998 and 1999 for lobbying. Meanwhile, Burt maintained a useful foothold in the Pentagon, serving on the influential Defense Policy Board.

"Rick Burt came to see me and said the IMF was being completely unreasonable in blocking the helicopter deal," Lissakers told me. "He wanted me to pressure the IMF country team, pressure them to approve the loan. His tone was bullying—the implication was that I was accountable to Congress and would suffer consequences. This was at a time when hospitals in Bucharest had no running water! I always regret I didn't throw him straight out of my office."

"She's full of shit, and that's on the record," responded Burt heatedly when I relayed Lissakers's comments. "That's not at all what I was doing. I was not pimping for this at all." He insisted that he himself always thought the helicopter deal was a bad idea, and was simply sounding out the IMF position. He also insisted that the $160,000 IEP Advisors was paid in 1998–99 was merely for "advice, not lobbying."

Daianu resigned and the helicopter deal was canceled, but Romania did finally make it into NATO, in 2004, along with six other countries. By that time, Lockheed had scored a major payoff with a $3.5 billion sale of F-16s to Poland, and the newly enlarged NATO had proved its military usefulness in the US-led coalition that bombed Serbia, a Russian ally, for seventy-seven days in 1999 on behalf of Kosovo separatists. "The Russians were humiliated in Kosovo," Jackson said, "and that was the first time they showed militant opposition to NATO."

Their protests made little difference. "'Fuck Russia' is a proud and long tradition in US foreign policy," Jackson pointed out to me. "It doesn't go away overnight." Consequently, no one in Washington appeared to care very much about the Russian reaction when NATO's eastward flow began spilling into the territory of the former Soviet Union, especially once George W. Bush was in the White House with Dick Cheney by his side.

With the momentum of expansion carrying NATO ever closer to the Soviet heartland, it was no longer realistic to presume Russian indifference. Yet the movement was hard to stop. Even farther to the east, in Georgia, a charismatic young US-trained lawyer, Mikheil Saakashvili, took power in 2003 and straightaway began offering a welcome embrace to Washington and pleading to join the alliance. To bolster his standing in the American capital, Saakashvili hired Randy Scheunemann, a Republican lobbyist and the executive director of the Committee for the Liberation of Iraq, a neocon group formed in 2002 under the chairmanship of none other than Bruce Jackson.

Privately, Washington players felt a little nervous about their hyperactive protégé, suspecting that he might get everyone into trouble. As one of them told me, Saakashvili "needed a course of Ritalin to shut him up." But in public, it was easy to get swept away. In 2005, George W. Bush stood in Tbilisi's Freedom Square and told the crowd they could count on American support:

> As you build a free and democratic Georgia, the American people will stand with you . . . As you build free institutions at home, the ties that bind our nations will grow deeper, as well . . . We encourage your closer cooperation with NATO.

Saakashvili worked hard at ingratiating himself with the friendly superpower, supplying a Georgian contingent for the US-led coalitions in Iraq and Afghanistan, and offering hospitality to various American intelligence operations in Georgia itself, where NSA interception facilities began appearing on suitably sited hilltops. Although he may have had less appeal among European leaders, in Washington the Georgian president basked in bipartisan favor among influential figures such as Richard Holbrooke, as well as White House aspirant Senator John McCain and his adviser (and Saakashvili lobbyist) Randy Scheunemann.

Unfortunately, the burgeoning relationship promoted a dangerous overconfidence on Saakashvili's part. By 2008, he was unabashedly provoking Moscow, apparently confident that he could win a war with his immense neighbor. Receiving Bruce Jackson, who by now was heading up yet another entity, the Project on Transitional Democracies, Saakashvili demanded immediate shipment of various weapons systems, including, remembers Jackson, "a thousand Stingers." Jackson said that would not happen. "Go fuck yourself," snapped the Georgian leader.

Matters came to a head at a NATO summit in Bucharest in April 2008. Vladimir Putin flew in to say that the alliance's expansion posed a "direct threat" to Russia. President Bush, accompanied by National Security Adviser Stephen Hadley, took Saakashvili aside and told him not to provoke Russia. Sources privy to the meeting tell me that Bush warned the Georgian leader that if he persisted, the United States would not start World War III on his behalf.

Bush had arrived in Bucharest eager for an agreement on rapid NATO membership for Georgia and Ukraine, but he backed off in the face of protests from European leaders. In an awkward compromise, NATO released a statement forswearing immediate membership, but also stating: "We agreed today that these countries will become members of NATO." Putin duly took note.

Buoyed by hubris and undeterred by warnings (possibly undermined by back-channel assurances from Dick Cheney that he had US support for a confrontation), Saakashvili pressed on, ultimately assaulting the separatist region of South Ossetia, which was disputed by Russia. Russian forces swiftly counterattacked and were soon deep in Georgian territory, making sure along the way to destroy all those US listening posts.

Despite this debacle, appetite for engagement on the fringes of Russia itself did not go away. Cheney and the rest of the Bush

Administration were shortly to make way for the new broom of Obama and his team—or nearly new. As is so often the case in important matters, policy proved to be bipartisan. Thus Dan Fried, a senior foreign policy official under Clinton and Bush, was still in office to welcome the Obama Administration, and currently supervises the sanctions regime directed at Russia for the State Department. Victoria Nuland, wife of Robert Kagan and chief of staff to Clinton's deputy secretary of state, Strobe Talbott, served Cheney as deputy national security adviser, then resurfaced as Hillary Clinton's spokesperson in the first Obama term before transitioning to assistant secretary of state for Europe in the second.

Reacting to the news that the United States had put $5 billion into democracy-building projects in Ukraine, Putin, whose popularity at home had been sagging, pressured Ukraine's elected president, Viktor Yanukovych, to forgo a trade agreement with the European Union. In its place he offered $15 billion in economic assistance. The rest, as they say, is history. When street protests in Kyiv threatened to overthrow the corrupt Yanukovych, Nuland hurried to the scene, distributed cookies to the protesters, and later incautiously discussed her plans for installing a new government on an open phone line ("that would be great, I think, to help glue this thing . . . and, you know, fuck the EU"), remarks that were intercepted and speedily leaked. Even a politician far less paranoid than the Russian leader might have found grounds for suspecting that the Americans were up to something, and Putin promptly responded by seizing control of Crimea. Since that moment, as news anchor Diane Sawyer announced in March, it has been "game on" for the United States and Russia.

For many of its original protagonists, NATO expansion has proved an unblemished success. "I see no empirical evidence that enlargement was threatening to Russia," Jackson told me firmly. "You can't prove that." On the other hand, he is no great enthusiast for the economic warfare against Russia levied by the Obama Administration in support of Ukraine. "The moral defense of international intervention is the improvement of the freedom and prosperity of the people in question," he wrote me recently. "I suspect sanctions will lead to the impoverishment of all concerned, most particularly the Ukrainians [whom] the sanctions policy purports to defend."

In any event, the vision of Augustine and his peers that an enlarged NATO could be a fruitful market has become a reality. By 2014, the twelve new members had purchased close to $17 billion worth of American weapons, while this past October Romania celebrated the arrival of Eastern Europe's first $134 million Lockheed Martin Aegis Ashore missile defense system.

The ebullience expressed by defense lobbyists at Mike Rogers's breakfast back in March has been amply justified. "Vladimir Putin has solved the sequestration problem for us because he has proven that ground forces are needed to deter Russian aggression," declared Congressman Mike Turner, an Ohio Republican and chair of an important defense subcommittee, in October. Meanwhile, the Bipartisan Policy Center, a Washington entity that numbers, inevitably, Norm Augustine among the panjandrums adorning its board of directors, sponsored a panel on "Ensuring a Strong US Defense for the Future." Michèle Flournoy, defense undersecretary for policy during Obama's first term, warned the panel, "You can't expect to defend the nation under sequestration." Fellow panelist and former Cheney adviser Eric Edelman, who preceded Flournoy in the Pentagon post, echoed her theme. Other speakers demanded that NATO members increase their defense budgets.

At the end of October 2014, as European economies quivered, thanks in part to the sanctions-driven slowdown in trade with Russia, the United States reported a gratifying 3.5 percent jump in gross domestic product for the quarter ending September 3. This spurt was driven, so government economists reported, by a sharp uptick in military spending.

Sustained American pressure on its European allies to boost their military budgets has brought resounding success. As of late 2020, NATO collective defense spending had hit $1.03 trillion, or *roughly twenty times Russia's military budget. Although Donald Trump was reviled for "alienating allies" by hectoring them to spend more, his demands for 2 percent increases in spending reflected bipartisan priorities, as was succinctly expressed by Democratic Senator Richard Durbin in late December 2020. In a Senate speech denouncing efforts to hold up the $740 billion defense authorization bill until the Senate agreed to grant $2,000 payments for poor Americans, he cited the more urgent necessity of providing support for "the Baltic states and Ukraine, especially in the face of continued, unforgivable, Russian aggression." The Pentagon got its money.*

7

Undelivered Goods

August 2015

How fostering co-optation of the Ukrainian swamp as a US ally spawned some very unappealing swamp creatures.

Arriving home from a recent trip to Ukraine, former Senate majority leader Tom Daschle reported his joy at witnessing "the Ukrainian people . . . coming together to rebuild their country from scratch." Ukrainians had, he wrote, moved him with their dreams of joining the European Union, fighting corruption and rebuilding their shattered economy, inspiring Daschle, now a highly paid lobbyist, to endorse the ominously strengthening Washington consensus on escalating the fighting with "$3 billion in lethal and nonlethal military assistance."

Daschle's trip was sponsored by the National Democratic Institute, an affiliate of the congressionally funded National Endowment for Democracy, headed by ur-neoconservative Carl Gershman, who some time ago identified Ukraine as "the biggest prize" for Russia and deployed considerable amounts of taxpayer dollars at his disposal to securing it for the West. However, it has been Assistant Secretary of State Victoria Nuland who has played the most active role in pursuit of the prize. Therefore, her interventions in Ukrainian politics and the realities of politics and business in that country deserve closer attention than they have so far received.

"Toria" Nuland has enjoyed a remarkable career, occupying a succession of powerful positions through changing administrations, despite her close neocon associations over the years both marital—her husband being leading neocon ideologue Robert Kagan—and political, notably as a national security adviser to former vice president Dick Cheney. In the buildup to the 2008 Russo-Georgia war, for example, Nuland, at the time ambassador to NATO, urged George Bush to accept both Georgia and Ukraine as NATO members. Since Georgia's then president and neocon favorite, Mikheil Saakashvili, had high hopes of drawing the United States in on his side in the coming conflict, this was a dangerous initiative. Fortunately, Bush, by that time leery of neocon advice, stood firm against her pleas.

Despite her ongoing proximity to power, Nuland attracted little public attention until the leak of an intercepted phone call gave the rest of us a taste of how she operates. Incautiously chatting on her cell on January 28, 2014, with US Ambassador to Ukraine Geoffrey Pyatt, as the Kyiv street protests against elected Ukrainian president Viktor Yanukovych gathered momentum, Nuland and the diplomat mulled over who should now rule the country. Their candidate was "Yats," the opposition politician Aseniy Yatsenyuk, as opposed to another opposition candidate, former world heavyweight boxing champion Vitali Klitschko, favored by various European powers. Nuland was determined to keep Klitschko out and, as she infamously remarked on that call, thereby "fuck the EU."

However, despite her enthusiasm for Yatsenyuk, Nuland was clearly well aware of who was really pulling the strings in Ukrainian politics: the oligarchs, who had assembled enormous fortunes out of the wreckage of the Soviet economy. Chief among these were those connected to the import of Russian natural gas, on which Ukraine was heavily dependent, most especially Dmitry Firtash, a multimillionaire and key supporter of the government Nuland hoped to displace. This may explain why, at the end of 2013, Firtash found himself the subject of a US international "wanted" notice, charged with attempting to bribe local officials in distant India. He happened to be in Vienna, and a request was accordingly submitted to the Austrian government for his extradition back to the United States to stand trial.

On the day the request was submitted, Victoria Nuland left Washington on an urgent visit to Ukraine. President Yanukovych appeared to be backtracking on a pledge to sign an association agreement with the European Union—the specific "biggest prize" cited by Gershman in a *Washington Post* op-ed the month before. If Yanukovych were to be persuaded to change his mind, threatening to put his sponsor Dmitry Firtash behind bars was a potent lever to apply. Four days later, Yanukovych signaled he was ready to sign, whereupon Washington lifted the request to shackle his billionaire ally.

A month later, Yanukovych changed course again, accepting a $15 billion Russian aid package. Street protests in Kyiv followed, eagerly endorsed by Nuland, who subsequently distributed cookies in gratitude to the demonstrators. Yanukovych fled Kyiv on February 22, and four days later the United States renewed the request to the Austrians to arrest Firtash. They duly did. Briefly imprisoned, Firtash posted the equivalent of $174 million bail and waited for a court to rule on his appeal against extradition.

Nevertheless, Firtash was still politically powerful enough in Ukraine to decide who should become president. The two leading candidates for the post were Petro Poroshenko, a chocolate-industry oligarch favored by Nuland, and Vitali Klitschko, the boxer she had successfully schemed to exclude from the premiership. Klitschko was very much under Firtash's control. Both men flew to the Austrian capital for a meeting with the oligarch, who negotiated a deal in which Klitschko stood down and left the way open for Poroshenko, while Klitschko became mayor of Kyiv.

Ukraine, meanwhile, was in chaos. The revolution that had brought anti-Russian nationalists to power in Kyiv was highly unwelcome in the Russian-speaking east, not to mention Moscow. Vladimir Putin capitalized on this to engineer the return of Crimea to Russian rule, and it appeared possible that he would similarly absorb eastern Ukraine. By April 2014, Russian-backed separatists had taken control of the Donbass, the steel and mining region, and were advancing westward toward the next big industrial center, Dnipropetrovsk, the domain of another oligarch, Igor Kolomoisky.

Kolomoisky had built his multibillion-dollar financial base partly thanks to his mastery of "raiding," the local version of mergers and acquisitions, involving methods that would make even the most hardened Wall Street financier turn pale. According to Matthew Rojansky, director of the Kennan Institute at the Woodrow Wilson Center for International Scholars, who has made a special study of the practice, "there are actual firms in Ukraine . . . registered with offices and business cards, firms [that specialize in] various dimensions of the corporate raiding process, which includes armed guys to do stuff, forging documents, bribing notaries, bribing judges."

Rojansky describes Kolomoisky as "the most famous oligarch-raider, accused of having conducted a massive raiding campaign over the roughly ten years up to 2010," building an empire based on banking, chemicals, energy, media and metals, and centered on PrivatBank, the country's largest bank, holding 26 percent of all Ukrainian bank deposits. At some point, Kolomoisky's business practices raised enough eyebrows in Washington to get him on the visa ban list, precluding his entry into the United States.

In April 2014, as the separatists advanced, Kolomoisky mobilized his workforce into a 20,000-man private army in two battalions, Dnipro-1 and Dnipro-2, and stemmed the tide. According to Wilson Center director Rojansky, Kolomoisky is "perceived as the bulwark and the reason why the whole Novorossiya project [Putin's plan to absorb most of eastern Ukraine] broke down at the border of the Donbass."

Stopping Putin in his tracks would clearly have earned the master raider merit in the eyes of policymakers in Washington and other Western capitals, which may just explain how it was that while Firtash was under the shadow of the US indictment, no one made too much of a fuss at the disappearance of an estimated

$2 billion in IMF aid for Ukraine that speedily exited the country via Kolomoisky's PrivatBank.

The international financial agency had rushed the money to Ukraine in April, in response to what IMF managing director Christine Lagarde called a "major crisis." She went on to hail the government's "unprecedented resolve" in developing a "bold economic program to secure macroeconomic and financial stability." Over the next five months the international agency poured the equivalent of $4.51 billion ($2.97 billion in "Special Drawing Rights"—the IMF's own currency) into the National Bank of Ukraine, the country's central bank. Much of this money was urgently needed to prop up the local commercial banks. In theory, the IMF appeared to require direct supervision of how the Ukrainian banks used the aid. In fact, it appears the banks got to select their own auditors.

As the largest bank, Kolomoisky's PrivatBank stood to garner the largest share of the international aid. Published estimates put this share as high as 40 percent. Despite the torrent of cash, the banks' situation did not improve; nine months into the program, the IMF announced, "As of end January 2015 . . . the banking system's capital adequacy ratio stood at 13.8 percent, down from 15.9 percent at end-June." Where had the money gone?

Although we hear much about corruption in countries such as Ukraine in general terms, a precise, detailed accounting of the means by which an impoverished country has been stripped of precious assets is not usually easy to come by. In this case however, thanks to investigative work by the Ukrainian anticorruption watchdog group Nashi Groshi ("Our Money"), we can actually watch the process by which the gigantic sum of $1.8 billion was smoothly maneuvered offshore, in the first instance to Privat-Bank accounts in Cyprus, and thence into accounts in Belize, the British Virgin Islands and other outposts of the international financial galaxy.

The scheme, as revealed in a series of court judgments of the Economic Court of the Dnipropetrovsk region monitored and reported by Nashi Groshi, worked in this way: Forty-two

Ukrainian firms owned by fifty-four offshore entities registered in Caribbean, American and Cypriot jurisdictions and linked to or affiliated with the Privat group of companies, took out loans from PrivatBank in Ukraine to the value of $1.8 billion. The firms then ordered goods from six foreign "supplier" companies, three of which were incorporated in the United Kingdom, two in the British Virgin Islands, one in the Caribbean statelet of St. Kitts & Nevis. Payment for the orders—$1.8 billion—was shortly afterward prepaid into the vendors' accounts, which were, coincidentally, in the Cyprus branch of PrivatBank. Once the money was sent, the Ukrainian importing companies arranged with PrivatBank Ukraine that their loans be guaranteed by the goods on order.

But the foreign suppliers invariably reported that they could not fulfill the order after all, thus breaking the contracts, but without any effort to return the money. Finally, the Ukrainian companies filed suit, always in the Dnipropetrovsk Economic Court, demanding that the foreign supplier return the prepayment and also that the guarantee to PrivatBank be canceled. In forty-two out of forty-two such cases the court issued the identical judgment: the advance payment should be returned to the Ukrainian company, but the loan agreement should remain in force.

As a result, the loan of the Ukrainian company remained guaranteed by the undelivered goods, while the chances of returning the advance payments from foreign companies remain remote. "Basically this transaction of $1.8 bill[ion] abroad with the help of fake contracts was simply an asset siphoning [operation] and a violation of currency legislation in general," explained Lesya Ivanovna, an investigator with Nashi Groshi in an email to me. "The whole lawsuit story was only needed to make it look like the bank itself is not involved in the scheme . . . officially it looks like PrivatBank now owns the products, though in reality [they] will never be delivered."

Thanks to the need to use the economic court as a legal fig leaf, the scheme operated in plain view. "There were no secret sources," Ivanovna told me. "We found this story while monitoring the court decisions registrar. It's open and free to search, so we read it on a daily basis." Other companies had used the same mechanism, she pointed out. "The major difference of this case is its immensity."

Despite this brazen raid on Ukraine's dwindling assets, no one in authority seemed to care very much. Ivanovna's group joined with an anticorruption NGO, Anti-Corruption Action Center (ANTAC), in a request to the Ukrainian General Prosecutor Office to open a criminal proceeding, but with no result. ANTAC's legal director, Antonina Volkotrub, tells me that there is currently no official investigation of the transactions, though her group has sued the prosecutor to start a criminal investigation.

Kolomoisky himself has, however, run into a small spot of bother with authorities. In March of this year he launched his most bold raid yet, sending a hundred armed "lawyers" to seize physical control of Ukrnafta, the principal Ukrainian oil company, and UkrTransNafta, which controls almost all oil pipelines in the country. This was a direct threat to the authority of Poroshenko, the oligarch/president, who enlisted ambassador Pyatt, Nuland's phone-mate, in a deal to remove his rival from the scene. "My understanding is that part of the deal whereby Kolomoisky gave up his attempt to take over control of Ukrnafta and UkrTransNafta and gave up governorship of Dnipropetrovsk and gave up having his pawn in control of Odessa," Rojansky told me, "was that the US ambassador came in as an intermediary guarantor and said if you do these things, we will take you off the visa bad list." So it came to pass. Kolomoisky flew unmolested to the United States, where he is reported to have been spending a lot of time watching basketball games, and with no one asking awkward questions about what happened to all that IMF money. (Nuland's friend Mikheil Saakashvili, the former president of Georgia who had worked so hard to draw the United States into conflict with Russia, took over the governorship of Odessa, with the United States paying his staff's salaries.)

As for Firtash, the State Department has been less forgiving. In April this year a Vienna court presided over by Judge Christoph

Bauer finally got around to hearing Firtash's appeal against the extradition request in the Indian bribery case. In a daylong hearing, a crowded courtroom received a fascinating tutorial on the inside story of recent Ukrainian political events, including the background to Washington's on-again-off-again with the Firtash extradition requests according to the status of Ukraine's EU negotiations, not to mention Firtash's role in the Poroshenko–Klitschko negotiations. Firtash's lawyers argued that the case had little to do with bribery in India and everything to do with United States meddling in Ukrainian politics. The judge emphatically agreed, handing down a withering verdict, stating that "America obviously saw Firtash as somebody who was threatening their economic interests." He also expressed his doubts as to whether two anonymous witnesses cited by the United States in support of its case "even existed." The State Department announced it was "disappointed" in the verdict and maintained its outstanding warrant for Firtash, should he leave Austria and travel to some country with a legal system more deferential to US demands.

Complex realities such as those related here do not intrude on official Washington pronouncements, where all is black and white, and the party line shifts inexorably closer to endorsing US military engagement in the Ukrainian quagmire. At least we should know who is taking us there.

Kolomoisky invested much of his ill-gotten gains in US businesses and real estate. In 2020 the Justice Department moved to seize some of them on grounds they were the fruits of multibillion-dollar thefts from his bank. The wily oligarch had meanwhile fostered the installation of former comedian Volodymyr Zelensky as president of Ukraine. Victoria Nuland was selected by President Joe Biden to be undersecretary of state for political affairs, the third most senior position in the Department.

8

The New Red Scare

December 2016

At one level, "Russiagate," the presumption that Russia had manipulated the 2016 election in favor of Donald Trump, was a stick deployed by the Democrats to excuse their defeat and torment Trump. At a deeper level, it was an exercise in threat inflation as traditionally practiced throughout the (first) Cold War.

"Welcome to the world of strategic analysis," Ivan Selin used to tell his team during the Sixties, "where we program weapons that don't work to meet threats that don't exist." Selin, who spent the following decades as a powerful behind-the-scenes player in the Washington mandarinate, was then the director of the Strategic Forces Division in the Pentagon's Office of Systems Analysis. "I was a twenty-eight-year-old wiseass when I started saying that," he told me , reminiscing about those days. "I thought the issues we were dealing with were so serious, they could use a little levity."

His analysts, a group of formidable young technocrats, were known as the Whiz Kids. Their iconoclastic reports on military budgets and programs, conveyed directly to the secretary of defense, regularly earned the ire of the Pentagon bureaucracy. Among them was Pierre Sprey, who later played a major role in developing the F-16 and A-10 warplanes. He emphatically confirmed his old boss's observation about chimerical threats. "It was true for all the big-ticket weapons programs," he told me recently. "But although we pissed off the generals and admirals, we couldn't stop their threat-inflating, and their nonworking weapons continued to be produced in huge quantities. Of course," he added with a laugh, "the art of creating threats has advanced tremendously since that primitive era."

Sprey was referring to the current belief that the Russians had hacked into the communications of the Democratic National Committee, election-related computer systems in Arizona and Illinois and the private emails of influential individuals, notably Clinton campaign chairman John Podesta—and then malignly leaked the contents onto the internet. This, according to legions of anonymous officials quoted without challenge across the media, was clearly an initiative authorized at the highest level in Moscow. To the *Washington Post*, the hacks and leaks were unquestionably part of a "broad covert Russian operation in the United States to sow public distrust in the upcoming presidential election and in US political institutions."

In early October, this assessment was endorsed by James Clapper, the director of national intelligence, as well as by the Department of Homeland Security. Though their joint statement expressed confidence that the Russian government had engineered the DNC hacks, it appeared less certain as to Moscow's role in the all-important leaks, saying only that they were "consistent with the methods and motivations of Russian-directed efforts." As for the most serious intrusion into the democratic process—the election-system hacks—the intelligence agencies took a pass. Although many of those breaches had come from "servers operated by a Russian company," the statement read, the United States was "not now in a position to attribute this activity to the Russian Government."

The company in question is owned by Vladimir Fomenko, a twenty-six-year-old entrepreneur based in Siberia and proprietor of King Servers. In a series of indignant emails, Fomenko informed me that he merely rents out space on his servers, which are scattered throughout several countries, and that hackers have on occasion used his facilities for criminal activities "without our knowledge." Although he has "information that undoubtedly will help the investigation," Fomenko complained that nobody from the US government had contacted him. He was upset that the FBI had "found it necessary to make a loud statement through the media" when he would have happily assisted them. Furthermore, these particular "criminals" had stiffed him $290 in rental fees.

As it happened, a self-identified solo hacker from Romania named Guccifer 2.0 had made public claim to the DNC breaches early on, but this was generally written off as either wholly false or Russian disinformation. During the first presidential debate, on September 26, Hillary Clinton blithely asserted that Vladimir Putin had "let loose cyber attackers to hack into government files, to hack into personal files, hack into the Democratic National Committee. And we recently have learned that, you know, that this is one of their preferred methods of trying to wreak havoc and collect information."

By "wreak havoc," Clinton presumably had in mind such embarrassing revelations as the suggestion by a senior DNC official that the party play the religious card against Bernie Sanders in key Southern races, or her chummy confabulations with Wall Street banks, or her personal knowledge that our Saudi allies have been "providing clandestine financial and logistic support to ISIL and other radical Sunni groups." It made sense, therefore, to create a distraction by loudly asserting a sinister Russian connection—a tactic that has proved eminently successful.

Donald Trump's rebuttal ("I don't think anybody knows it was Russia that broke into the DNC . . . It could be somebody sitting on their bed that weighs 400 pounds, OK?") earned him only derision. But a closer examination of what few facts are known about the hack suggests that Trump may have been onto something.

CrowdStrike, the cybersecurity firm that first claimed to have traced an official Russian connection—garnering plenty of free publicity in the process—asserted that two Russian intelligence agencies, the FSB and the GRU, had been working through separate well-known hacker groups, Cozy Bear and Fancy Bear. The firm contended that neither agency knew that the other was rummaging around in the DNC files. Furthermore, one of the hacked and leaked documents had been modified "by a user named Felix Dzerzhinsky, a code name referring to the founder of the Soviet Secret Police." (Dzerzhinsky founded the Cheka, the Soviet secret police and intelligence agency, in 1917.) Here was proof, according to another report on the hack, that this was a Russian intelligence operation.

"OK," wrote Jeffrey Carr, the CEO of cybersecurity firm Taia Global, in a derisive blog post on the case. "Raise your hand if you think that a GRU or FSB officer would add Iron Felix's name to the metadata of a stolen document before he released it to the world while pretending to be a Romanian hacker." As Carr, a rare skeptic regarding the official line on the hacks, explained to me, "They're basically saying that the Russian intelligence services are completely inept. That one hand doesn't know what the other hand is doing, that they have no concern about using a free Russian email account or a Russian server that has already been known to be affiliated with cybercrime. This makes them sound like the Keystone Cops. Then, in the same breath, they'll say how sophisticated Russia's cyberwarfare capabilities are."

In reality, Carr continued, "It's almost impossible to confirm attribution in cyberspace." For example, a tool developed by the Chinese to attack Google in 2009 was later reused by the so-called Equation Group against officials of the Afghan government. So the Afghans, had they investigated, might have assumed they were being hacked by the Chinese. Thanks to a leak by Edward Snowden, however, it now appears that the Equation Group was in fact the NSA. "It doesn't take much to leave a trail of bread crumbs to whichever government you want to blame for an attack," Carr pointed out.

Bill Binney, the former technical director of the NSA, shares Carr's skepticism about the Russian attribution. "Saying it does not make it true," he told me. "They have to provide proof . . . So let's see the evidence."

Despite some esoteric aspects, the so-called Russian hacks, as promoted by interested parties in politics and industry, are firmly in the tradition of Cold War threat inflation. Admittedly, practitioners had an easier task in Ivan Selin's day. The Cold War was at its height, America was deep in a bloody struggle against the communist foe in Vietnam, and Europe was divided by an Iron Curtain, behind which millions chafed under Soviet occupation.

Half a century later, the Soviet Union is long gone, along with the international communist movement it championed. Given that Russia's defense budget is roughly one tenth of America's, and that its military often cannot afford the latest weapons Russian manufacturers offer for export, resurrecting this old enemy might seem to pose a challenge to even the brightest minds in the Pentagon. Yet the Russian menace, we are informed, once again looms large. According to Defense Secretary Ashton Carter, Russia "has clear ambition to erode the principled international order" and poses "an existential threat to the United States"—a proclamation endorsed by a host of military eminences, including Gen. Joseph Dunford, the chairman of the Joint Chiefs of Staff; his vice-chairman, Gen. Paul Selva; and NATO's former Supreme Allied Commander, Gen. Philip Breedlove.

True, relations with Moscow have been disintegrating since the Bush Administration. Yet Russia achieved formal restoration to threat status only after Putin's takeover of Crimea in February 2014 (which followed the forcible ejection, with US encouragement, of Ukraine's pro-Russian government just a few days earlier). Russia's intervention in Syria, in the fall of 2015, turned the chill into a deep freeze. Still, the recent accusation that Putin has been working to destabilize our democratic system has taken matters to a whole new level, evoking the Red Scare of the 1950s.

At the core of the original Cold War threat was the notion that the Soviets, notwithstanding the loss of 20 million lives and the utter devastation of their country in World War II, somehow maintained a military technologically equal to that of the United States, and far greater in numbers. Portraying the United States as militarily vulnerable might have seemed tricky. There was, after all, the nation's million-man army, its 900-ship navy, its 15,000-plane air force, and a strategic nuclear arsenal guaranteed, as its commander, Gen. Curtis LeMay, announced in a 1954 briefing, to reduce Russia to a "smoking, radiating ruin in two hours."

Nevertheless, public belief in the Soviet Union as an existential threat (not that the phrase existed then) was undimmed. The enemy to be held in check appeared awesome. No less than 175 Soviet and satellite divisions were reportedly poised on NATO's eastern border, vastly outnumbering the puny twenty-five NATO divisions defending Western Europe. US military officials regularly delivered somber warnings that the Soviets were also close to overtaking us in the quality of their military hardware. In 1956, when the Soviet defense minister, Georgy Zhukov, informed a visiting US delegation that its estimate of Soviet military strength was "too high," the visitors brushed this aside as obvious disinformation. They returned home, as one of them wrote later, convinced that "the Soviets were rapidly reaching the point where they could successfully challenge our technical superiority."

Zhukov was telling the truth. Soviet military units were to a large extent undermanned, badly trained and ill equipped—those menacing divisions in East Germany had only enough ammunition for a few days of fighting. An exhaustive 1968 study by the Systems Analysis Office concluded that the two sides in Europe were actually equal in numbers. But since this dose of reality ran counter to the official story, it had no effect on military planning, and certainly none on defense spending.

The "missile gap," conceived by the Air Force and heavily promoted by John F. Kennedy as he ran for the White House in 1960, stands out as a preeminent example of Cold War threat inflation. Kennedy, briefed by the CIA on President Eisenhower's orders, knew perfectly well that no such gap existed—except in America's favor. He campaigned on the lie nonetheless, and once in office, he felt it necessary to spend billions of dollars on 1,000 Minuteman ICBMs. (In accord with Selin's maxim, a large percentage of the missiles were inoperable thanks to a faulty guidance system.)

So it continued. Throughout the 1960s, '70s and '80s, the Soviet threat reliably prompted infusions of cash into the defense complex, to the gratification of its many functionaries, not least the congressmen and senators who were amply rewarded for their role in lubricating the process. Meanwhile, the "American threat" was performing a similar role on the other side of the Iron Curtain, sustaining the Soviet military's grip on the commanding heights of a comparatively impoverished domestic economy. Thus, the Soviets eagerly matched the US missile buildup until they, too, had the ability to lay waste to the planet several times over.

Maintaining these huge forces on hair-trigger alert, ready to launch on a few minutes' notice, was an intricate business, requiring radar arrays, high-powered computers, and elaborate communication networks. Though profitable for participants, these systems had potentially catastrophic consequences. In November 1979, for example, Zbigniew Brzezinski, President Carter's national security adviser, was awoken at three in the morning with the news that the NORAD headquarters in Colorado had detected Russian nuclear missiles streaming toward the United States; they would begin detonating in a matter of minutes. A second call moments later confirmed the report. Brzezinski was on the point of calling Carter, who would have had three minutes to decide whether to precipitate an all-out nuclear war, when a third call announced it had all been a mistake. A NORAD computer had inexplicably started running a software program simulating a Russian attack. Another false alert occurred the following year, this one generated by a single malfunctioning computer chip. The Soviets, meanwhile, developed the Perimeter system, by which alerts of an incoming attack would *automatically* trigger a counterstrike.

A decade later, the end of the Cold War and the collapse of the Soviet Union appeared to consign the long-standing threat of nuclear annihilation to the ashcan of history. Europe was (almost) stripped of tactical nuclear weapons, and the United States and Russia agreed to reduce their strategic arsenals to 6,000 warheads on either side. American nuclear bombers (though not missiles) were taken off alert. Although the Russians had inherited the remains of the Soviet arsenal, they could not afford to maintain or update decaying systems. In the words of Bruce Blair, a leading authority on nuclear weaponry who once served as a Minuteman launch-control officer, our perennial opponent "effectively disarmed."

Unsurprisingly, there was much optimistic talk of a "peace dividend" for the American taxpayer. If the threat propelling all that spending over the years had disappeared, surely defense budgets could and should be slashed. Our fighting forces did indeed shrink—by 1997, half the Air Force's tactical fighter wings had been disbanded, while the Army had lost half its combat units, and the Navy more than a third of its ships. Overall military spending, on the other hand, remained extremely high. As Franklin "Chuck" Spinney, then an analyst at the Defense Department and long an acute observer of such trends, noted presciently in 1990: "The much smaller post–Cold War military will require a Cold War budget to keep it running." Spinney was overoptimistic: allowing for inflation, defense spending has never once fallen below the Cold War average.

This mismatch, astonishing to the uninitiated, was in fact a classic example of a hallowed Pentagon maneuver known as the "bow wave." When afflicted by rare but irksome intervals of budgetary hardship, the services launch research-and-development projects, initially modest in cost, that lock in commitments to massive spending down the road. A post-Vietnam downturn had spawned the B-2 bomber and the MX intercontinental missile. Now the post–Cold War drought incubated the F-22 and F-35 fighter programs, not to mention a fantasy-laden Army project, replete with computers and sensors, called Future Combat Systems. The cost of these projects would explode in later years, even when there were no tangible results. The F-22 was canceled early in its planned production run, while the Army project never got off the drawing board. The F-35 program staggers on, with an ultimate budget now projected at $1.5 *trillion*.

All this was achieved without much sign of a viable enemy, despite hopeful invocations of the Chinese military as a potential "peer competitor." In any case, steps were being taken to remedy that deficiency. The United States casually violated promises made in the Soviet Union's dying days not to expand NATO into Eastern Europe—an initiative prompted and certainly exploited by US arms manufacturers smarting from the outbreak of peace and in need of fresh markets. A possible downside to this trend surfaced in 2008, when Georgian president Mikheil Saakashvili, an enthusiastic petitioner for NATO membership, provoked hostilities with Russia in expectation, reportedly encouraged by Vice President Cheney, of US military support. "Misha was trying to flip us into a war with Russia," Bruce P. Jackson, a former Lockheed Martin vice president who had been key to the NATO expansion effort, recently explained to me. President Bush proved reluctant to blow up the world on behalf of his erstwhile protégé, and Saakashvili was left to his fate.

Initially, the Obama Administration appeared disposed to warmer relations with Moscow. Secretary of State Hillary Clinton presented her Russian counterpart with a "reset" button. According to Vali Nasr, a former State Department official, the new direction was largely prompted by a desire to gain Russian cooperation for tougher sanctions against Iran. In pursuit of this goal, Nasr later wrote,

> Obama stopped talking about democracy and human rights in Russia . . . abandoned any thought of expanding NATO farther eastward, [and] washed his hands of the missile defense shield that had been planned for Europe.

These amicable gestures also extended to a 2010 nuclear-arms-control agreement. New START, as it was called, cut the number of strategic nuclear-missile launchers deployed by either side and limited the number of warheads to 1,550. Commendable as this might seem, there was less to the agreement than met the eye. The treaty reduced the number of deployed Minuteman ICBMs from

450 to 400, along with the same quantity of deployed warheads. Yet this slimmed-down complement of missiles, constituting only part of our nuclear arsenal, still represents 8,000 times the explosive force meted out at Hiroshima. The fifty missiles taken out of service were by no means destroyed, merely stored away against the day when they might be needed, in which case they could be reloaded in their old silos—which would be kept "warm," ready for reuse.

In fact, this modest effort at trimming the nuclear arsenal came at a high price, which we will be paying for many years to come. As the administration struggled to gain ratification for the treaty, key Republicans, led by Senator Jon Kyl of Arizona, demanded a commitment to the "modernization" of our nuclear forces. This clashed somewhat with Obama's 2009 pledge to take "concrete steps toward a world without nuclear weapons." Nonetheless, he caved and accepted the trade-off. Though the president protested that he was merely taking steps to maintain and secure the existing nuclear arsenal, modernization turned out to mean the wholesale replacement of almost every component of the force with new weapons, and at vast cost.

The Navy has therefore been promised a fleet of twelve ballistic-missile-launching nuclear submarines, loaded with newly developed missiles, at an estimated price of $100 billion. The Air Force will acquire 642 new ICBMs at a supposed cost of $85 billion (a price tag that will, like that of the naval program, inevitably increase). In addition, the Air Force is getting a long-range nuclear bomber, the cost of which it has brazenly classified with the excuse that such details would reveal technical secrets to the enemy. The shopping list also includes several nuclear warheads that are essentially new designs. Meanwhile, command-and-control systems are being developed for an array of satellites (costing up to $1 billion each), whose purpose is to make the business of fighting a nuclear war more manageable.

Those new warheads have allowed the nation's nuclear laboratories (better described as nuclear weapons factories) to elbow their way to the trough. Thus the Los Alamos lab in New Mexico plans to expand its facility for producing plutonium "pits"—the fissile core at the heart of a nuclear weapon. Instead of an annual total of ten such pits, Los Alamos now plans to manufacture eighty, at a cost of some $3 billion. This is despite the fact that the United States has roughly 15,000 pits in storage, most of which will be in working order for another century. In a fine example of the pervasive power of the military-industrial complex, Tom Udall of New Mexico, among the most liberal members of the Senate, has felt it necessary to support this inane scheme.

Reliable estimates indicate that "modernization" will ultimately deplete the public purse by $1 trillion. Justifying such spending might have been tough in the immediate aftermath of the Soviet collapse. But times have changed. "We are investing in the technologies that are most relevant to Russia's provocations," Brian McKeon, principal deputy undersecretary for policy at the Department of Defense, told Congress in December 2015. In other words, Moscow has resumed its customary role as budget prop and bogeyman—and one with a modernization plan of its own.

On the face of it, the Russians have plenty to modernize. American bomber pilots "need around 200 hours of flight training a year in order to remain proficient in everything from takeoff to landing to flying the plane," Bruce Blair told me. "Back in the '90s, all the Russian pilots were receiving just ten hours of flight training per year. The last time I checked, they were up to eighty or ninety hours." Blair also cited the Russian deployment of mobile early-warning radars around the borders to compensate for the "drastic decline of their missile-attack early-warning system over the past two decades. They have not yet managed to put up a satellite network."

True, the Russians have been digging underground bunkers for their military and civilian leadership, including one to house the general staff at their wartime headquarters south of Moscow. They are developing a big intercontinental ballistic missile, the RS-28 Sarmat, and another missile, the Bulava, for a new class of submarine. They are also reported to be designing a nuclear-armed underwater drone, allegedly capable of zipping across the ocean and exploding in an American harbor. One might even argue, as Blair does, that the "operational posture" of the Russian military, which essentially collapsed after 1989, has "been fixed, more or less."

A Russian military "more or less" back in working order doesn't sound much like an existential threat, nor like one in any shape to "erode the principled international order." That has not deterred our military leadership from scaremongering rhetoric, as typified by Philip Breedlove, who stepped down as NATO's commander in May. Breedlove spent much of his three-year tenure issuing volleys of alarmist pronouncements. On various occasions throughout the Ukrainian conflict, he reported that 40,000 Russian troops were on that nation's border, poised to invade; that regular Russian army units were operating inside Ukraine; that international observers were reporting columns of Russian troops and heavy weapons entering Ukraine. These claims proved to be exaggerated or completely false. Yet Breedlove continued to hit the panic button. "What is clear," he told Washington reporters in February 2015, "is that right now, it is not getting better. It is getting worse every day."

In reality, the fighting had almost completely died down at that point. There was still no sign of the armored Russian invaders Breedlove had unblushingly described. This in no way fazed the general, whose off-duty relaxation runs to leather-clad biker jaunts. His private emails, a portion of which were pilfered and released by a hacker organization called DC Leaks (rapidly and inevitably billed as a Kremlin tool), revealed him to be irritated by Obama's dovishness and eager to pressure the White House for a change of policy. "I think POTUS sees us as a threat that must be minimized," he complained to a Washington friend in a 2014 email.

Breedlove's largely spurious claims, which were echoed by the US Army commander in Europe, Lt. Gen. Ben Hodges, reportedly caused considerable agitation in Berlin, where officials let it be known that they considered such assertions "dangerous propaganda" without any foundation in fact. *Der Spiegel*, citing sources in Washington, insisted that such statements were by no means off the cuff, but had clearance from the Pentagon and White House. The aim, according to William Drozdiak, a senior fellow at the Brookings Institution's Center on the United States and Europe, was to "goad the Europeans into jacking up defense spending"—and the campaign seems to have worked. Several NATO members, including Germany, have now begun raising their defense spending to the levels demanded by the United States.

Russian actions, when interpreted as threateningly aggressive, have been a boon to the defense establishment. But talking up Russian *capabilities* is no less important for nurturing defense budgets in the long term—in case the Kremlin's foreign policy should take on an inconveniently peaceful turn. So, just as those US generals returned home from a desolate Russia in the mid-1950s convinced that Soviet weapons makers were about to challenge American technical superiority, Russian weapons are today receiving glowing reviews from US military leaders.

Last June, for example, Vice Adm. James Foggo, commander of the Sixth Fleet, told the *National Interest* that the Russians had upped their game on submarine warfare. He singled out for praise the *Severodvinsk*, a 13,800-ton behemoth. Foggo also noted that the Russians were "building a number of stealthy hybrid diesel-electric submarines and deploying them around the theater." In the same article, Alarik Fritz, a senior official with the Center for Naval Analyses and an adviser to Foggo, described these hybrid vessels as some of the most dangerous threats faced by the US Navy: "They're a concern for us and they're highly capable—and they're a very agile tool of the Russian military."

A closer look reveals something less impressive. The sinister-sounding description "hybrid diesel-electric" refers to a submarine equipped with a small nuclear reactor that is used to power up the electric batteries that drive the boat while it is underwater. (On the surface, it relies on diesel power.) Despite the admiral's casual reference to "a number" of such boats, the Russians have built just one, the *Sarov*. It was laid down in 1988 and entered service in 2008, after which they apparently decided to build no more. In any case, the design concept sounds strange— as the batteries need topping up, the reactor, described by engineers as a "nuclear teakettle," is switched on and off. This would be a cumbersome and noisy process, the opposite of stealthy. In any event, there is little sign of a surge in Russian submarine building, which seems to be proceeding very, very slowly. The dreaded *Severodvinsk*, laid down in 1993, took twenty-one years to be built and enter active service. The *Sarov*, that "very agile tool" of the Evil Empire, took twenty years.

Similar distortion proliferates in depictions of the Russian and, for that matter, the Chinese air force. (China has yet to be raised to "existential" threat status—maybe because we owe them so much money.) *Air Superiority 2030 Flight Plan*, published by the USAF this year, asserts that the service's "projected force structure in 2030 is not capable of fighting and winning against [the expected] array of potential adversary capabilities." Unsurprisingly, this gloomy forecast is followed by an urgent plea for more money. In contrast, Pierre Sprey, who may certainly be considered an authority on fighter design, observes that even the latest Russian fighters are "huge, awfully short-ranged and relatively unmaneuverable, except at low speeds—which is good for air shows and nothing else. Their 'latest' models are basically the same old machines, such as the MiG-29, which has been around for years, with a few trendy add-ons. But they've realized that you can sell more airplanes abroad if you change the number, so the MiG-29 has become the MiG-35, and so on."

Needless to say, Russia's land forces are being accorded a status no less ominous than its subs and planes. "The performance of Russian artillery in Ukraine," according to Robert Scales, a retired Army general who is esteemed by many of his peers as a military intellectual, "strongly demonstrates that, over the past two decades, the Russians have gotten a technological jump on us." The Russians' T-14 Armata tank is similarly hailed in the defense press as a "source of major concern for Western armies."

In one sense, the new Red Scare has had the desired and entirely predictable result. Defense spending, though hurt by troop wind-downs in Iraq and Afghanistan, is now exhibiting renewed vigor. Introducing its upcoming $583 billion budget in 2016, the Pentagon specifically cited "Russian aggression" as a rationale for spending. NATO allies have meanwhile pledged to increase their defense spending to 2 percent of GDP.

Yet despite all the rhetoric, practical responses to the "existential threat" have been curiously modest. Even with 480,000 troops, the US Army generates surprisingly little fighting power. According to its chief of staff, this force is hard pressed to field more than a third of its "ready" 4,500-man brigades, overwhelmingly light infantry, that can deploy and fight in less than a month. "These are paltry numbers for a force that approaches nearly a half-million," Douglas Macgregor, a former colonel and pungent commentator on defense topics, wrote me recently. To achieve "this stellar result," added Macgregor, the US Army has eleven four-star generals scattered throughout the world.

A loudly proclaimed plan to bolster NATO's eastern defenses against those aggressive Russians has turned out to mean sending a battalion—700 troops!—to Poland and each of the allegedly threatened Baltic republics. In addition, the United States will rotate one armored brigade into and out of Eastern Europe. Aerial reinforcements to the Baltics have been similarly miserly: small contingents of fighters deployed for limited periods before returning home.

It is not as if the military lacks sufficient cash. The Army budget alone, some $150 billion, is more than twice Russia's spending for the entire armed forces. The ratios for the other services are similarly unbalanced. The answer would seem to lie in the military's priorities, thanks to which actual defense needs take second place to more urgent concerns, such as the perennial interservice battle for budget share, as well as the care and feeding of defense contractors (who will doubtless employ all those four-star generals once they retire).

This approach, of course, generates a staggering amount of waste. Many of the headline scandals, such as the $200 million F-35 fighter that could not fly within twenty-five miles of a thunderstorm, have become notorious—but the list is long. The Army in particular has spawned an impressive list of procurement projects, including helicopters, radios and armored troop carriers, that have come to nothing. The Future Combat Systems referred to above is said to have been launched by Gen. Eric Shinseki, the Army chief of staff, as a kind of pre-emptive strike on the taxpayer's wallet. "If I don't buy something new," he reportedly declared, "no one on the Hill will believe that the US Army is changing." The project ultimately absorbed $20 billion with nothing whatsoever to show for it.

There would seem to be one major difference between the fine art of threat inflation as practiced during the Cold War and the current approach. In the old days, taxpayers at least got quite a lot for their money, albeit at inflated prices: the 900 ships, the 15,000 planes and so forth. Things are different today. The so-called global war on terror, though costing more than any American conflict apart from World War II, has been a comparatively lackadaisical affair. Iraq at its height absorbed one fifth the number of troops sent to Vietnam, while Air Force sorties ran at one eighth the earlier level. Though the weapons cost more and more, we produce fewer and fewer of them. For example, the Air Force originally told us they were buying 749 F-22 fighters at a cost of $35 million each. They ended up with 187 planes at $412 million apiece. The trend persists across the services—and sometimes, as in the case of the Army's Future Combat Systems, no weapons are produced at all.

This may be of comfort to those who worry at the prospect of war. Yet the threat inflation that keeps the wheels turning can carry us toward catastrophe. Among the token vessels deployed to reassure Eastern European NATO countries have been one or two Aegis Destroyers, sent to patrol the Baltic and Black Seas.

The missiles they carry are for air defense. Yet the launchers can just as easily carry nuclear or conventional cruise missiles, without any observer being able to tell the difference.

Bruce Blair, who spent years deep underground waiting to launch nuclear missiles and now works to abolish them, foresees frightening consequences. As he told me: "Those destroyers could launch quite a few Tomahawk cruise missiles that can reach all the way to Moscow. You could lay down a pretty severe attack on Russian command-and-control from just a couple of destroyers." This, he explained, is why the Russians have been aggressively shadowing the ships and buzzing them with fighter planes at very close quarters.

"Now the Russians are putting in a group of attack submarines in order to neutralize those destroyers," Blair continued. "And we're putting in a group of P-8 antisubmarine airplanes in the area in order to neutralize the submarines." Quite apart from the destroyers, he continued, "are the B-2 and B-52 missions we fly over the Poles, which looks like we're practicing a strategic attack. We fly them into Europe as shows of reassurance. We're in a low-grade nuclear escalation that's not even necessarily apparent to ourselves." Excepting a few scattered individuals in intelligence and the State Department, he continued, "so few people are aware of what we're getting into with the Russians." Nobody is paying attention on the National Security Council, Blair said, and he added, "No one at Defense."

Trump was never forgiven for his heretical statements about the desirability of friendly relations with Russia, despite the resolutely anti-Russian initiatives pursued by his administration. Russian intelligence authorship of the Democratic Party hack was soon accepted as holy writ by journalists and politicians. No one ever explained why Russian cyber-agents would go to such lengths to leave evidence implicating themselves. Vladimir Fomenko, never contacted by the FBI, is still waiting for his $290.

PART III
War on Terror

9

A Special Relationship

January 2016

A terrorist bomb in Kabul blows apart a number of civilians. When a dedicated US foreign service officer reports the event, he is reprimanded. The bomber, it turns out, is on the CIA payroll— a typical episode in a never-ending story. The embrace and support of militant Islamic fundamentalism has long been the dirtiest open secret of US foreign policy, never entirely concealed but continually obscured by half-truths and outright lies. Meanwhile, the strategy of mixing Islam with politics in pursuit of a "much more potent explosive brew," in the words of one cold-hearted protagonist, has left bloody disaster in its wake.

One morning early in 1988, Ed McWilliams, a Foreign Service officer posted to the United States Embassy in Kabul, heard the thump of a massive explosion from somewhere on the other side of the city. It was more than eight years after the Russian invasion of Afghanistan, and the embassy was a tiny enclave with only a handful of diplomats. McWilliams, a former Army intelligence operative, had made it his business to venture as much as possible into the Soviet-occupied capital. Now he set out to see what had happened.

It was obviously something big: although the explosion had taken place on the other side of Sher Darwaza, a mountain in the center of Kabul, McWilliams had heard it clearly. After negotiating a maze of narrow streets on the south side of the city, he found the site. A massive car bomb, designed to kill as many civilians as possible, had been detonated in a neighborhood full of Hazaras, a much-persecuted minority.

McWilliams took pictures of the devastation, then headed back to the embassy. But his prompt dispatch describing the outrage was received with extreme disfavor in Washington—not because someone had launched a terrorist attack against Afghan civilians, but because McWilliams had reported it. The bomb, it turned out, had been the work of Gulbuddin Hekmatyar, the mujahedeen commander who received more CIA money and support than any other leader of the Afghan rebellion. The attack, the first of many, was part of a CIA-blessed scheme to "put pressure" on the Soviet presence in Kabul. Informing the Washington bureaucracy that Hekmatyar's explosives were being deployed to kill civilians was therefore entirely unwelcome.

"Those were Gulbuddin's bombs," McWilliams, a Rhode Islander with a gift for laconic understatement, told me recently. "He was supposed to get the credit for this." In the meantime, the former diplomat recalled, the CIA pressured him to "report a little less specifically about the humanitarian consequences of those vehicle bombs."

I tracked down McWilliams, now retired to the remote mountains of southern New Mexico, because the extremist Islamist groups currently operating in Syria and Iraq called to mind the extremist Islamist groups whom we lavishly supported in Afghanistan during the 1980s. Hekmatyar, with his documented fondness for throwing acid in women's faces, would have had nothing to learn from Al Qaeda. When a courageous ABC News team led by my wife, Leslie Cockburn, interviewed him in 1993, he had beheaded half a dozen people earlier that day. Later, he killed her translator.

In the wake of 9/11, the story of US support for militant Islamists against the Soviets became something of a touchy subject. Former CIA and intelligence officials like to suggest that the agency simply played the roles of financier and quartermaster.

In this version of events, the dirty work—the actual management of the campaign and the dealings with rebel groups—was left to Pakistan's Inter-Services Intelligence (ISI). It was Pakistan's fault that at least 70 percent of total US aid went to the fundamentalists, even if the CIA demanded audited accounts on a regular basis.

The beneficiaries, however, have not always been content to play along with the official story. Asked by the ABC News team whether he remembered Charlie Wilson, the Texas congressman later immortalized in print and onscreen as the patron saint of the mujahedeen, Hekmatyar fondly recalled that "he was a good friend. He was all the time supporting our jihad." Others expressed the same point in a different way. Abdul Haq, a mujahedeen commander who might today be described as a "moderate rebel," complained loudly during and after the Soviet war in Afghanistan about American policy. The CIA "would come with a big load of ammunition and money and supplies to these [fundamentalist] groups. We would tell them: 'What the hell is going on? You are creating a monster in this country.'"

American veterans of the operation, at the time the largest in CIA history, have mostly stuck to the mantra that it was a Pakistani show. Only occasionally have officials let slip that the support for fundamentalists was a matter of cold-blooded calculation. Robert Oakley, a leading player in the Afghan effort as ambassador to Pakistan from 1988 to 1991, later remarked, "If you mix Islam with politics, you have a much more potent explosive brew, and that was quite successful in getting the Soviets out of Afghanistan."

In fact, the CIA had been backing Afghan Islamists well before the Russians invaded the country in December 1979. Zbigniew Brzezinski, Jimmy Carter's national security adviser, later boasted to *Le Nouvel Observateur* that the president had "signed the first directive for secret aid to the opponents of the pro-Soviet regime in Kabul" six months *prior* to the invasion. "And that very day," Brzezinski recalled, "I wrote a note to the president in which I explained to him that in my opinion this aid was going to induce a Soviet military intervention." The war that inevitably followed killed a million Afghans.

Other presumptions proved to be less accurate, including a misplaced faith in the martial prowess of our fundamentalist clients. As it turned out, the Islamists were not really the ferocious anti-Soviet warriors their backers claimed them to be. McWilliams, who left Kabul in 1988 to become special envoy to the Afghan rebels, recalled that Hekmatyar was more interested in using his US-supplied arsenal on rival warlords. (On occasion, he tortured them as well—another fact the envoy was "discouraged" from reporting.) "Hekmatyar was a great fighter," McWilliams remembered, "but not necessarily with the Soviets."

Even after the Russians left, in February 1989, the agency's favorite Afghan showed himself incapable of toppling the Soviet-supported regime of Mohammad Najibullah. Hekmatyar's attack on the key city of Jalalabad, for example, was an embarrassing failure. "Oakley bragged in the weeks leading up to this offensive [that] it was going to be a great success," said McWilliams, who had passed on warnings from Abdul Haq and others that the plan was foolhardy, only to be told, "We got this locked up." To his disgust, the Pakistani and American intelligence officials overseeing the operation swelled its ranks with youthful cannon fodder. "What they wound up doing was emptying the refugee camps," McWilliams told me. "It was a last-ditch effort to throw these sixteen-year-old boys into the fight in order to keep this thing going. It did not work." Thousands died.

Anxious as they might have been to obscure the true nature of their relationship with unappealing Afghans like Hekmatyar, US officials were even more careful when it came to the Arab fundamentalists who flocked to the war in Afghanistan and later embarked on global jihad as Al Qaeda. No one could deny that they had been there, but their possible connection to the CIA became an increasingly delicate subject as Al Qaeda made its presence felt in the 1990s. The official line—that the United States had kept its distance from the Arab mujahedeen—was best expressed by Robert Gates, who became director of the CIA in 1991. When the agency first learned of the jihadi recruits pouring into Afghanistan from across the Arab world, he later wrote, "We examined ways to increase their participation, perhaps in the form of some sort of 'international brigade,' but nothing came of it."

The reality was otherwise. The United States was intimately involved in the enlistment of these volunteers—indeed, many of them were signed up through a network of recruiting offices in the United States. The guiding light in this effort was a charismatic Palestinian cleric, Abdullah Azzam, who founded Maktab al-Khidamat (MAK), also known as the Afghan Services Bureau, in 1984, to raise money and recruits for jihad. He was assisted by a wealthy young Saudi, Osama bin Laden. The headquarters for the US arm of the operation was in Brooklyn, at the Al-Kifah Refugee Center on Atlantic Avenue, which Azzam invariably visited when touring mosques and universities across the country.

"You have to put it in context," argued Ali Soufan, a former FBI agent and counterterrorism expert who has done much to expose the CIA's post–9/11 torture program. "Throughout most of the 1980s, the jihad in Afghanistan was something supported by this country. The recruitment among Muslims here in America was in the open. Azzam officially visited the United States, and he went from mosque to mosque—they recruited many people to fight in Afghanistan under that banner."

American involvement with Azzam's organization went well beyond laissez-faire indulgence. "We encouraged the recruitment of not only Saudis but Palestinians and Lebanese and a great variety of combatants, who would basically go to Afghanistan to perform jihad," McWilliams insisted. "This was part of the CIA plan. This was part of the game."

The Saudis, of course, had been an integral part of the anti-Soviet campaign from the beginning. According to one former CIA official closely involved in the Afghanistan operation, Saudi Arabia supplied 40 percent of the budget for the rebels. The official said that William Casey, who ran the CIA under Ronald Reagan, "would fly to Riyadh every year for what he called his 'annual hajj' to ask for the money. Eventually, after a lot of talk, the king would say OK, but then we would have to sit and listen politely to all their incredibly stupid ideas about how to fight the war."

Despite such comments, it would seem that the US and Saudi strategies did not differ all that much, especially when it came to routing money to the most extreme fundamentalist factions. Fighting the Soviets was only part of the ultimate goal. The Egyptian preacher Abu Hamza, now serving a life sentence in a federal prison in Colorado on terrorism charges, visited Saudi Arabia in 1986, and later recalled the constant public injunctions to join the jihad: "You have to go, you have to join, leave your schools, leave your family." The whole Afghanistan enterprise, he explained, "was meant to actually divert people from the problems in their own country." It was "like a pressure-cooker vent. If you keep [the cooker] all sealed up, it will blow up in your face, so you have to design a vent, and this Afghan jihad was the vent."

Soufan agreed with this analysis. "I think it's not fair to only blame the CIA," he told me. "Egypt was happy to get rid of a lot of these guys and have them go to Afghanistan. Saudi Arabia was very happy to do that, too." As he pointed out, Islamic fundamentalists were already striking these regimes at home: in November 1979, for example, Wahhabi extremists had stormed the Grand Mosque in Mecca. The subsequent siege left hundreds dead.

Within a few short years, however, the sponsoring governments began to recognize a flaw in the scheme: the vent was two-way. I heard this point most vividly expressed in 1994, at a dinner party on a yacht cruising down the Nile. The wealthy host had deemed it safer to be waterborne owing to a vigorous terror campaign by Egyptian jihadists. At the party, this defensive tactic elicited a vehement comment from Osama El-Baz, a senior security adviser to Hosni Mubarak. "It's all the fault of those stupid bastards at the CIA," he said, as the lights of Cairo drifted by. "They trained these people, kept them in being after the Russians left, and now we get this."

According to El-Baz, MAK had been maintained after the Afghan conflict for future deployment against Iran. Its funding, he insisted, came from the Saudis and the CIA. A portion of that money had been parked at the Al-Kifah office in Brooklyn, under the supervision of one of Azzam's acolytes—until the custodian was himself murdered, possibly by adherents of a rival jihadi. (Soufan confirmed the murder story, stating that the sum in question was about $100,000.)*

A year before my conversation with El-Baz, in fact, the United States had already been confronted with the two-way vent. In 1993, a bomb in the basement of one of the World Trade Center towers killed six people. (The bombers had hoped to bring down both structures and kill many thousands.) A leading member of the plot was Mahmud Abouhalima, an Afghanistan veteran who had worked for years at the recruiting center in Brooklyn. Another of Azzam's disciples, however, proved to be a much bigger problem: Osama bin Laden, who now commanded the loyalty of the Arab mujahedeen recruited by his mentor. In 1996, the CIA set up a special unit to track down bin Laden, led by the counterterrorism expert Michael Scheuer. Now settled in Afghanistan, the Al Qaeda chief had at least theoretically fallen out with the Saudi regime that once supported him and other anti-Soviet jihadis. Nevertheless, bin Laden seemed to have maintained links with his homeland—and some in the CIA were sensitive to that fact. When I interviewed Scheuer in 2014 for my book *Kill Chain*, he told me that one of his first requests to the Saudis was for routine information about his quarry: birth certificate, financial records and so forth. There was no response. Repeated requests produced nothing. Ultimately, a message arrived from the CIA station chief in Riyadh, John Brennan, who ordered the requests to stop—they were "upsetting the Saudis."

Five years later, Al Qaeda, employing a largely Saudi suicide squad, destroyed the World Trade Center. In a sane world, this disaster might have permanently ended Washington's long-standing taste for mixing Islam with politics. But old habits die hard.

---

* Azzam was assassinated in 1989 in Peshawar, Pakistan, by a sophisticated car bomb. Though there was a wide range of credible suspects, his widow was convinced that the CIA had commissioned the killing.

In the spring and summer of last year, a coalition of Syrian rebel groups calling itself Jaish al-Fatah—the Army of Conquest—swept through the northwestern province of Idlib, posing a serious threat to the Assad regime. Leading the charge was Al Qaeda's Syrian branch, known locally as Jabhat al-Nusra (the Nusra Front). The other major component of the coalition was Ahrar al-Sham, a group that had formed early in the anti-Assad uprising and looked for inspiration to none other than Abdullah Azzam. Following the victory, Nusra massacred twenty members of the Druze faith, considered heretical by fundamentalists, and forced the remaining Druze to convert to Sunni Islam. (The Christian population of the area had wisely fled.) Ahrar al-Sham meanwhile posted videos of the public floggings it administered to those caught skipping Friday prayers.

This potent alliance of jihadi militias had been formed under the auspices of the rebellion's major backers: Saudi Arabia, Turkey and Qatar. But it also enjoyed the endorsement of two other major players. At the beginning of the year, Al Qaeda leader Ayman al-Zawahiri had ordered his followers to cooperate with other groups. In March, according to several sources, a US–Turkish–Saudi "coordination room" in southern Turkey had also ordered the rebel groups it was supplying to cooperate with Jaish al-Fatah. The groups, in other words, would be embedded within the Al Qaeda coalition.

A few months before the Idlib offensive, a member of one CIA-backed group had explained the true nature of its relationship to the Al Qaeda franchise. Nusra, he told the *New York Times*, allowed militias vetted by the United States to appear independent, so that they would continue to receive American supplies. When I asked a former White House official involved in Syria policy if this was not a de facto alliance, he put it this way: "I would not say that Al Qaeda is our ally, but a turnover of weapons is probably unavoidable. I'm fatalistic about that. It's going to happen."

Earlier in the Syrian war, US officials had at least maintained the pretense that weapons were being funneled only to so-called moderate opposition groups. But in 2014, in a speech at Harvard, Vice President Joe Biden confirmed that we were arming extremists once again, although he was careful to pin the blame on America's allies in the region, whom he denounced as "our largest problem in Syria." In response to a student's question, he volunteered that our allies

> were so determined to take down Assad and essentially have a proxy Sunni–Shia war, what did they do? They poured hundreds of millions of dollars and tens, *thousands* of tons of weapons into anyone who would fight against Assad. Except that the people who were being supplied were al-Nusra and Al Qaeda and the extremist elements of jihadis coming from other parts of the world.

Biden's explanation was entirely reminiscent of official excuses for the arming of fundamentalists in Afghanistan during the 1980s, which maintained that the Pakistanis had total control of the distribution of US-supplied weapons and that the CIA was incapable of intervening when most of those weapons ended up with the likes of Gulbuddin Hekmatyar. Asked why the United States of America was supposedly powerless to stop nations like Qatar, population 2.19 million, from pouring arms into the arsenals of Nusra and similar groups, a former adviser to one of the Gulf States replied softly: "They didn't want to."

The Syrian war, which has to date killed upward of 200,000 people, grew out of peaceful protests in March 2011, a time when similar movements were sweeping other Arab countries. For the Obama Administration, the tumultuous upsurge was welcome. It appeared to represent the final defeat of Al Qaeda and radical jihadism, a view duly reflected in a *New York Times* headline from that February: AS REGIMES FALL IN ARAB WORLD, AL QAEDA SEES HISTORY FLY BY. The president viewed the killing of Osama bin Laden in May 2011 as his crowning victory. Peter Bergen, CNN's terrorism pundit, concurred, certifying the Arab Spring and the death of bin Laden as the "final bookends" of the global war on terror.

Al Qaeda, on the other hand, had a different interpretation of the Arab Spring, hailing it as entirely positive for the jihadist cause. Far from obsessing about his own safety, as Obama had suggested, Zawahiri was brimful of optimism. The "tyrants" supported by the United States, he crowed from his unknown headquarters, were seeing their thrones crumble at the same time as "their master" was being defeated. "The Islamic project," declared Hamid bin Abdullah al-Ali, a Kuwait-based Al Qaeda fund-raiser, would be "the greatest beneficiary from the environment of freedom."

While the revolutions were ongoing, the Obama Administration settled on "moderate Islam" as the most suitable political option for the emerging Arab democracies—and concluded that the Muslim Brotherhood fitted the bill. This venerable Islamist organization had originally been fostered by the British as a means of countering leftist and nationalist movements in the empire. As British power waned, others, including the CIA and the Saudis, were happy to sponsor the group for the same purpose, unmindful of its long-term agenda. (The Saudis, however, always took care to prevent it from operating within their kingdom.)

The Brotherhood was in fact the ideological ancestor of the most violent Islamist movements of the modern era. Sayyid Qutb, the organization's moving spirit until he was hanged in Egypt in 1966, served as an inspiration to the young Zawahiri as he embarked on his career in terrorism. Extremists have followed Qutb's lead in calling for a resurrected caliphate across the Muslim world, along with a return to the premodern customs prescribed by the Prophet.

None of which stopped the Obama Administration from viewing the Brotherhood as a relatively benign purveyor of moderate Islam, not so different from the type on display in Turkey, where the Brotherhood-linked AKP party had presided over what seemed to be a flourishing democracy and a buoyant economy, even if the country's secular tradition was being rolled back. As Mubarak's autocracy crumbled in Egypt, American officials actively promoted the local Brotherhood; the US ambassador,

Anne Patterson, reportedly held regular meetings with the group's leadership. "The administration was motivated to show that the US would deal with Islamists," the former White House official told me, "even though the downside of the Brotherhood was pretty well understood."

At the same time that it was being cautiously courted by the United States, the Brotherhood enjoyed a firm bond with the stupendously rich ruling clique in Qatar. The tiny country was ever eager to assert its independence in a neighborhood dominated by Saudi Arabia and Iran. While hosting the American military at the vast Al Udeid Air Base outside Doha, the Qataris put decisive financial weight behind what they viewed as the coming force in Arab politics. They were certain, the former White House official told me, "that the future really lay in the hands of the Islamists," and saw themselves "on the right side of history."

The Syrian opposition seemed like an ideal candidate for such assistance, especially since Assad had been in the US crosshairs for some time. (The country's first and only democratically elected government was overthrown by a CIA-instigated coup in 1949 at the behest of American oil interests irked at Syria's request for better terms on a pipeline deal.) In December 2006, William Roebuck, the political counselor at the American Embassy in Damascus, sent a classified cable to Washington, later released by WikiLeaks, proposing "actions, statements and signals" that could help destabilize Assad's regime. Among other recommended initiatives was a campaign, coordinated with the Egyptian and Saudi governments, to pump up existing alarm among Syrian Sunnis about Iranian influence in the country.

Roebuck could count on a receptive audience. A month earlier, Condoleezza Rice, the secretary of state, testified on Capitol Hill that there was a "new strategic alignment" in the Middle East, separating "extremists" (Iran and Syria) and "reformers" (Saudi Arabia and other Sunni states). Undergirding these diplomatic euphemisms was something more fundamental. Prince Bandar bin Sultan, who returned to Riyadh in 2005 after many years as

Saudi ambassador in Washington, had put it bluntly in an earlier conversation with Richard Dearlove, the longtime head of Britain's MI6. "The time is not far off in the Middle East," Bandar said, "when it will be literally *God help the Shia*. More than a billion Sunnis have simply had enough." The implications were clear. Bandar was talking about destroying the Shiite states of Iran and Iraq, as well as the Alawite (which is to say, Shia-derived) leadership in Syria.

Yet the Saudi rulers were acutely aware of their exposure to reverse-vent syndrome. Their corruption and other irreligious practices repelled the jihadis, who had more than once declared their eagerness to clean house back home. Such fears were obvious to Dearlove when he visited Riyadh with Tony Blair soon after 9/11. As he later recalled, the head of Saudi intelligence shouted at him that the recent attacks in Manhattan and Washington were a "mere pinprick" compared with the havoc the extremists planned to unleash in their own region: "What these terrorists want is to destroy the House of Saud and to remake the Middle East!"

From these statements, Dearlove discerned two powerful (and complementary) impulses in the thinking of the Saudi leadership. First, there could be "no legitimate or admissible challenge to the Islamic purity of their Wahhabi credentials as guardians of Islam's holiest shrines." (Their record on head-chopping and the oppression of women was, after all, second to none.) In addition, they were "deeply attracted toward any militancy which can effectively challenge Shia-dom." Responding to both impulses, Saudi Arabia would reopen the vent. This time, however, the jihad would no longer be against godless Communists but against fellow Muslims, in Syria.

By the beginning of 2012, Saudi Arabia, Qatar, Turkey and the United States were all heavily involved in supporting the armed rebellion against Assad. In theory, American support for the Free Syrian Army was limited to "nonlethal supplies" from both the State Department and the CIA. Qatar, which had successfully packed the opposition Syrian National Council with members of the Muslim Brotherhood, operated under no such restrictions. A stream of loaded Qatari transport planes took off from Al Udeid and headed to Turkey, whence their lethal cargo was moved into Syria.

"The Qataris were not at all discriminating in who they gave arms to," the former White House official told me. "They were just dumping stuff to lucky recipients." Chief among the lucky ones were Nusra and Ahrar al-Sham, both of which had benefited from a rebranding strategy instituted by Osama bin Laden. The year before he was killed, bin Laden had complained about the damage that offshoots such as Al Qaeda in Iraq, with its taste for beheadings and similar atrocities, had done to his organization's image. He directed his media staff to prepare a new strategy that would avoid "everything that would have a negative impact on the perception" of Al Qaeda. Among the rebranding proposals discussed at his Abbottabad compound was the simple expedient of changing the organization's name. This strategy was gradually implemented for the group's newer offshoots, allowing Nusra and Ahrar al-Sham to present themselves to the credulous as kinder, gentler Islamists.

The rebranding program was paradoxically assisted by the rise of the Islamic State, a group that had split off from the Al Qaeda organization partly in disagreement over the image-softening exercise enjoined by Zawahiri. Although the Islamic State attracted many defectors and gained territory at the expense of its former Nusra partners, its assiduously cultivated reputation for extreme cruelty made the other groups look humane by comparison. (According to Daveed Gartenstein-Ross, a senior fellow with the Foundation for Defense of Democracies, many Nusra members suspect that the Islamic State was created by the Americans "to discredit jihad.")

Saudi Arabia, meanwhile, driven principally by its virulent enmity toward Iran, Assad's main supporter, was eager to throw its weight behind the anti-Assad crusade. By December 2012, the CIA was arranging for large quantities of weapons, paid for by the Saudis, to move from Croatia to Jordan to Syria.

"The Saudis preferred to work through us," explained the former White House official. "They didn't have an autonomous capability to find weapons. We were the intermediaries, with some control over the distribution. There was an implicit illusion on the part of the US that Saudi weapons were going to groups with some potential for a pro-Western attitude." This was a curious illusion to entertain, given Saudi Arabia's grim culture of Wahhabi austerity as well as Secretary of State Hillary Clinton's flat declaration, in a classified cable from 2009, that "donors in Saudi Arabia constitute the most significant source of funding to Sunni terrorist groups worldwide."

Some in intelligence circles suspect that such funding is ongoing. "How much Saudi and Qatari money—and I'm not suggesting direct government funding, but I am suggesting maybe a blind eye being turned—is being channeled towards ISIS and reaching it?" Dearlove asked in July 2014. "For ISIS to be able to surge into the Sunni areas of Iraq in the way that it's done recently has to be the consequence of substantial and sustained funding. Such things simply do not happen spontaneously." Those on the receiving end of Islamic State attacks tend to agree. Asked what could be done to help Iraq following the group's lightning assaults in the summer of 2014, an Iraqi diplomat replied: "Bomb Saudi Arabia."

However the money was flowing, the Saudis certainly ended up crafting their own Islamist coalition. "The Saudis never armed al-Nusra," recalled the Gulf State adviser. "They made the calculation that there's going to be an appetite for Islamist-leaning militias. So they formed a rival umbrella army called Jaish al-Islam. That was the Saudi alternative—still Islamist, but not Muslim Brotherhood."

Given that Jaish al-Islam ultimately answered to Prince Bandar, who became the head of Saudi intelligence in 2012, there did not appear to be a lot of room for Western values in the group's agenda. Its leader, Zahran Alloush, was the son of a Syrian religious scholar. He talked dutifully about the merits of tolerance to Western reporters, but would revert to such politically incorrect themes as the mass expulsion of Alawites from Damascus when addressing his fellow jihadis. At the same time, Saudi youths have poured into Syria, ready to fight for any extremist group that would have them, even when those groups started fighting among themselves. Noting the huge numbers of young Saudis on the battle lines in Syria, a Saudi talk-show host lamented that "our children are fighting on both sides"—meaning Nusra and the Islamic State. "The Saudis," he exclaimed, "are killing one another!"

The determination of Turkey (a NATO ally) and Qatar (the host of the biggest American base in the Middle East) to support extreme jihadi groups became starkly evident in late 2013. On December 6, armed fighters from Ahrar al-Sham and other militias raided warehouses at Bab al-Hawa, on the Turkish border, and seized supplies belonging to the Free Syrian Army. As it happened, a meeting of an international coordination group on Syria, the so-called London Eleven, was scheduled for the following week. Delegates from the United States, Europe and the Middle East were bent on issuing a stern condemnation of the offending jihadi group.

The Turks and Qataris, however, adamantly refused to sign on. As one of the participants told me later, "All the countries in the room [understood] that Turkey's opposition to listing Ahrar al-Sham was because they were providing support to them." The Qatari representative insisted that it was counterproductive to condemn such groups as terrorist. If the other countries did so, he made clear, Qatar would stop cooperating on Syria. "Basically, they were saying that if you name terrorists, we're going to pick up our ball and go home," the source told me. The US delegate said that the Islamic Front, an umbrella organization, would be welcome at the negotiating table—but Ahrar al-Sham, which happened to be its leading member, would not. The diplomats mulled over their communiqué, traded concessions, adjusted language. The final version contained no condemnation, or even mention, of Ahrar al-Sham.

Two years later, Washington's capacity for denial in the face of inconvenient facts remains undiminished. Addressing the dominance of extremists in the Syrian opposition, Leon Panetta, a former CIA director, has blamed our earlier failure to arm those elusive moderates. The catastrophic consequences of this very approach in Libya are seldom mentioned. "If we had intervened more swiftly in Syria," Gartenstein-Ross says, "the best-case scenario probably would have been another Libya. Meaning that we would still be dealing with a collapsed state and spillover into other Middle Eastern states and Europe."

Even as we have continued our desultory bombing campaign against the Islamic State, Ahrar al-Sham and Nusra are creeping closer and closer to international respectability. A month after the London Eleven meeting, a group of scholars from the Brookings Institution published an op-ed making the case for Ahrar al-Sham: "Designating [the] group as a terrorist organization might back-fire by pushing it completely into Al Qaeda's camp." (The think tank's recent receipt of a multiyear, $15 million grant from Qatar was doubtless coincidental.)

Over the past year, other distinguished figures have voiced support for a closer relationship with Al Qaeda's rebranded extensions. David Petraeus, another former head of the CIA, has argued for arming at least the "more moderate" parts of Nusra. Robert Ford, a former ambassador to Syria and a vociferous supporter of the rebel cause, called on America to "open channels for dialogue" with Ahrar al-Sham, even if its members had on occasion slaughtered some Alawites and desecrated Christian sites. Even *Foreign Affairs*, an Establishment sounding board, has echoed these notions, suggesting that it was time for the United States to "rethink its policy toward al-Qaeda, particularly its targeting of Zawahiri."

"Let's be fair to the CIA," said Benazir Bhutto, the once and future prime minister of Pakistan, back in 1993, when the consequences of fostering jihad were already becoming painfully clear to its sponsors. "They never knew that these people that they were training to fight Soviets in Afghanistan were one day going to bite the hand that fed them."

Things are clearer on the ground. Not long ago, far away from the think tanks and briefing rooms where policies are formulated and spun, a small boy in the heart of Nusra territory was telling a filmmaker for Vice News about Osama bin Laden. "He terrified and fought the Americans," he said reverently. Beside him, his brother, an even smaller child, described his future: "To become a suicide fighter for the sake of God." A busload of older boys was asked which group they belonged to. "Al Qaeda, Al Qaeda," they responded cheerfully.

Although the CIA operation in aid of Jihadis in Syria, code-named "Timber Sycamore" with a lifetime budget exceeding $1 billion, was allegedly wound down in 2017, US policy objectives remained essentially unchanged. Despite Trump's rhetorical support for disengagement, US diplomats and military officials ignored his confused directives and extracted his agreement for continued US military occupation of Syrian oil fields. In addition, US officials put heavy pressure on the Syrian Kurds to ally with Islamist groups. Kurdish negotiators who refused were physically assaulted. Consistent with a theme expressed throughout this book, a US company financially linked to leading Republican politicians was awarded the exclusive rights to extract the (stolen) oil. Biden has stoutly maintained Trump's Syrian policy, in all its cruelty.

10

Acceptable Losses

September 2016

If the essential function of the US government is to buy arms at home and sell arms abroad, then war crimes must inevitably ensue. The Yemeni war proves the case.

Just a few short years ago, Yemen was judged to be among the poorest countries in the world, ranking 154th out of the 187 nations on the UN's Human Development Index. One in every five Yemenis went hungry. Almost one in three was unemployed. Every year, 40,000 children died before their fifth birthday, and experts predicted the country would soon run out of water.

Such was the dire condition of the country *before* Saudi Arabia unleashed a bombing campaign in March 2015, which has destroyed warehouses, factories, power plants, ports, hospitals, water tanks, gas stations and bridges, along with miscellaneous targets ranging from donkey carts to wedding parties to archaeological monuments. Thousands of civilians—no one knows how many—have been killed or wounded. Along with the bombing, the Saudis have enforced a blockade, cutting off supplies of food, fuel and medicine. A year and a half into the war, the health system has largely broken down, and much of the country is on the brink of starvation.

This rain of destruction was made possible by the material and moral support of the United States, which supplied most of the bombers, bombs and missiles required for the aerial onslaught. (Admittedly, the United Kingdom, France and other NATO arms exporters eagerly did their bit.) US Navy ships aided the blockade. But no one that I talked to in Washington suggested that the war was in any way necessary to our national security. The best answer I got came from Ted Lieu, a Democratic congressman from California who has been one of the few public officials to speak out about the devastation we were enabling far away. "Honestly," he told me, "I think it's because Saudi Arabia asked."

The principal targets of the Saudi bombers (augmented by a coalition of Arab allies) have been a tribal group from the north of Yemen, adjacent to the Saudi border, who follow Zaidism, an offshoot of Shia Islam. Though it is distinct from the variant of Shiism practiced in Iran, the connection was destined to excite the suspicions of the fervently anti-Iranian Saudi regime.

So, almost forty years ago, the Saudis planted an outpost of their own extreme Wahhabi sect in the heart of Zaidi territory. The emissary sent to found the madrassa was Muqbil al-Wadie, a leader of the 1979 assault on Mecca's Grand Mosque, who had until that moment been rotting in a Saudi prison. As has been their habit, the Saudis solved their own terrorism problem by exporting it.

The intrusive enterprise, which attracted a growing stream of militant Sunnis, eventually provoked a reaction among the local Zaidis in favor of their Shia tendencies. Accordingly, under the leadership of Hussein al-Houthi, they sought religious instruction from Iran in the form of teachers and literature, which were duly supplied, much to Riyadh's irritation.

For many years, this Iranian connection was treated with equanimity by Yemen's president, Ali Abdullah Saleh. Following 9/11, however, he came under pressure from Washington to play his part in the war against Al Qaeda, which had been active in Yemen since the late 1990s. Saleh found this mission unappealing, given the terrorist group's connections with some of the country's most powerful political forces. According to Abdul-Ghani al-Iryani, an activist whose family has long played a leading role in the nation's politics, Saleh suggested to the Americans that he first deal with the Shiite troublemakers in the north. "From day one," Iryani told me, "the Houthis were presented as an Iranian client, a terrorist movement." This policy, unsurprisingly, was greeted with favor in Riyadh, and reciprocated with commensurate financial largesse.

Privately, US officials were doubtful of the Iranian connection, even at the beginning of Saleh's campaign against the group in 2004. "The fact that after five years of conflict there is still no compelling evidence of that link must force us to view this claim with some skepticism," wrote the US ambassador to Yemen, Stephen Seche, in a classified 2009 cable later released by Wiki-Leaks. Nevertheless, the Americans were eager to secure Saleh's cooperation against Al Qaeda. They did little to restrain him in his war with the Houthis, as they came to be called following the death of Hussein al-Houthi in 2004.

In 2009, hoping for a final victory, Saleh managed to involve the Saudis directly by eliciting their permission to send Yemeni troops across the border to attack the Houthis from the rear. In response, a small force of Houthis invaded Saudi Arabia. Adding to the complications, Yemen now became embroiled in Saudi court politics: Khalid bin Sultan, the prince who effectively controlled the defense ministry, moved to assert dominance at the expense of a rival prince at the interior ministry, using the Houthi incursion as an excuse. Promptly declaring the southern portion of the country a "killing zone," he mobilized the entire Saudi military. The air force carpet bombed the border region, including Saada, the Houthi heartland.

The result, however, was a humiliating setback for the House of Saud. Their ground troops were bested by the Houthis and suffered numerous casualties. The aerial campaign was no more impressive. "It was not a moment of glory for the Saudi Air Force," according to David Des Roches, who formerly oversaw Saudi-related policy at the Pentagon and is now an associate professor at the National Defense University. "They were basically just dropping rounds in the desert." A senior UN diplomat put it to me more bluntly: "They lost."

Saleh's own offensive was equally ineffectual, and the Houthis were left to fight another day. Meanwhile, Yemen's ill fortune proved a blessing, not for the last time, for the US defense establishment. The Obama Administration was already bent on expanding arms sales as part of its drive to boost exports, and now manna fell from heaven. Shocked by their poor performance against the Houthi guerrillas, the Saudis embarked on a massive weapons-buying spree.

At the top of their shopping list were eighty-four specially modified Boeing F-15 jets, along with around 170 helicopters. They also purchased a huge quantity of bombs and missiles— notably, 1,300 cluster bombs sold by the Textron Corporation at a cost of $641 million. Fortunately for Textron, neither the United States nor Saudi Arabia had endorsed the Convention on Cluster Munitions, a 2008 treaty already signed by more than one hundred nations, which banned these weapons on the grounds that they caused "unacceptable harm" to civilians.

This enormous deal totaled $60 billion: the largest arms sale in US history. The scale of the transaction says much about America's relationship with the House of Saud. The bond was forged at a 1945 meeting between President Franklin Roosevelt and King Abdulaziz, with both parties agreeing that Saudi Arabia would guarantee the United States cheap oil in return for American military protection. Both sides largely kept to the bargain. The Saudis even subsidized the price of oil exported to the United States—at least until 2002, when they abandoned the policy out of irritation at George W. Bush's plan to topple the Sunni regime in Iraq.

America's adherence to its side of the deal is most concretely manifested in a housing compound a dozen or so miles outside Riyadh. Eskan Village is home to 2,000 Americans, military and civilian, dedicated to the security of the regime. For the US military, it is a gratifyingly lucrative arrangement. Some inhabitants of the compound supervise the arming and training of the Saudi National Guard—a mission that has so far generated $35 billion in US military sales. Others are attached to the US Military Training Mission to Saudi Arabia, which services the regular armed forces. According to its website, this group is charged with enhancing American national security "through building the capability and capacity of the Saudi Arabian Armed Forces"—a task that absolutely includes acting as an "advocate for US business to supply defense goods and services to the SAAF." In other words, the Saudis host a sales team dedicated to selling them weapons. Furthermore, they fund its upkeep, paying roughly $30 million a year for the privilege.

As Des Roches reminded me, the US government is the official vendor for weapons sales on behalf of corporations such as Boeing and Textron, levying a surcharge of 7 percent for the service. "Seven percent of [$60 billion] is a significant amount of money," he observed. "That basically covers US government operating expenses to run things like training for the Bolivian armed forces in counternarcotics, and stuff like that. Up until very, very recently, the Saudis pretty much subsidized everything. People do not realize how much benefit we get from our interaction with them."

This long relationship has sunk deep roots in the US defense establishment, especially since close acquaintance with the free-spending Saudi hierarchy can lead to attractive postretirement opportunities. David Commons, for example, the Air Force general who directed the military mission from 2011 to 2013, was responsible for what he calls the "management and execution" of the huge 2010 arms sale. It should come as no surprise, therefore, that on his return from Saudi Arabia he turned to commerce, where his Middle Eastern connections could be put to good use. First he chaired the Sharaka Group, offering "knowledge, experience and tenacity" in navigating the "maze" of Saudi bureaucracy. Next he cofounded Astrolabe Enterprises, which, by his account, helps the Saudis buy American weapons. "If they need a capability," he told me, "we are there."

One capability of which the Saudis are certainly in need is keeping their expensive toys in working order, a lucrative prospect for firms such as Astrolabe. By 2015, the maintenance contract for the F-15s alone was worth $2.5 billion. Almost all the technically demanding work on the highly complex plane, especially on its electronics, appears to require the services of American contract workers. This has led to something of a gold rush for mechanics and engineers. TS Government Solutions, of Lake Elsinore, California, is currently looking for maintenance mechanics "in support of RSAF F-15 platform throughout Saudi Arabia . . . VERY lucrative comp plan." There are no less than 1,471 openings listed on the website of ManTech International, of Fairfax, Virginia, the recipient of a $175 million F-15 maintenance contract. "Every time I looked at someone doing something technical on an F-15, it was an American contractor," Chet Richards, a former Air Force Reserve colonel who served several tours as an air attaché in Riyadh, told me. "These are really, really complex systems. We have trouble keeping them flying in our own air force."

Other features of the US–Saudi security relationship are more obscure, such as the "secret" CIA drone base deep in the southwestern desert, which became operational in 2011 and has been periodically rediscovered by the media in subsequent years. Dedicated to launching drone strikes against Al Qaeda in Yemen, it was a fruit of Saleh's delicate balancing act, whereby he tacitly endorsed the ongoing US assassination campaign against Al Qaeda leaders while avoiding direct action against the group himself. Indeed, even as the drones regularly incinerated Al Qaeda members along with innocent bystanders and the occasional wedding party, Saleh not only declined to arrest the terrorists but on occasion provided them with safe houses in Sanaa. Ignorant of (or perhaps unconcerned by) this double-dealing, Washington continued to indulge the wily Yemeni leader with copious aid and training missions.

This comfortable arrangement became unstuck in early 2011, when the so-called Arab Spring reached Yemen. The populace united in massive demonstrations against the president's dictatorial and corrupt rule. Wounded in an unsuccessful assassination attempt, Saleh eventually resigned in favor of his vice president, the former army general Mansour Hadi. Endorsed by both the

United States and Saudi Arabia, Hadi ran for election in 2012 and won with 99 percent of the vote—hardly a surprise, given that he was the only candidate. He quickly launched a "national dialogue" with the aim of reconciling Yemen's many tribal and regional factions. This failed to mollify the Houthis, who felt (somewhat reasonably, according to Ambassador Seche) that they were being dealt out of the new arrangements. In September 2014 they marched into Sanaa and, not long afterward, placed Hadi under house arrest.

Meanwhile, there had been ructions north of the border. King Abdullah died in January 2015, at the age of ninety, and was succeeded by his seventy-nine-year-old half-brother, Prince Salman. Suffering from dementia, Salman reportedly could function at meetings only by reading prepared talking points off a monitor masked by a vase of flowers. It soon became apparent that real power had devolved to his twenty-nine-year-old son, Prince Mohammed bin Salman, who in short order took control of the defense ministry as well as the royal household.

The Saudi regime has traditionally ruled by consensus. A previous king, Fahd, once told an American envoy that he had made only one decision in fifty years: inviting the Americans to expel Saddam Hussein from Kuwait in 1990. But Mohammed cut through the venerable system of checks and balances, imposing decisions that were, according to one former American diplomat with long experience of the Saudis, "bold, not to say rash."

Given his nation's long-standing readiness to see "a Persian under every khat bush," as the diplomat put it, Mohammed was eager to try out his expensive new weapons. He could crush the Houthis with a quick campaign and thereby shore up his own position at the expense of potential rivals in the ruling family.

On March 26, 2015, having secured a request for intervention from Hadi, the Royal Saudi Air Force went into action. The United States announced it was supplying "logistical and intelligence support." Five days later, the Saudi-led coalition imposed a comprehensive air and sea blockade of Houthi-held areas, including Hudaydah, the principal port serving northern Yemen.

For a population that relied on imports for at least 90 percent of its food, not to mention almost all other essentials such as fuel, cooking gas and medicine, the effect would be devastating.

Following standard practice in modern air campaigns, initial strikes targeted the Yemeni Air Force and air defenses, using high-tech bombs and missiles that allegedly guarantee precise accuracy. The Saudis may even have believed the arms merchants' sales pitches: a few days after the bombing began, a senior Saudi diplomat assured UN officials that the use of "very precise weapons" would prevent any collateral damage among the civilian population. In any event, the Saudis had little need to fear diplomatic censure at the United Nations. A Security Council resolution effectively demanding unconditional surrender from the Houthis passed with American support.

US diplomatic cover would be unstintingly maintained as the war raged on. In September, six months into the bombing, the Dutch government sponsored a resolution in the UN Human Rights Council calling for an independent and unfettered investigation into war crimes committed by all sides in Yemen. The Saudis strenuously objected, demanding that any such investigation be left in the hands of the deposed President Hadi, who was living in exile in Riyadh. The United States declined to support the Dutch, effectively killing the idea. In an officially cleared background interview, I asked a senior State Department official why the United States had acted as it did.

"The Yemenis didn't want it," he replied, by which he meant Hadi.

"Does the United States usually do what Mr. Hadi wants or doesn't want?" I asked.

"Well, when we agree with him, yes," he answered with a smirk.

In fact, the Obama Administration's support for the Yemeni adventure was never in doubt, if only because it had much bigger diplomatic fish to fry—most notably, the nuclear deal with Iran, the centerpiece of Obama's foreign policy agenda, which was impending at the time the war began. "The negotiations were not complete," I was told by William Luers, a former senior diplomat deeply involved in back-channel talks with the Iranians. "The opposition from Israel and the Gulf to the Iran deal was very strong." Under the circumstances, he suggested, Obama could ill afford to alienate his Arab partners—and surely the Yemeni conflict wouldn't last long. "Once they were involved in support of the Saudis," Luers said, "they couldn't back out."

Civilians began to die early on the day the war started. Among the first were three young sons of Yasser al-Habashi, a grocery-store owner whose home on the outskirts of Sanaa was hit by a bomb around two in the morning on March 26. Habashi himself woke up in a hospital after thirteen days in a coma. "There is nothing left of my house that I lived in," he said later, "and on top of all this, three of my children were killed."

Five days into the assault, the attackers leveled Yemen's largest cement factory, killing at least ten people, most of them employees preparing to head home on a bus. A further thirty-one workers died when bombers struck the Yemany Dairy and Beverage factory on the coast. A strike on a refugee camp at Mazraq, full of people who had fled the bombing in Saada and elsewhere, killed forty-five and injured 200 more.

The Saudis' education in aerial targeting had been the best that money could buy. A week before the war began, they had approached John Brennan, an old friend from his days as CIA station chief in Riyadh and now the agency's director, with a list of more than a hundred potential targets. Reporters were later told that American defense and intelligence officials had reviewed the list and suggested some amendments, removing targets of little military value and others that might endanger civilians. In addition, the United States agreed to help man the coalition's joint operations center with a liaison group that would advise the Saudis on how to hit their targets most effectively. The group would also ensure that US Air Force tankers were on hand to refuel bombing sorties, a duty they performed more than 700 times by February 2016—charging, of course, for the gas.

As reports of civilian casualties and Houthi advances seeped into the media, administration officials began to nurture some misgivings. On April 7, two weeks into the war, Tony Blinken, the deputy secretary of state, arrived in Riyadh, the first State Department official to meet one-on-one with the hyperactive and increasingly powerful Prince Mohammed. Blinken's public message was one of unqualified support for the war. "Saudi Arabia is sending a strong message to the Houthis and their allies that they cannot overrun Yemen by force," he told reporters. "As part of that effort, we have expedited weapons deliveries [and] increased our intelligence sharing."

In private, however, Blinken had an urgent question for his hosts. According to diplomatic sources, he asked: What were they actually trying to accomplish in this war? "Eliminate all traces of Iranian influence in Yemen," the Saudis answered blithely. American officials blenched at the prospect of a Houthi-extermination campaign, but they gave their blessing to what seemed like a more modest goal: preventing a Houthi takeover of all of Yemen and restoring the "elected president" to power.

Indeed, as Iryani explained to me, the allies had put all their chips on Hadi. "The Saudis and Americans believed that once the bombing started, Hadi would be able to rally loyal elements in the army and regain control," he said. "But it turned out that the entire military was with Saleh. Hadi had no influence at all." So the war went on, with the Houthis and Saleh's forces advancing steadily despite the bombing.

In August, after visiting Sanaa and Aden, Peter Maurer, the head of the International Red Cross, declared that "Yemen after five months looks like Syria after five years." Maurer attributed this not only to the fighting and bombing but to the ongoing blockade. A day earlier, coalition planes had bombed the vital port of Hudaydah, carefully targeting cranes and other necessary equipment.

The port city of Mukalla, however, was left completely unmolested, despite the fact that it was now controlled by Al Qaeda, the object of so many US drone attacks in previous years. The takeover, in April 2015, had been a peaceful one. Saudi-backed forces evacuated the city with barely a shot fired. Al Qaeda would continue to occupy the city and most of eastern Yemen, enriching itself in the process, over the following year. In bitter fighting for the city of Taiz in February 2016, Al Qaeda fighters formed a crucial component of the Saudi-backed anti-Houthi forces.

In Washington, I asked an intelligence official in close touch with the Yemeni situation what the Saudi plan had been at the outset. "Plan?" he replied in exasperated tones. "There *was* no plan. No plan at all. They just bombed anything and everything that looked like it might be a target. Trucks on a highway—that became a military convoy. Buildings, bridges, anything. When they *did* find a military target, they bombed it, and then went back and bombed it again."

There may have been a certain military logic to the repeated strikes on the mountains surrounding Sanaa, into which Saleh had burrowed ammunition dumps over the years. Still, these attacks were catastrophic for people living in nearby neighborhoods. On April 20, 2015, a powerful bunker-buster bomb hit one such dump on Faj Attan mountain, setting off a massive explosion that wrecked houses over a wide area, including Iryani's. "The mountain exploded," he told me soon afterward. "About 1,000 people were killed or injured. All the children I know are traumatized. Everyone I know knows someone who's died."

For hundreds or thousands of strikes, there was less excuse, or none at all. In mid-April of 2015, for example, there appears to have been a concerted attempt to destroy all the gas stations in Saada, which was already being heavily attacked. Thanks to the blockade, fuel was scarce, and drivers would spend hours or days waiting in line to fill up. That was how at least five people died and twenty-three were injured on April 15—the number of victims is actually unclear, since so many were burned beyond recognition. Several weeks later, on May 8, the coalition declared that the entire 4,000-square-mile governorate of Saada was now a "military target," and therefore open to indiscriminate attack. In the weeks and months to come, much of the province's ancient capital city was reduced to rubble, a fate shared by towns and villages across the north, where cluster bombs were heavily used.

"I witnessed about a thousand air strikes," recalled Tariq Riebl, an aid worker with a major international humanitarian organization who traveled extensively in Yemen from June to September last year. "Some of them were very close. I almost burst my eardrum in one." In Sanaa, he said, the strikes were relentless, lasting up to five hours. "You'd have that four to six times a day. It would start randomly. It was the middle of the night, middle of the day, morning, night, afternoon, anytime. Consistently on holidays, on Fridays, in the middle of prayer time, market days."

Crowded markets appear to have had a particular attraction for the targeteers. Human Rights Watch documented a dozen such attacks across northern Yemen, including five in Saada alone. On May 12, for example, three bombs, five minutes apart, hit a market in the Houthi-controlled town of Zabid, killing at least sixty civilians. Another attack killed sixty-five on July 4. In the deadliest market attack to date, on March 15, 2016, two bombs in the village of Mastaba killed at least ninety-seven people, including twenty-five children. Many of the victims died as they fled the scene of the first strike only to be hit by the second, a notable example of the double-tap technique frequently employed during the campaign. "When the first strike came, the world was full of blood," Mohammed Yehia Muzayid, a cleaner at the market, told Belkis Wille, a researcher for Human Rights Watch. "People were all in pieces, their limbs were everywhere. People went flying. Most of the people, we collected in pieces, we had to put them in plastic bags. A leg, an arm, a head. There wasn't more than five minutes between the first and second strike. The second strike was there, at the entrance to the market. People were taking the injured out, and it hit the wounded and killed them."

Metal fragments retrieved from the scene were revealed to be from US-manufactured GBU-31 satellite-guided bombs, 1,000 of which were included in a $1.29 billion weapons sale to the Saudis in November 2015. I asked the senior State Department official if there was ever any consideration of refusing such deals. He responded by suggesting that supplying high-tech precision weapons was essentially a humanitarian gesture: "If you want the Saudis to be able to limit collateral damage, then it's not particularly useful *not* to give them the weapons that would be most effective in doing that."

Congressman Lieu thought this a "very lame excuse" when I quoted it to him. "The law of war doesn't say, 'Hey, we have the precision-guided-munitions exception.' It says, 'You cannot target or kill civilians.'"

Lieu could be considered an authority on this topic, since he is a colonel in the Air Force Reserve and spent four years as an active-duty JAG lawyer, instructing military personnel on the law of war. He was convinced that the Saudis and their allies were in violation of those very statutes. He was especially concerned by the use of cluster bombs, which he categorized as a "war crime if you drop them on civilians."

Six months into the war, Lieu wrote to the chairman of the Joint Chiefs of Staff, Gen. Joseph Dunford Jr., asking if he believed that Yemeni civilians were being deliberately targeted. The answer was classified, but it seems reasonable to assume it was negative. Belkis Wille has a more complicated view. She told me she would often spot some kind of military installation near a bombed civilian site, which may have been the intended target. On the evening of July 24, for example, the coalition bombed a housing compound for workers of the Mokha power plant, in the southwest corner of Yemen. Sixty-five people were killed, including ten children. At least forty-two more were wounded, several of them critically. Wille concluded that the intended target was a military air defense base, which had been empty for many years, according to unanimous local testimony. More to the point, the base was half a mile away, and easily distinguishable from the compound. "There may have been a lack of good military intelligence," she told me. "But the end result was an incredibly high rate of sloppiness and recklessness."

Others are less forgiving. Tariq Riebl concluded that the civilian targets were not an accident. "Let's be very clear," he told me.

"The civilian targeting is absolutely astounding. I've seen hospitals, mosques, marketplaces, restaurants, power plants, universities, residential houses, just bombed, office buildings, bombed. Everything is a target. In Saada, there were dead donkeys on the side of all the main roads because the Saudis were hitting donkey carts. In Hajjah, the water tank in one of the towns got hit, and it sits on a lonesome little hill. There was nothing there. When you're hitting a donkey cart or you're hitting a water tank, what is your rationale? Is that donkey cart transporting a Scud missile? What is the thinking here from a military perspective?"

According to Ahmed Assiri, a brigadier general in the Saudi Army and a coalition spokesman, the "work" was not "random." Occasional "mistakes" were due solely to "human error." In a January 31 press conference, Assiri addressed the particular case of the Doctors Without Borders hospital in Hayden, destroyed last October by air strikes—one of three of the organization's facilities to be hit during the war—leaving 200,000 people in the region without access to lifesaving medical care. The group had repeatedly relayed the hospital's GPS coordinates to the Saudis, most recently three days before the strike, and prominently displayed their logo on the roof.

An otherwise unidentified "frontline observer," explained Assiri, had spotted a target that was "of high value" and relayed the news to a patrolling coalition attack plane. This target, presumably an individual, moved closer to the hospital, and the pilot, seizing an opportunity, attacked. "But there were side effects," Assiri continued, "causing the collapse of a big part of the hospital." (In fact, it was utterly demolished.) It seems that the frontline observer did not check with the command center as to whether the hospital was a restricted target—and in any case, the pilot overlooked the logo on the roof, "which was very small and cannot be seen by eye." (A spokesman for the organization, Tim Shenk, assured me that the logo "clearly identified" the hospital.)

From the professional perspective of Des Roches, the Saudis and their partners have not done badly at all. "Twenty-eight hundred [killed] for a yearlong bombing campaign?" he told me, using a UN figure from January. "That's one night in Hamburg in World War II." In fact, the number of civilians killed from the air in a year, he suggested, bore favorable comparison with NATO's record in the 1999 air campaign against Serbia, the so-called Kosovo War, in which some 500 civilians died from allied air strikes in barely three months. The Saudis, in his view, were "showing restraint. They're showing a degree of technical expertise."

As of February 2016, the Saudis noted that the coalition had flown more than 46,500 sorties over Yemen. By July, sixty-nine strikes studied in detail by Amnesty International and Human Rights Watch had killed 913 civilians, at least. As of June, the World Health Organization reported nearly 6,500 dead and more than 31,400 injured, on the basis of information from hospitals around the country. But Doctors Without Borders officials insist that they alone have treated more than 37,000 people with war-related injuries. In any case, more than half the population lacked access to any health care, let alone hospitals.

"As you can of course imagine, those numbers are an under-estimation, as people might not bother to take their killed relatives to the hospital just to be counted," observed Alvhild Strømme, a WHO spokesperson, in a candid email. "I am sure there are many more, especially killed, but also wounded."

Just over a year after the onslaught began, the Saudis and Houthis called a halt, declaring a cease-fire and beginning peace talks. Bitter fighting has continued in parts of the country, espe-cially around Taiz, where the Saleh-allied Houthi forces, themselves no angels, have nonchalantly shelled civilian areas. Though air strikes slowed, they have continued into the summer, inflicting a steady toll of civilian deaths. Al Qaeda was meanwhile permitted to evacuate Mukalla with all its equipment. Disappearing into the countryside, the terrorist group began a series of deadly bombing attacks. UN officials talked of a "humanitarian catastro-phe" and issued a call for $1.8 billion in emergency funds. By July, the United States had contributed $148 million, just over 8 percent of the requested amount. Meanwhile, weapons sales to Saudi Arabia over the course of the Obama Administration had topped $111 billion.

The country is in ruins, like Abdul-Ghani al-Iryani's own house. "Yemen," he told me sadly as the explosions continued, "is such a small part of the US–Saudi relationship."

The war ground on for years. US and European arms companies made money. The ongoing war crime was so undeniable that even the US Senate voted to end support for the war. Trump predictably vetoed the initiative. Biden, on assuming office, promised to end support for "offensive" Saudi operations and imposed a temporary freeze on weapons sales to the kingdom. At that point, according to UN estimates, 233,000 Yemenis had died due to the war.

11

Crime and Punishment

October 2017

The sanctioning of mass murder in Yemen in exchange for vast and profitable arms sales was only one feature of the ongoing devil's bargain with Saudi Arabia. It seems that the relationship also allows for obscuring the truth about mass murder in the US.

Meeting with the leaders of NATO countries in May, President Trump chastised them sternly for their shortcomings as allies. He took the time, however, to make respectful reference to the ruler of Saudi Arabia, Salman bin Abdulaziz Al Saud, whom he had just visited at the start of his first overseas trip as president. "I spent much time with King Salman," he told the glum-looking cluster of Europeans, calling him "a wise man who wants to see things get much better rapidly."

Some might find this fulsome description surprising, given widespread reports that Salman, who took the throne in January 2015, suffers from dementia. Generally seen wearing a puzzled look, the king has been known to wander off in the middle of conversations, as he reportedly did once while talking with President Obama. When speaking in public, he depends on fast-typing aides whose prompts appear on a discreetly concealed monitor.

Whatever wisdom Trump absorbed from his elderly royal friend, the primary purpose of his trip to Riyadh, according to a former senior US official briefed on the proceedings, was cash—both in arms sales and investments in crumbling American infrastructure, such as highways, bridges and tunnels. The Trump Administration is "desperate for Saudi money, especially infrastructure investments in the Rust Belt," the former official told me. An influx of Saudi dollars could generate jobs and thus redound to Trump's political benefit. As a cynical douceur, the Saudis, derided by Trump during his campaign as "people that kill women and treat women horribly," joined the United Arab Emirates in pledging $100 million for a women's-empowerment initiative spearheaded by Ivanka Trump. A joyful president took part in the traditional sword dance and then helped launch a Saudi center for "combating extremism."

This was not the first time the Saudis had dangled the prospect of massive investments to leverage US support. "Mohammed bin Salman made the same pitch to the Obama people," the former official told me. "'We're going to invest all this money here, you're going to be our great economic partner, etc.' Because the Trump Administration doesn't know much about foreign affairs, they were really seduced by this."

The president certainly viewed the visit as a huge success. "We made and saved the USA many billions of dollars and millions of jobs," he tweeted as he left Saudi Arabia. The White House soon trumpeted $110 billion in weapons sales and billions more in infrastructure investments, with the total purportedly rising to $350 billion.

Yet amid the sword dances and flattery, a shadow lingered over the occasion: 9/11. After years of glacial legal progress, the momentous charge that our Saudi allies enabled and supported the most devastating act of mass murder on American soil may now be coming to a resolution. Thanks to a combination of court decisions, congressional action and the disclosure of long-sequestered government records, it appears increasingly likely that our supposed friend and peerless weapons customer will finally face its accusers in court.

Over the years, successive administrations have made strenuous efforts to suppress discussion of Saudi involvement in the

September 11 attacks, deploying everything from abusive security classification to the judiciary to a presidential veto. Now, at last, we stand a chance of discovering what really happened, largely because of a court case.

In re Terrorist Attacks on September 11, 2001, which grew out of a suit filed in 2002 on behalf of bereaved family members and other victims of the attacks, includes a charge of direct Saudi government involvement in 9/11. It also claims that Riyadh directly funded the creation, growth and operations of Al Qaeda worldwide. The Saudis, though scorning the accusation, have been striving ever more desperately to prevent the case from advancing through the legal system. To that end, they have employed to date no fewer than fifteen high-powered Washington lobbying firms.

The task is growing more urgent because the kingdom, long confident of essentially unlimited wealth, is facing money problems. Oil prices are in a slump and likely to stay there. The war in Yemen, launched in 2015 by Salman's appointed heir, Mohammed bin Salman, drags on, costing an estimated $200 million a day, with no end in sight. To alleviate his cash-flow problems, the young prince is set on raising as much as $2 trillion by floating the state-owned oil company, Saudi Aramco, on international stock markets. That is part of the reason the 9/11 lawsuit poses such a threat—it raises the possibility that much-needed cash from the stock sale might never find its way to Riyadh. "They're afraid they're going to get a default judgment against them, and some of their domestic assets will be seized," the former senior official explained to me.

To Sharon Premoli, one of the more than 6,500 plaintiffs in the lawsuit, that is precisely the goal. On September 11, she had been at her desk at a financial services software company, on the eightieth floor of the North Tower of the World Trade Center, when American Airlines Flight 11 slammed into the building thirteen floors above her. Fleeing the area, she had almost reached safety when the South Tower came crashing down, propelling her into a plate-glass window. Coming to, she found herself lying on top of a dead body. Like many other survivors, she has developed an encyclopedic knowledge of the legal issues around the case, not to mention the world of terrorism and Saudi connections thereto. A multibillion-dollar award "would certainly stop the Saudis from financing terrorism," she told me. "That's the whole point of this. It is all about money. If you can cut that off, that would make a serious impact on the dissemination of this rabid ideology around the world."

Premoli was more fortunate than Peter Owens, a forty-two-year-old bond trader at Cantor Fitzgerald, twenty-four floors above her, who had no chance of escape. He left behind a wife and three children. "It's kind of sad to look forward to the anniversary," Kathy Owens told me recently. Each September gives her hope that the recurring news peg will inspire journalists to explore the case. "We started a war because of 9/11—more than one war—and the wars are still going on," she said. "Every war we start now, we say it's because of 9/11. It manages so much of our lives. They keep fighting the war on terror, but we are giving the Saudis a pass, despite all of this evidence."

There has always been evidence—in abundance. The Joint Inquiry Into Intelligence Community Activities Before and After the Terrorist Attacks of September 11, 2001 began work in February 2002. Congressional investigators soon uncovered numerous failures by the FBI and CIA. The degree of cumulative incompetence was breathtaking. Most egregiously, the CIA had been well aware that two known Al Qaeda operatives, Nawaf al-Hazmi and Khalid al-Mihdhar, were en route to the United States, but the agency had refused to tell the FBI. The FBI, meanwhile, had multiple reports in its San Diego office on locally based Saudis suspected of terrorist associations, but failed to take action.

San Diego looms large in the recorded history of 9/11, though not because it was the focal point of the plot. While preparing for the operation, the future hijackers had been dispersed around the country, in such places as New Jersey and Florida. The reason we know so much about the West Coast activities of the hijackers is largely because of Michael Jacobson, a burly former FBI lawyer and counterterrorism analyst who worked as an investigator for the Joint Inquiry. Reviewing files at FBI headquarters, he came across a stray reference to a bureau informant in San Diego who had known one of the hijackers. Intrigued, he decided to follow up in the San Diego field office. Bob Graham, the former chairman of the Senate Intelligence Committee, told me recently that Robert Mueller, then the FBI director (and now the special counsel investigating connections between Russia and the Trump campaign) made "the strongest objections" to Jacobson and his colleagues visiting San Diego.

Graham and his team defied Mueller's efforts, and Jacobson flew west. There he discovered that his hunch was correct. The FBI files in California were replete with extraordinary and damning details, notably the hijackers' close relationship with Omar al-Bayoumi, a Saudi living in San Diego with a no-show job at a local company with connections to the Saudi Ministry of Defense and Aviation. The FBI had investigated his possible connections to Saudi intelligence. A couple of weeks after the two hijackers flew into Los Angeles from Malaysia, in February 2000, he had driven up to the city and met with Fahad al-Thumairy, a cleric employed by his country's Ministry of Islamic Affairs who worked out of the Saudi Consulate. Thumairy, reported to be an adherent of extreme Wahhabi ideology—he was later denied a US visa on grounds of jihadi connections—was also an imam of the King Fahad mosque in Los Angeles County, which the hijackers had visited soon after their arrival.

After meeting with Thumairy, Bayoumi had driven across town to a Middle Eastern restaurant where he "accidentally" encountered and introduced himself to Hazmi and Mihdhar. He invited them to move to San Diego, found them an apartment, paid their first month's rent, helped them open a bank account, and introduced them to members of the local Saudi community, including his close friend Osama Bassnan.

During the time Bayoumi was catering to the hijackers' needs, his salary as a ghost employee of the aviation company got a 700 percent boost; it was cut when they left town. That was not his only source of extra funds: After Hazmi and Mihdhar arrived in San Diego, Bassnan's wife began signing over to Bayoumi's wife the checks she received from the wife of the Saudi ambassador in Washington. The total value reportedly came to nearly $150,000.

Jacobson also found evidence, noted but seemingly ignored by the bureau, that Hazmi had worked for a San Diego businessman who had himself been the subject of an FBI counterterrorism investigation. Even more amazingly, the two hijackers had been close with an FBI informant, Abdussattar Shaikh. Hazmi had actually lived in his house after Mihdhar left town. Shaikh failed to mention his young Saudi friends' last names in regular reports to his FBI case officer, or that they were taking flying lessons. Understandably, the investigators had a lot of questions for this man. Nevertheless, Mueller adamantly refused their demands to interview him, even when backed by a congressional subpoena, and removed Shaikh to an undisclosed location "for his own safety." Today, Graham believes that Mueller was acting under orders from the White House.

Another intriguing document unearthed by the investigators in San Diego was a memo from July 2, 2002, discussing alleged financial connections between the September 11 hijackers, Saudi government officials and members of the Saudi royal family. It stated that there was "incontrovertible evidence that there is support for these terrorists within the Saudi Government."

Back in 2002, Graham himself was already coming to the conclusion that the 9/11 attacks could not have been the work of a stand-alone terrorist cell. As he later wrote, "I believed almost intuitively that the terrorists who pulled off this attack must have had an elaborate support network, abroad and in the USA," with expenses far exceeding the official estimate of $250,000. "For that reason," he continued, "as well as because of the benefits that come with the confidentiality of diplomatic cover, this infrastructure of support was probably maintained, at least in part, by a nation-state."

I asked Graham whether he believed that a careful search of the FBI files in Florida and elsewhere would yield similarly explosive disclosures. He told me that the inquiry would have doubtless discovered whom the hijackers were associating with in those places, and where that money came from. Fifteen years on, Graham still regretted not having pursued the possibility of revelatory FBI files in those other locations "aggressively." Instead, he lamented, the inquiry ended up "with San Diego being the microscope through which we've been looking at this whole plot."

Even the comparatively comprehensive accounts of the San Diego phase of the plot may be missing some telling leads. FBI records detailed the close connections between Bayoumi, the hijackers and a local imam, Anwar al-Awlaki.* Awlaki apparently served as the hijackers' spiritual mentor. He soon moved to Northern Virginia, and when Hazmi and another hijacker arrived in the neighborhood in April 2001 to begin their final preparations, he served in that capacity again, and also found them an apartment. Many investigators, including Graham, concluded that Awlaki was not only aware of the developing plot but very much a part of it.

But before that, Awlaki reportedly served as a senior official of a "charity"—viewed by the FBI as a terrorist fund-raising operation—founded by Abdul Majid al-Zindani, a Saudi-backed cleric in Yemen. Zindani had been the spiritual mentor of Osama bin Laden himself. He also founded a powerful Yemeni political party and headed Iman University in Sanaa, often described as a jihadi recruiting hub. Both of these enterprises were supported by Saudi money.

In 2004, the US government listed Zindani as a "specially designated global terrorist" and a supporter of Al Qaeda. This in no way interfered with his travels to Saudi Arabia, however. As recently as this February, Zindani was observed in the company of prominent clerics in Mecca. Among those who have drawn attention to this in published reports is Michael Jacobson, who

---

* Several years later, Awlaki would become notorious as a recruiter of terrorists; he was deemed so dangerous that President Obama ordered his execution by drone in Yemen, in 2011.

after service with the 9/11 inquiries returned to counterterrorism analysis with the US Treasury. Currently, he is at the State Department. When I called him to discuss Zindani's relationship with the Saudis, he quickly replied, "I can't talk about that," and ended the conversation with the words, "Good luck."

After a mere ten months, in December 2002, the Joint Inquiry team presented its report to the CIA for declassification. The agency demanded numerous cuts, only a few of which, in Graham's view, were justified. But one section had been censored in its entirety: a twenty-eight-page summary, written by Jacobson, of the evidence relating to Saudi government support for the hijackers. It was the only area on which the Bush White House absolutely refused to relent. "The president's loyalty apparently lay more with Saudi Arabia than with America's safety," Graham told me bitterly. To highlight the degree of censorship, he made sure that the published version of the report included the blacked-out pages, much to the irritation of the intelligence community.

The report concluded that the FBI, in light of its lamentable performance, deserved to be drastically reformed. But many questions remained unanswered. The 9/11 families, now emerging as a powerful lobby, called for a more sweeping probe. In November 2002, Congress had authorized another bipartisan panel, a National Commission on Terrorist Attacks upon the United States. The initial choice of chairperson for the new probe, Henry Kissinger, drew outrage from 9/11 families, particularly a formidable foursome of well-informed widows known as the Jersey Girls, who questioned his impartiality given his suspected professional ties to prominent Saudis. Rather than divulge his Saudi client list, Kissinger quit. Ultimately, the White House selected in his place two retired politicians—Tom Kean, the former governor of New Jersey, and Lee Hamilton, who had represented Indiana in the House. Neither, especially Hamilton, showed much inclination to challenge the Bush Administration's preferred version of events.

For the post of executive director, Kean and Hamilton appointed Philip Zelikow, a historian and national security scholar with strong connections to the Bush Administration. (He had served on the Bush transition team and prepared an important policy paper for his friend Condoleezza Rice, the national security adviser.) A forceful personality, Zelikow maintained strict day-to-day control of the investigation. According to *The Commission*, by the former *New York Times* reporter Philip Shenon, Dana Lesemann, a Justice Department lawyer who had worked on the prior congressional investigation before transferring to the commission staff, asked for Zelikow's permission to review the redacted twenty-eight pages. In Shenon's account, he refused. Bucking his orders, she obtained them anyway, whereupon she was promptly fired.*

Despite these obstacles, commission staffers did energetically pursue leads uncovered by the original probe. They were therefore frustrated when telling indications of a Saudi connection were largely excluded or downplayed in the main text of the final report. The staffers were, however, able to smuggle much of what they had uncovered into endnotes at the back of the document—an act of small-print, guerrilla-style resistance. For example, Jacobson and a colleague flew to Riyadh to interview Fahad al-Thumairy, the cleric from the Saudi Consulate in Los Angeles subsequently banned from the United States as a suspected terrorist. During the interview, with Saudi officials in attendance, Thumairy denied any connection to the plot—in fact, he disclaimed ever having met Bayoumi or the hijackers. The investigators concluded that he was "lying" and "dangerous." The main text of the report mentions both the allegations and his denials, without coming to any particular conclusion. But lengthy endnotes specify the numerous phone calls between Thumairy and Bayoumi over several years, as well as evidence that Thumairy's occasional chauffeur had driven Hazmi and

---

* Asked to comment, Zelikow denied the account and said that Lesemann, who had a security clearance, had been fired for "violating her security agreement." He declined to elaborate further, citing what he called a "privacy issue." Lesemann died in March 2017.

Mihdhar, at Thumairy's request, on sightseeing trips to Sea World and other spots.

The main conclusion from the final report was that there was "no evidence that the Saudi government as an institution or senior Saudi officials individually funded the organization." The Saudi authorities were so pleased by this verdict that they posted the quote on the website of their Washington embassy. The published version of the report was a bestseller, nominated for a National Book Award, and hailed by the novelist John Updike as the greatest masterpiece written by a committee since the King James Bible.

So far as the US government and most of the media were concerned, there was no need for further investigation. But the Bush Administration didn't reject the notion that a nation-state had been behind the attacks. They merely offered up a different nominee for the role: Iraq. In the absence of any evidence to back this up, interrogators at Guantánamo were tasked, according to a 2008 report by the Senate Armed Services Committee, to torture detainees into admitting to such a link.

The 9/11 families, however, had no interest in letting the kingdom off the hook. Nor did their lawyers. These included Ron Motley, of the South Carolina firm Motley Rice. He had recently scored the largest civil settlement in history—some $246 billion from America's tobacco companies—and was eager for a fresh challenge. Also enlisted in the multiple suits were Jim Kreindler, the New York aviation lawyer who had won more than $2 billion from Muammar Qaddafi in the Pan Am Flight 103 case, and Stephen Cozen of Cozen O'Connor, specialists in recovering money for insurance companies.

The 9/11 suit as it now stands is a compilation of many such suits. It cites evidence of direct support for the attacks by Saudi officials such as Thumairy, Bayoumi and Bassnan. It also lays out the case for the intimate involvement of the Saudi government in the creation and expansion of Al Qaeda. Whereas the 9/11 Commission Report began its narrative with Osama bin Laden, *In re Terrorist Attacks* goes back to the foundation of the Al Saud family's rule and its alliance with the puritanical and intolerant

Wahhabi sect. In the 1970s, and then again in the early 1990s, violent challenges to the family's legitimacy, fostered by its corruption and backsliding from the fundamentalist creed, persuaded the ruling princes to appease the clerics by giving them further leeway, and massive amounts of money, to export their extremist agenda.

For example, according to internal Al Qaeda documents seized by US forces in 2002, a man named Abdullah Omar Naseef was simultaneously the head of one such Saudi "charity," the Muslim World League, and a member of the Majlis al-Shura, the kingdom's consultative assembly, which is entirely appointed by the government. Naseef not only met with bin Laden and leaders of Al Qaeda at the time of its founding but reportedly agreed that the league's offices would be used as a platform for the new organization. He then proceeded to appoint senior Al Qaeda figures to run league offices in such key outposts as Pakistan and the Philippines, the latter position being entrusted to bin Laden's brother-in-law. Another group, the International Islamic Relief Organization, is meanwhile said to have funded terrorist training camps in Afghanistan, from which the 9/11 hijackers graduated, and in Pakistani-controlled Kashmir, for the evident use of terrorist groups such as Lashkar-e-Taiba.

Should there have been any doubt about the connection between these Wahhabi missionary groups and the Saudi government, they were dispelled by the groups themselves. In documents filed between 2002 and 2005, some formally declared themselves to be organs of the state. They could thus shelter behind the principal Saudi defensive fortification in the case: the immunity enjoyed by foreign countries against being sued in US courts, granted by the Foreign Sovereign Immunity Act.

For years, this appeared to be a sound strategy, in large part because of the 9/11 Commission's concluding blanket absolution of the Saudi government. In 2005, US District Judge Richard Casey dismissed the case against the kingdom itself and many of the individual defendants, on the grounds that they were covered by sovereign immunity.

Casey's judgment was upheld by the US Court of Appeals for the Second Circuit in 2008, prompting an appeal to the Supreme Court in 2009, just as Barack Obama entered the White House. Candidate Obama had talked derisively about Bush's "buddying up to the Saudi royal family and then begging them for oil." President Obama's Justice Department almost immediately informed the Supreme Court that the Saudis were in no way liable. Shortly thereafter, Obama flew to Riyadh, where he was royally entertained and duly bedecked with the gold chain and medal of the Order of King Abdulaziz, an honor also conferred on Presidents Clinton, Bush and Trump. "Goodness gracious," he exclaimed when presented with the costly bauble, "that's something there!"

"The mystery to me is Obama," remarked Graham. He could, he said, understand Bush's rationale for covering up the Saudi connection in order to bolster the case for war with Iraq. But Obama's refusal to address the issue, which included a multiyear reluctance to release the twenty-eight pages, mystified him. Meeting with officials on Obama's National Security Council, he found them "very non-forthcoming. 'You've got all the files,'" he told them. "'Go back and verify what I've just said and see if you hold the same opinion about the Saudis that you have just stated.' Either they didn't want to find out the facts, or if they found them out, they ignored them."

Similarly uninterested in the facts, at least as Graham saw them, was the 9/11 Review Commission authorized by Congress in 2014 to examine the progress of reforms recommended by the original commission and recheck its conclusions on the attacks. Three commissioners were appointed to the task by the FBI director, James Comey: Reagan's former attorney general, Edwin Meese; the former Democratic congressman Tim Roemer; and Bruce Hoffman, a terrorism expert and former RAND official. This inquiry, working with the "full cooperation" of the FBI, upheld the conclusions of the original commission in full. No one from this commission contacted Graham.

In reality, the Obama Administration was well aware that Saudi Arabia was a supporter of terrorism, though it kept the information to itself. Only through WikiLeaks did we learn of Secretary of State Hillary Clinton's classified cable, circulated to department officials in December 2009, stating as fact that "donors in Saudi Arabia constitute the most significant source of funding to Sunni terrorist groups worldwide." Saudi Arabia was of course also a significant source of funding to the US defense industry. Two years after the classified cable, Clinton aide Jake Sullivan emailed her the "good news" that the kingdom had just signed a $30 billion order for Boeing F-15 fighters. "Not a bad Christmas present," observed someone else on the same email thread.

However, while the administration and the intelligence agencies maintained the tradition of protecting the Saudis, the long-stalled legal case against the kingdom was coming back to life. One major stumbling block remained: the Foreign Sovereign Immunity Act. Faced with this legal bulwark, the families and their lawyers resolved to get Congress to change the law. The resulting legislation, the Justice Against Sponsors of Terrorism Act (JASTA), was crafted to blow away the Saudis' immunity from prosecution.

Kathy Owens was among the widows and other plaintiffs crowding the corridors of Congress in May 2016 to push for the bill. For the first decade after the attack, she had paid little attention to the lawsuit, adding her name only at her father's urging. Then she happened to pick up a magazine excerpt from Anthony Summers and Robbyn Swan's book on 9/11, *The Eleventh Day.* "It woke me up," she told me. "What? There was Saudi involvement and possibly our government was onto it, and nothing was being done about it, and things were being kept secret?" Learning about JASTA from a website run by Sharon Premoli, Owens started making trips to Washington.

The government warned that the proposed law could inspire similar legislation abroad, allowing foreigners to sue America, and Americans (though JASTA did not apply to individuals). The president's press secretary pushed this argument, as did State Department officials. Prominent former national security experts dispatched warnings to Congress. Even the Dutch parliament weighed in, apparently swayed by the State Department's pronouncements.

"It was a bogeyman they threw out in every setting," one of the senior lawyers involved in the lawsuit told me, explaining that the government had been raising the same objection on previous occasions. Yet "we haven't seen any floodgate of claims against the United States." In the view of this attorney, who has spent most of his life since 9/11 working on the case, the Obama Administration was merely "feigning" concern. "They're not dumb. They had to understand that these arguments didn't hold water."

There was one foreign state threatening to strike back at the United States if JASTA became law. Visiting Washington in March 2016, before Congress began voting on the measure, Saudi Foreign Minister Adel al-Jubeir explicitly warned that his government might sell its portfolio of "$750 billion" in US Treasury bonds, thereby crashing the market in government securities, should JASTA become law. (The figure was a wild exaggeration—US Treasury figures showed that the real amount was $117 billion.)

Even with all the threats and warnings, the House passed the bill that September, whereupon Obama announced he would veto it, which he duly did. The battle resumed with greater intensity as both sides prepared another vote. "President Obama, you can't hide! We'll get Congress to override," protesters chanted outside the White House.

Despite frantic efforts by the administration, and ranks of lobbyists for the Saudis, the Senate crushed Obama's veto, 97 to 1. It was the first and only time Obama suffered such an indignity. Reportedly, he was "furious." Meanwhile, bipartisan pressure to release the censored twenty-eight pages in Graham's original report had been building for some time, led by congressmen such as the Democrat Stephen Lynch and the Republican Walter Jones. Jones, once a fervent hawk, had turned sharply dovish, through guilt, as he told me, over voting for the Iraq war on the basis of "lies." (He writes a letter of condolence to the family of every single casualty of the wars in Iraq and Afghanistan.) Jones, Lynch and others on both sides of the aisle held regular press conferences about the twenty-eight pages "to keep a drumbeat going to give the 9/11 families the complete truth."

With the exception of that committed group, Owens was not impressed by what she found on Capitol Hill. Most of the senators and representatives she met didn't seem to care who was behind 9/11. "They just didn't want to be seen as voting against the 9/11 families. So they would vote yes for it, and then try to sabotage it behind the scenes . . . Washington is an ugly place." Encouraging this assessment was her discovery that at the very moment they were voting almost unanimously for the bill, a significant number of senators from both parties were quietly circulating and signing a letter citing "concerns" regarding JASTA's "potential unintended consequences" to "the national security and foreign policy of the United States." In effect, they were suggesting that the law they had just been seen enthusiastically supporting be weakened.

Front and center in this sorry initiative were Senators John McCain and Lindsey Graham, who, following the override, introduced amendments purportedly designed to "fix" JASTA. One of the 9/11 lawyers coolly appraised this tactic as "demonstrably the brainchild of Saudi lawyers here in Washington. They don't fix JASTA; they're designed to gut JASTA." The lawyer speculated that the Saudis' lobbyists hadn't told their clients that "even if amendments like that were to be enacted, this litigation would continue." The lobbyists' interests, he suggested, lay in keeping the fight going as long as possible. "I think that you've got dozens of retainers out there that people would like to extend into the very distant future."

Meanwhile, after JASTA became law, dozens of veterans across the country received invitations to a "cool trip." At no cost to themselves, they would fly to Washington, stay at the luxurious Trump Hotel—and tell Congress how the law endangered them and others who had fought in Iraq and Afghanistan by potentially opening them to lawsuits. The entire operation was sponsored by the Saudi government. However, according to multiple accounts by veterans who made the trip, they were not informed beforehand of the Saudi involvement as required by the Foreign Agents Registration Act. They discovered the connection only by accident. Scott Bartels, who served two tours in Iraq, described his experience to me. "We were told that a veterans' advocacy group [had] brought us there to propose a fix to JASTA," he said. "If anyone in Congress asked us what group we were from, or who we were associated with, then we were to simply say we were an independent group of concerned veterans here on our own, because JASTA posed a threat to veterans."

Jason Johns, a lobbyist for Qorvis, which brought Bartels and some 140 others to Washington, denied that the veterans were ever misinformed as to who was paying the tab. He also insisted to me that his failure to mention the Saudis in various written materials distributed to the veterans did not violate the law. (Justice Department guidelines specifically stipulate that all such material must state the name of the "foreign principal.") Three of Johns's colleagues in the veterans-against-JASTA effort echoed his argument that no laws had been broken. It was, in any case, a highly profitable enterprise for the organizers. Johns himself received $100,000, while the Trump Hotel billed Qorvis $270,000 for lodging, refreshments and parking. In total, Saudi payments to their lobbyists during the JASTA fight ran to at least $1.3 million a month.

At the same time, another legal barrier, erected years before by George W. Bush, had already crumbled. Yielding to mounting pressure, Congress finally released the infamous twenty-eight pages in July 2016, albeit with many passages still censored. At long last, the discoveries unearthed by Jacobson and his colleagues in San Diego could be incorporated in the lawsuit. Though salient details, such as Omar Bayoumi's role in assisting the hijackers, had previously been bruited, many new ones came to light, such as the actions of Saleh al-Hussayen, a Saudi cleric and government employee who had suddenly moved to Hazmi and Mihdhar's hotel the night before the attacks. Hussayen was "deceptive" about his relationship with the attackers when interviewed by the FBI and feigned a seizure to evade further questioning. Taken to the hospital, he escaped and fled the country. The world also learned about Mohammed al-Qudhaeein, another Saudi government agent whose "profile is similar to that of al-Bayoumi." While on his way to a party at the Saudi Embassy in Washington, Qudhaeein researched ways to get into an American Airlines cockpit. (Thanks to a tip from a friendly government archivist, Kathy Owens meanwhile unearthed another long-censored document that had been quietly declassified. It reveals an Al Qaeda member's flight certificate enclosed in a Saudi Embassy envelope.)

Even before the release of these documents, some with a vested interest in the official story had already begun circling the wagons. Tom Kean and Lee Hamilton penned an op-ed in *USA Today* misleadingly asserting that the twenty-eight pages consisted merely of "raw, unvetted material," and stated that 9/11 Commission staff had access to the classified pages and pursued the leads before absolving the Saudi government. In their motion to dismiss the lawsuit, filed on August 1, 2017, Saudi Arabia's D.C. lawyers, Kellogg, Hansen, Todd, Figel & Frederick, hewed to much the same posture. Employing the assertive bluster common to such documents, they derided the relevance of the missing pages, invoked the findings of the 9/11 Commission as gospel, scorned assertions regarding Saudi government collusion with Al Qaeda, and challenged the very notion that JASTA would allow the lawsuit against the Saudi government to proceed. Naturally, they demanded that the suit be dismissed.

Ironically, the newly released pages also resonated among a group of lawyers very far removed from the JASTA plaintiffs, but no less embroiled in the story of the attacks. In a courtroom in Guantánamo Bay, Cuba, attorneys employed by the Defense Department were defending five of the original 9/11 conspirators, who were facing charges in a military court. Now these attorneys demanded that portions of the twenty-eight pages still being withheld by the government—a total of three pages—be made available to the defense. (The military judge rejected the motion in an order that was, naturally, withheld from the public at large.) Edwin Perry, who is defending Walid bin Attash, pointed out that his client and the other defendants were being held wholly responsible for the attacks. If there was information, he argued, that identified "other individuals more responsible," then the government should make it known.

It seems a reasonable request.

In February 2021, the Biden administration released an intelligence report naming Mohammed Bin Salman, crown prince of Saudi Arabia, as responsible for the death of former US resident Jamal Khashoggi. But the government still refused to release the FBI's findings in Operation Encore, a secret probe of Saudi involvement in the 9/11 mass killings that was concluded in 2016. The 9/11 lawsuit is still pending in the New York District Court.

12

Money Trail

November 2015

The record shows America's Afghan war was nothing other than a prolonged and entirely successful operation—to loot the US taxpayer. At least a quarter of a million Afghans, not to mention 3,500 US and allied troops, paid a heavier price.

In November 2015, the Special Inspector General for Afghanistan Reconstruction (SIGAR) released a report that outlined how the Pentagon spent nearly $43 million on building a gas station in the Afghan provincial town of Sheberghan. Though comparable stations in Pakistan cost only $500,000, the report cited Pentagon claims that it could provide no explanation for the enormous cost of the project.

The compressed natural gas (CNG) automobile filling station was constructed under the auspices of something called the Task Force for Business and Stability Operations (TFBSO), an $800 million project to which the Pentagon "appears determined to restrict or hinder SIGAR access." There was no indication that the Task Force, which answered directly to the secretary of defense, had conducted a feasibility study before building the station. If they had, the SIGAR report remarked drily, they "might have noted that Afghanistan lacks the natural gas transmission and local distribution infrastructure necessary to support a viable market for CNG vehicles. [Additionally,] it appears that the cost of converting a gasoline-powered car to run on CNG may be prohibitive for the average Afghan. TFBSO's contractor, CADG, stated that conversion to CNG costs $700 per car . . . *The average annual income in Afghanistan is $690.*"

For the most part, the inspector's regular reports of such fiascos have become part of the background noise in Washington, irksome reminders to the bureaucracy of the scandalous waste that has been the $100 billion–plus US program to "reconstruct" Afghanistan. To find out more, I visited the man responsible for this sustained exercise in truth telling, in his office in Pentagon City, a prosperous district a few minutes' drive from the Pentagon itself, in which almost every office tower is jammed with corporations large and small feeding at the national security trough.

John Sopko is a lawyer and a veteran investigator for Congress and government, appointed to the job in 2012. He heads a team of 200 investigators and support staff, more than a quarter of them in Afghanistan. When he visits the country, he moves with a large security detail, since he is considered a high-value target— though not necessarily by the Taliban.

Where did the one hundred and something billion dollars go?
One hundred and ten billion, I think, is where our best guesstimate is. It may even be higher now. The [cost of] the total conflict there is over a trillion dollars. The actual fighting of the war over the last thirteen to fourteen years cost a lot more than reconstruction. War fighting is more expensive. Reconstruction is relatively cheap if it's done right. A lot of it was lost, fraud, waste and abuse. I don't know what percentage. We just don't have the time or the ability to calculate the loss, but a significant amount of that number is lost.

When you go there, do you see 110 billion dollars' worth of reconstruction? Could you put a price on what you do see?
No, I can't. We keep finding horror stories all the time. A lot of it was just stolen.

When you get into a war it's like you're on steroids, everything is just crazy, people are shooting at you. When you're on steroids, when you're in Afghanistan, you're spending more on AID [the Agency for International Development] than the next four countries combined. But the head of AID only visited Afghanistan twice. He rarely focused on it. He was more interested in something else; other issues were more important to him. It wasn't a priority.

The way we reward people in the government is not based on saving money. If you're a procurement officer your reward is on how much money you procure, how much money you put on contract. If you have a reward system in place, if you have a human resources system that rotates people out every six months, what do you expect is going to happen? Welcome to my world. It was a disaster ready to happen, and it happened. We wasted a lot of money. It wasn't that people were stupid, and it wasn't that people didn't care; it's just the system almost guarantees failure.

See this airplane here? [*Gesturing toward a plastic model of a twin-engine transport plane sitting on his office windowsill.*] That's a model of the G222. It was an airplane we purchased out of an Italian boneyard for . . . They were almost scrap. We purchased it for 400, 500 million dollars. We sent twenty of them over to Afghanistan. They were the wrong plane for the country, the altitude, the weather. They were basically referred to as death traps. They couldn't fly over there. The Afghans couldn't be trained on them. When I first saw them, they were sitting outside the airport in Kabul just rusting with trees growing through them. They were eventually turned into—when we started the investigation—scrap. We got three cents on the dollar. That's a 400, 500 million–dollar investment. We don't know the exact figure. No one has been fired for purchasing that airplane.

Now, you've worked in some major news-gathering organizations. If you lost 300 million dollars, do you think somebody would maybe say, "Gee, maybe it's time for you to move on"? Maybe you're not going to get your bonus this year. But this is the way the government works. If there's one critical thing, it's personal accountability in the government. You've got to fire some people. You can't always give them awards. Because it's cheap to give an award if everybody gets an award. It's like kids' soccer games when you had toddlers. Everybody gets a medal.

An unknowable quantity was just stolen. How much of that money came back here?
I can't really say for sure. A lot did come back here. A lot of it went to other places. You're getting into an area of classified information, but it's amazing the countries that the money has gone to, and that's all I can say. Everybody talks about Dubai because that's a flight away, so bulk cash got to Dubai, and then it went from there. But money also went to a lot of other countries.

How much of the money never left here?
Quite a bit. I don't have the percentage, but quite a bit ended up in the coffers of consultants, firms here, and it never got to Afghanistan, and that is a true complaint about our assistance program: high overhead costs. Again, nobody is minding the store. We also get instances where we do financial audits and we can't find any records to support the costs to the US government. We just had one of 130, 135 million dollars.

What was that for?
It was for Afghan National Security Forces training in the eastern part of the country. [*The contract was with Jorge Scientific, recipient of $1 billion in contracts.*]
    They just didn't have any records, so for 130-some million dollars they couldn't support where the money went. The prime contractor said, "It's not our problem, it's the subcontractor's," because they basically subbed the job out to somebody else. But we said: "No, no, no, under Contracting 101, going back to the 1860s, you're supposed to be responsible. You can't contract away, you've got to provide the records." So they said, "Well go to Guernsey; that's where our subcontractor is located." We said, "No, no, no, we're not going to Guernsey, we're just going to question where this $130 million went." We've had instances

where we've questioned costs and they said, "Oh, a flood or a fire," or, you know, "Somebody lost the records." Our concern is, when you can't support the record, can't support a cost, that it could just be fraudulent.

But of all of this, is there anything in particular that stands out for sort of the enormity of the waste?
I think this airplane, the G222, stands out. Not just the enormity but, I think, just the silliness. Another enormity—and this is for a different issue—this has to do with personal accountability. We just issued a report on what we call the 64K, the 64,000-square-foot building in Camp Leatherneck where three generals on the ground said, "We don't need it, we don't want it, we're not going to use it, don't build it." They were overruled by a general sitting back in a comfortable office, not in the fog of war, but back in Kuwait or Qatar or wherever he was, and he said, "Well, since it was supplemental appropriations it would be unwise or imprudent to ignore the wishes of Congress." So we spent $36 million on a building that was totally built, never used, and has been turned over to the Afghans. As far as we know, it's empty. That's another example: no accountability. When we referred it to the Pentagon—because we can't punish the general and the other people—the Pentagon said, "We didn't think that was a problem." Senator McCain has gone ballistic on it, and Senator Grassley and McCaskill and all saying: "What are you talking about? You just wasted $36 million. Nobody's accountable?"

Another example I like to cite for just how we don't understand Afghanistan: somebody came up with a brilliant idea in the Department of Agriculture that Afghans really should eat more soy. So they spent $36 million on creating a soy program. The Afghans don't grow soy, they don't eat soy, they don't like the taste of soy. But we spent $36 million doing this. We were kind of putting our value system, you know, "You should have a low-carb diet," onto the Afghans. It was a total disaster from the beginning to the end.

Would things have worked better if there had just been less money? Was the problem too much money?

Yeah, too much money, too fast, too small a country with too little oversight. It was like the four "too"s. That's the problem. Number two: the experts we didn't really listen to, Afghan experts, people who knew Afghanistan. Afghanistan is not the same as Iraq. We had too many people who said, "Oh, I did this in Iraq." They're two different countries. Afghanistan is a totally different mindset.

We didn't listen to our own experts, we didn't stick with a strategy that had buy-in from not only the international community but the Afghans. We didn't consider the corruption issue. We didn't consider sustainability. The Afghans only raise about $2 billion a year, and it's 8 to 10 billion dollars to keep the government afloat. So we basically have built a government for Afghanistan that they can't afford on their own. Why build something if you know they can't sustain it? We didn't really consider that. Because again, the incentives were: build something big, cut a ribbon, put money on contract, get your reward and then go to the next assignment. That's the problem. It was almost guaranteed to fail because of these inherent problems with the US government.

The one success story in Afghanistan for thirteen years is opium. That is a growth industry. Now we spent $8 billion to fight opium, and if you use any metrics, we failed. Number of people being arrested is down, the number of hectares under cultivation is up; every year it's going up. The amount of interdiction of drugs is down. The amount of drug addiction in Afghanistan is up. So every metric that you would normally use in fighting narcotics has been a total failure.

When you go to Afghanistan, do you have security?

Yeah, I have a lot of security. [One time] when the State Department security guy was briefing me, I said, "Look I'm not going to question you, you're a security expert, but somebody really wants to hurt me?" He said, "Mr. Sopko, are you talking about inside the embassy or outside the embassy?"

Have you encountered any outrage in the government about what you've been saying and reporting back here in Washington?
Well, there's pushback from a lot of people: I'm unfair. Why am I identifying people by name? Or, "You don't understand the situation, it's a war." We should waste money on a war, we can't be accountable?

Nobody has gotten fired in Afghanistan for all of the problems I've exposed.

No one?
Nope. Call up DOD, call up State, see if anybody has gotten fired. I bet you no one has lost a promotion. I bet you no one has lost a bonus.

The so-called "Afghan Papers" a series of documents compiled by Sopko's team, was released through a Freedom of Information Act request in 2019. They revealed that US military and civilian officials had long known, despite what they said in public, that the war was a hopeless cause. They did not acknowledge, of course, that the war's trillion-dollar budget constituted a victory in itself.

13

Mobbed Up

April 2018

In every war, the US Air Force seeks to destroy "critical nodes" essential to the enemy's war effort. In World War II, it was German ball-bearing factories. In Vietnam it was the Ho Chi Minh Trail. In Afghanistan, for a time, it was heroin laboratories, but like the earlier iterations of the strategy, this one proved futile, highlighting in the process the near-total, as well as complacent, ignorance of the western forces about the country in which they were fighting.

Lance Bunch has had an impressive year. In July 2017, the Air Force colonel was promoted to brigadier general while serving as the principal military assistant to James Mattis, the secretary of defense. His job put him at the epicenter of all US national security issues—and among the most pressing for Mattis at that moment was Afghanistan.

The pre-presidential Donald Trump had repeatedly questioned the need for US forces to stay in the country. The military leadership felt otherwise, and once Trump was elected, they argued that he should send more troops and hang on for the long haul. This meant beating back efforts by Steve Bannon to hold Trump to his earlier isolationist instincts. H. R. McMaster, the national security adviser, reportedly even showed the president a '70s-era photo of miniskirted women in Kabul as indication that the

Afghans were not beyond redemption. Ultimately, the generals carried all before them. Late in August, Trump announced, implausibly, that he had "studied Afghanistan in great detail and from every conceivable angle" and concluded that the top brass should have the open-ended commitment they demanded.

"We will also expand authority," said the commander in chief, "for American armed forces to target the terrorist and criminal networks that sow violence and chaos throughout Afghanistan." For Bunch, this feature of the plan would have particular significance. The following month, he was awarded his own command position: director of Future Operations at the American headquarters in Kabul. This was a brand-new unit (inevitably reduced to the acronym FUOPS) established to implement the new targeting strategy.

Three months into the job, General Bunch briefed the Pentagon press corps via video link on the novel features of his mission. "Before," he explained, "we could only target essentially in defense or in close proximity to Afghan forces that were in contact. Now, with our new authorities, we're able to target networks, not just individual fighters."

In other words, air power commanders could now operate autonomously, selecting and striking targets without reference to ground operations—the core doctrine of the US Air Force ever since it began its fight for independence from the Army between the world wars. Central to this approach is the idea of "critical nodes," elements in an enemy system that, when identified and destroyed, will cause that system to collapse. Accordingly, Bunch explained, his command would now target the Taliban in their "so-called safe zones, command-and-control nodes, illicit revenue–generating ventures and their logistical networks." Among these, the drug trade had been classified as especially vital, supposedly generating $200 million a year—60 percent of the Taliban's annual budget. If his campaign went according to plan, proclaimed the ebullient young general, "the future of Afghanistan is one free of terror, corruption and narcotic production."

The campaign, in fact, was already in process. The attacks had begun on the night of November 19, in Helmand Province, Afghanistan's most bountiful opium-growing region, deemed by Bunch the Taliban's "economic engine." The US commander in the country, Gen. John Nicholson, gave his own briefing in the immediate aftermath, supplying a running commentary for successive videos of individual strikes. One video featured the demolition of a "Taliban narcotics production facility" in the town of Musa Qala.

"As you look at this strike," Nicholson told the crowd of journalists, "you're going to see that inside this compound are multiple structures, and we destroy only two of them while leaving the third standing, which we did to avoid collateral damage." The images followed the familiar pattern of such PR displays. A peaceful vista of assorted structures, apparently unpopulated, is violently interrupted by a silent flash that gives way to a cloud of thick, black smoke.

By the time Bunch made his remarks, three weeks after the campaign began, twenty-five such "narcotics production facilities" had been attacked. He noted the impact in very precise terms: the drug kingpins had lost $80 million in merchandise, and the Taliban had consequently been deprived of $16 million in "direct revenue," meaning taxes on that merchandise.

Such certainty is questionable. Mike Martin, who spent years in Afghanistan as a British Army officer and then as a political adviser to the British forces, commented derisively to me: "Not long ago, the United States had over 100,000 troops in the country, plus a huge concentration of CIA and other intelligence resources. At that point, they couldn't understand what was going on: Mullah Omar had been dead for two years before they found out. Today, they have a footprint one fifteenth the size, so do they understand? They don't have a clue."

Nicholson had proudly touted the intelligence efforts preceding the air strikes, which had involved "hundreds of analysts," as well as drones, satellites and spy planes "soaking the area for hundreds of hours to then find, pinpoint, [and] assess the targets." What was missing from all this, Martin told me, was "human intel-ligence, which gives you context." Without such context, he said, the video and signals were meaningless "pinpricks."

For that matter, neither Nicholson's audience nor those hundreds of analysts poring over pictures of the target area for weeks before the strike could have known for sure who or what might have been inside those buildings that night. As it happened, one house in Musa Qala had contained the sleeping family of a local opium trader, Hajji Habibullah. All of them were killed, including Habibullah, his wife and six children, one of them just a year old. There was no mention of this collateral damage in US media coverage of the attacks, which was by and large uncritical and unquestioning of official claims that the Taliban had suffered a severe financial setback.

In any case, the claims of severe economic damage were highly dubious. According to information collected by local researchers for David Mansfield, a senior fellow at the London School of Economics, considered by many to be among the world's greatest experts on the Afghan opium economy, the results of the raid were considerably less impressive than advertised. Of the nine buildings hit in Musa Qala, for example, two were reportedly empty. Six were indeed used for cooking opium into heroin—but they, too, were probably empty at the time of the attack, since traders would be loath to leave valuable inventory in a lockup overnight. The following day, according to these on-the-ground reports, it was business as usual at the local drug bazaar. Prices for opium and heroin were unchanged, as were the wages demanded by workers in the "production facilities," which consisted of little more than a few oil drums, a hot plate and a connection to a water source. Children playing in the ruins found little trace of opium. Meanwhile, the unhappy fate of the Habibullah family was attract-ing wide publicity in the region, generating considerable outrage. (A military spokesperson in Kabul claimed that "There have been no validated instances of civilian casualties related to our strikes against enemy financial targets." He added that before air strikes, analysts are "able to tell if drugs labs are active or not.")

Mansfield has spent much of the past twenty years investigating the realities of the Afghan opium trade, traveling to the most remote and dangerous areas of the country. In a recent conversation, he pointed out that even if the destroyed labs had indeed been full of narcotics, the claims regarding the value of the merchandise were completely implausible, as was the argument that the Taliban would have collected $16 million in taxes. Such a claim presumed that the Taliban was an efficient, monolithic organization exacting unquestioning obedience from a compliant population. "The idea that the Taliban runs a tax system that the IRS would be proud of, in remote rural areas of a country that doesn't have a centralized government and never has had a centralized government," he told me, "just doesn't make sense."

In any case, Mansfield argued, intelligence assumptions about such fundamental issues as the opium tax rate have long been wildly off. If the Taliban had been due to collect $16 million from the traffickers' $80 million, that would suggest a rate of 20 percent. But Mansfield's own research indicates that the figure is much smaller and varies according to the bargaining skills on either side. Displaying a refreshing affection for hard data collected firsthand, he calculated that the true tax rate for a farmer's opium crop is a maximum of 3 percent, while the heroin rate is 1.5 percent. Not that everyone pays the full whack. "Everything is negotiable in Afghanistan," Mansfield said, especially since the farming communities are well armed and liable, if pushed too far, to eject the militia or strike a deal with a more accommodating Taliban commander.

Furthermore, Mansfield argued that the $80 million figure cited by Bunch was equally implausible. Even in the (unlikely) event that all the merchandise was high-value heroin, currently priced at $1,100 a kilo in the bazaars, the twenty-five demolished labs would have had to contain an average of three tons of product apiece, worth more than $3 million. As Mansfield saw it, the numbers simply didn't add up, in this case or in others. In his commentary on another attack video, this time of a building being obliterated by 2,000-pound bombs from a B-52, Nicholson stated confidently that there had been no fewer than "fifty barrels of opium," worth "millions of dollars," destroyed. Yet if Mansfield's pricing information is correct, those fifty barrels, as he reported in a paper for the LSE, "would have been worth at most $190,750, if converted to heroin, and no more than $2,863 to the Taliban in tax." Overall, he concluded, "The idea that the Taliban are reliant on opium for the war makes no sense whatsoever."

Rational or not, it is a proposition that has long appealed to Western politicians looking for excuses to occupy Afghanistan. Explaining his logic for joining the American invasion after 9/11, British prime minister Tony Blair assured Parliament that "the Al Qaeda network and the Taliban regime are funded in large part on the drugs trade." In fact, the Taliban government had effectively banned poppy growing the year before, and Al Qaeda was largely Saudi-funded. When the burgeoning crops that soon followed the regime's overthrow began attracting international attention, Blair successfully solicited the lead role for Britain in combating this supposed source of Taliban revenue. In Washington, too, bureaucrats at the State Department's International Narcotics and Law Enforcement Affairs division (known in Washington as Drugs and Thugs) were quick to promote the notion of the Taliban as a drug-fueled enterprise, as did the United Nations Office on Drugs and Crime.

The State Department had already developed a taste for such operations. On the other side of the world, the United States was sponsoring Plan Colombia, premised on a similar theory that the FARC insurgency was dependent on the cocaine business. The government used that as a rationale for spraying toxic herbicide across crops and people in coca-growing regions. William Wood, who as US ambassador to Colombia forcefully pushed the narco-terrorism narrative, moved to head the Kabul embassy in 2007, bringing equal zeal for this approach to his new posting.

For its part, the US military was initially reluctant to treat the conflict in Afghanistan as a drug war, as was the CIA. "Attacking the drug trade," Michael Hayden, the director of the CIA, told

Congress in 2006, "actually feeds the instability that you want to overcome." Indirectly at least, the Agency had skin in the game; at the time, it was paying a healthy retainer to Ahmed Wali Karzai, President Hamid Karzai's half-brother and a major player in the local narcotics business.

For those American officials who considered fighting narcotics as key to combating the Taliban and stabilizing Afghanistan, Gul Agha Sherzai, who had been appointed the governor of Nangarhar Province in 2005, was a welcome and indeed exciting ally. "Their attitude was, 'He's a real tough guy, and he's our friend,'" recalls Matthew Hoh, a senior civilian adviser in the province during those years who later quit the State Department in protest at the futility of the war. "They were thrilled to know him. He was 'our Tony Soprano.'" Burly, famed for his record as an anti-Soviet guerrilla commander in the '80s, Sherzai earned the nickname Bulldozer for his ability to deliver, especially on projects cherished by the Americans.

Most importantly, as US officials increasingly fixated on opium as the source of Taliban revenues, he was hailed for ridding his own province of the crop. In 2008, the UN declared Nangarhar "poppy free"—an achievement that earned Sherzai $10 million from a Good Performers Initiative fund set up by the United States and Britain to encourage communities fighting narcotics. Ambassador Wood, known as Chemical Bill for his eagerness to import toxic spraying to the poppy fields, nominated Nangarhar as a "model province." American aid soon swelled to a torrent. Even presidential candidate Barack Obama dropped by in July 2008 and was so charmed that he invited Sherzai to his inauguration.

The reality was a little different. In his previous role as the governor of his native Kandahar, Sherzai had earned a well-deserved reputation for corruption and cruelty, as well as garnering a healthy income from his extensive involvement in the local opium business. Sarah Chayes, who arrived in Kandahar in 2001 as a journalist, later founded an NGO to help Afghans find an alternative to opium farming and ultimately served as a senior adviser to the chairman of the Joint Chiefs of Staff, well understood the reality behind America's favorite Afghan governor. "He was deeply involved in poppy in Kandahar," she recalled recently, and when appointed governor of Nangarhar, "what he did was move into processing." So while Sherzai was basking in plaudits for stamping out opium growing (and impoverishing farmers in the process), he was manufacturing heroin.

"Those rewarding him should have known," Chayes told me. "This was not just the Afghan rumor mill." Her sources, she said, were at NATO headquarters in Kabul, meaning intelligence. "It was utterly typical of the double games we put up with and rewarded and thus became guilty of ourselves." Queried for his reaction, Sherzai, who currently serves as Afghanistan's minister of border and tribal affairs, responded with copies of glowing testimonials from American officials going back to his Nangarhar days. Speaking through a representative, he further insisted that he had "fought against opium cultivation" in the '90s and that he had "kept doing that his whole life," even during his tenure as governor of Kandahar.

There is a truism about Afghanistan that gets updated every year. Currently it runs: America has not been in Afghanistan for sixteen years; it has been in Afghanistan for one year, sixteen times. The complete lack of institutional memory may help to explain why the fervor of the anti-opium crusade keeps waxing and waning with policy shifts in Washington. The military, for example, had at first declined to play a major role—but then got on board after counterinsurgency doctrine (COIN) had supposedly helped to best Al Qaeda in Iraq. Applying COIN thinking to Afghanistan, they concluded that Afghan farmers should be weaned from growing opium, thereby lessening Taliban influence. To that end, the military eradicated crops whenever possible and induced farmers to grow something legal and supposedly profitable, such as wheat (though this is normally a subsistence crop in the country). However, Richard Holbrooke, appointed by President Obama to oversee Afghan policy, soon surmised that eradicating crops on which farmers depended for a living was a poor way to win support, and got that stopped, at least for a while. He also questioned the assumption that the Taliban depended on narcotics for funding, brandishing CIA reports that traced much of the group's money back to our allies in the Gulf oil kingdoms.

Despite these zigzagging shifts in policy, the universal assumption, at least among Western officials and media, was that the United States and its allies were supporting a legitimate Afghan government, albeit one marred by corruption, against a cohesive Taliban insurgency controlled from Pakistan. More complicated narratives were not welcome. One officer who served multiple tours in the country told me that new arrivals were never clued in as to what was really driving the conflict in the area: land disputes, tribal feuds, competition in the drug business. "It was: 'Welcome to Afghanistan, here's where you do your laundry, there's the chow hall. Do a check-fire of your weapon, then go out to your deployment area.' There was no turnover of institutional knowledge whatsoever."

This particular officer did make considerable efforts to understand what was going on, and eventually concluded that "Taliban" was "not really a useful term anymore." In reality, he concluded, the conflict in Helmand Province, where he was posted, was fundamentally driven by a long-standing clash between at least two powerful tribes, the Alizai (led by Sher Mohammed Akhundzada) and the Barakzai (led by Malim Mir Wali). Most pertinently, the rival leaders were rumored to head competing drug cartels. "Most of the violence that I saw was not really Taliban-driven," the officer said, "but cartel-driven." As he came to understand, each drug lord was constantly seeking to gain greater access to the opium crop at the expense of the other, principally by influencing local police chiefs and government officials. "I think these two individuals and others like them in Afghanistan use 'Taliban' to cover their tracks. They will say, 'There's terrible things going on, and I blame the Taliban, or I blame Pakistan,' when they are the ones actually doing it. So on any given day, violence will either remain on the border between their two territories or else push into one or the other's area."

My informant added that the drug lords were expert at manipulating American commanders. "You find no greater friend to the American than Sher Mohammed Akhundzada," he explained. "He speaks English, he rolls out the red carpet, he puts on a feast, and so everybody falls in love with him, never believing that he's into anything bad. Same thing with Malim Mir Wali. If you go to see him, he's going to give you the best rice, the best bread, the best chai, and you believe he's the key to the future. They are master manipulators and excellent politicians."

In fact, he recalled, there was a period when British troops in Helmand, influenced by Mir Wali, were assaulting Akhundzada's territory, while the Americans, under Akhundzada's spell, were doing precisely the opposite. They were carrying out "operations that were making our allies' lives harder and vice versa because we were caught in the middle of a civil war between two mafia families."

To Martin, such manipulating is a familiar story. He quickly recalled other cases in which these mafiosi had exploited outside powers to serve their own ends. Mir Wali, for example, had a profitable line in picking up local men, handing them over to the Special Forces and collecting the $2,000 bounty being offered for Taliban fighters. Some were sent to Guantánamo and languished there for years. Akhundzada, for his part, was removed from his post as the governor of Helmand after an antinarcotics squad discovered nine tons of opium in his office—a stash, as he later told Martin, that he had stolen from Mir Wali. Having revoked Akhundzada's governorship, Hamid Karzai nonetheless appointed him a senator in the Afghan parliament. Yet even with this stake in the central government, the wily drug lord hedged his bets by sending several thousand members of his private army to fight the Western and Afghan forces as "Taliban." Mir Wali, who also sported Taliban colors when it suited him, was a fellow member of parliament at the time.

Martin was a rarity among Westerners in the country in that he spoke fluent Pashto, the language of southern Afghanistan. After leaving the military, he spent years unraveling, through patient conversations with hundreds of locals, the real history of the war in Helmand, going all the way back to the '70s. His research, infinitely more detailed than that of the American officer quoted above but leading to similar conclusions, is laid out in *An Intimate War: An Oral History of the Helmand Conflict, 1978–2012*—an astonishing chronicle of feuds, betrayals, greed, manipulation, cruelty and (so far as the Americans and the British are concerned) stupidity and ignorance.

At one point, for example, Martin and his unit were asked by a district governor in Helmand to drive the Taliban out of a neighboring village, which they duly did, reinstalling the Afghan government police. He subsequently discovered that the "Taliban" were in fact a village militia formed to drive away the police— members of the governor's tribe—who had been robbing people and raping local boys. Furthermore, this was the governor's second stint as a local strongman: he had been chief of police under the Russians twenty years before. The "Taliban" whom he had sent the British to attack had been anti-Soviet resistance fighters in the earlier war.

As Martin recounts, such double-dealing agendas were the norm. The Helmandis adopted whatever label—police, Taliban, government militia—seemed most expedient at the time. Even when knowledgeable Westerners informed their superiors of the true state of affairs, as Sarah Chayes did when she heard of Obama's visit to Sherzai ("I cringed and tried to convey why that was exactly the wrong thing to do"), the government-versus-insurgency narrative was almost impossible to shake loose. Hence Martin's comment when I solicited his reaction to the recent strikes on the narcotics facilities: "How can they tell the difference between Taliban labs and government labs? Surely the intelligence came from drug factions pushing their own agenda. If you try and explain some of the complexities to Western officials and tell them, 'You're making things worse,' their faces go blank." (A military spokesperson said, "We are unaware of any report that says that the government of the Islamic Republic of Afghanistan is involved in the narcotics trade. The US military does not protect corrupt officials.")

One spectacular example of making things worse can be found in the explosive growth in the 2017 Afghan opium harvest: an eye-catching 87 percent increase over 2016. It was this bumper crop that did much to bolster the American designation of the Taliban as a narco-insurgency and launch the subsequent targeting campaign. According to Mattis, enemy advances and crop growth were closely connected: "As the Taliban surged, we watched the poppy surge right along with it. There's no surprise here—the intelligence community had warned us about this, so it's exactly what we were told would happen."

But why did Helmand farmers really grow so much more opium all of a sudden? In a supreme irony, the root cause would appear to be a multimillion-dollar effort by the United States and Britain to wean them *away* from opium. Agriculture in the region has traditionally been confined to areas irrigated by the Helmand River as it flows southwest from the Hindu Kush toward the Iranian border. But in the '50s, Washington had fostered a large-scale irrigation project that produced more fertile land—along with tribal disputes over ownership that underlie much of today's unrest and violence.

In recent decades, much of that land had been given over to opium. Beginning in 2008, the Americans and British began an ambitious project known as the Helmand Food Zone. The aim was to persuade farmers to shift from opium to wheat by means of inducements (seeds and fertilizer) and force (the prompt destruction of opium crops). Needless to say, the scheme was beset with problems, such as difficulties in seed distribution, which involved a major effort by overstretched British forces traveling over mine-strewn roads. Nevertheless, over most of the designated territory, amber waves of grain did begin to replace the poppy flowers. By 2012, the opium crop in the zone was one quarter of what it had been four years earlier. USAID alone had spent almost half a billion dollars in Helmand, but it did seem the project was working.

Opium, however, is a labor-intensive crop, while wheat is not. This meant that the farmers growing wheat had no need for the laborers and sharecroppers they had previously required. No one had thought about what might happen to the men who had worked on the opium plantations and were now without a live-lihood. For many, the solution was to move to the dry desert north of the Boghra Canal (built by the Americans in the '50s), drill wells and start planting opium. According to Mansfield, the population in that region went from almost zero in 2008 to 250,000 eight years later. Land was cheap to rent or buy, and planters were free of the unwelcome attentions of the US and Afghan government forces. Thus, as opium production declined in the Helmand Food Zone—to the delight of the project's sponsors and supporters, such as Senator Dianne Feinstein—the desert began to bloom. By 2012, opium production in the newly worked land exceeded the amount by which it had declined in the Food Zone.

Life in this desert paradise was not without challenges: early on, there were several years of bad harvests. In response, the farmers began switching from diesel pumps, which required expensive fuel and maintenance, to solar-powered Chinese models. Once purchased, these were essentially free to run and appeared to guarantee a limitless supply of water (although the long-term effects are likely to be catastrophic, since the northern Helmand water table is steadily sinking). Thanks to green energy, the farmers were soon pumping so much water that large ponds began appearing all across what had been desert only a year or so earlier. Mansfield recalls seeing these on aerial imagery and thinking: "What's this? Afghans are getting into swimming in a big way?" To further boost yield, growers also turned to a wide range of herbicides, including such locally labeled brands as Zanmargai ("Suicide Bomber") and Cruise (as in cruise missile).

Back in the Food Zone, meanwhile, all was not well. Though the presence of Western armies had for a while helped to suppress opium farming, the Afghan government had done little to endear itself to the local population, who complained angrily of every-thing from official corruption in wheat-seed distribution to bribery in the eradication program. Once the foreign troops pulled out in 2014, along with the hefty sums they had been injecting into the local economy, Afghan units were expelled from much of the area. Few farmers in the zone had been able to make an adequate living out of promoted alternatives like cotton or wheat. Now they eagerly began planting poppy again, thereby adding their bumper 2017 crop to the one sprouting in the new plantations.

In sum, the net effect of the most intensive effort ever to curb opium in Afghanistan was that the local crop almost doubled. Predictably, the actual reasons for this explosion went unexplored in official pronouncements, even as interested bureaucratic parties defaulted to familiar tropes regarding Taliban control of the business, which was now claimed to extend to processing. "I pretty firmly feel they are processing all the harvest," declared William Brownfield, the assistant secretary for drugs and law enforcement (another graduate of the Colombian program), in an August 2017 interview. "Where was the evidence for that?" asked David Mansfield. "He *felt* it?" Nevertheless, Brownfield's data-free hunch was now being translated into policy as the military, long dubious as to the merits of targeting labs from the air, finally signed on, and the bombs began to fall.

"It's very hard for people to integrate truth into the narrative," Martin told me in a long Skype conversation from Ethiopia, where he was en route to Somalia. We had been discussing the intricacies of tribal politics in Helmand and how such knowledge was essential to an understanding of the situation. But absorbing, for example, the twists and turns of Barakzai tribal history, or exactly how a farmer negotiates tax payments with the Taliban, does not fully reveal the story of the current war in Afghanistan. That requires some additional knowledge of the various cultures and subcultures at play on both sides—American as well as Afghan—and what really motivates them.

For example, Air Force publicity about the initial drug-lab raids emphasized the role played by the F-22 Raptor, a fifth-generation stealth fighter supposedly capable of evading enemy radar and costing, once all charges are included, in excess of $400 million per plane. When asked why it had been necessary to include this plane in the attacking force, Bunch invoked its ability to carry the GBU-39 Small Diameter Bomb, "which allowed us to be extremely precise, yet still target the Taliban narcotics labs and not cause any undue collateral damage."

But that particular bomb, which is in fact destructive over a wide area, can be carried by other planes. There were more weighty reasons to send the Raptor all the way from its base in Qatar (requiring multiple and expensive aerial refuelings along the way) to destroy a $500 drug lab. Though in service for twelve of the sixteen years we have been at war in Afghanistan, the plane has hitherto played no combat role, prompting potentially awkward questions about the worth of such expensive high-technology projects in modern warfare. It turns out that the groundwork is currently being laid for a *sixth*-generation fighter, projected to enter service a decade or so from now, which will be equipped with many novel and inevitably costly features. Highlighting the relevance of high-tech machines, and the budgets they justify, was therefore a powerful incentive for the Air Force to put the Raptor on display.

While the Air Force's zealous promotion of its bombing doctrine helps to explain why the United States apparently now believes that Afghanistan can be pacified from 20,000 feet, other features of American military culture, often unknown to outsiders, have also had their effect on the country. I'm told that the Marines, for example, pushed for a major role in Afghanistan partly because most of the force that had earlier been sent to Iraq had come from units based on the East Coast. Now the West Coast Marines wanted a chance to earn their share of battle honors, promotions and so forth.

Afghans who find bombs landing on their heads may not necessarily understand that at least some of their plight is a byproduct of US military personnel practices, notably the competition-based system for promotions. "If you get violent," the US officer quoted above explained to me, "if you call in an airstrike, not only do you get a combat ribbon and possibly an award for valor, but it also makes your report a *combat* report. When you have multiple combat reports and others do not, you're more competitive for promotion and assignment to prestigious billets." So even though the best course of action might be nonviolent, the culture is predisposed toward violence. "When you suggest doing something else," the officer told me, "guys will say: 'You're overthinking this. These people just need to be killed.'"

General Nicholson has said that the strategy endorsed by Trump last summer puts our side "on a path to win" in Afghanistan. He is at least the eighth senior American commander to pledge impending victory in those sixteen years of war. He will doubtless not be the last.

In the event, the anti–drug lab campaign didn't last long, being abandoned shortly after this article appeared. America's Afghan war continued, though, with strong bipartisan support. To prevent Trump from withdrawing remaining US forces, Congress voted to withhold the money required for bringing the troops home. Afghan entrepreneurs meanwhile discovered that a native plant, ephedra, freely available across otherwise barren mountain regions, was ideally suited for making methamphetamine. A prosperous industry emerged, and locally produced supplies of the drug were soon reaching markets in Europe and beyond. Finally, in 2021, President Biden ordered the withdrawal of all US troops.

14

A Very Perfect Instrument

September 2013

How mass starvation became America's favorite weapon, controlled by an obscure bureaucracy eager to advance its own influence and power.

At the beginning of World War I, Britain set up a blockade designed, according to one of its architects, Winston Churchill, to "starve the whole population of Germany—men, women and children, old and young, wounded and sound—into submission." By January 1918, the country's food supply had been reduced by half and its civilians were dying almost at the same rate as its soldiers. When the war finally ended eleven months later, the Germans assumed the blockade would be lifted and they would be fed again.

Instead the blockade went on, and was even tightened. By the following spring, German authorities were projecting a threefold increase in infant mortality. In March 1919, Gen. Herbert Plumer, commander of British occupation forces in the Rhineland, told Prime Minister David Lloyd George that his men could no longer stand the sight of "hordes of skinny and bloated children pawing over the offal" from the British camps.

In a later memoir, the economist John Maynard Keynes, at the time the chief adviser to the British Treasury, attributed this collective punishment of the civilian population most profoundly to a cause inherent in bureaucracy. The blockade had become by that time a very perfect instrument. It had taken four years to create and was Whitehall's finest achievement; it had evoked the qualities of the English at their subtlest. Its authors had grown to love it for its own sake; it included some recent improvements which would be wasted if it came to an end; it was very complicated, and a vast organization had established a vested interest. The experts reported, therefore, that it was our one instrument for imposing our peace terms on Germany, and that once suspended it could hardly be re-imposed.

Not until five months after the armistice did the Allies allow Germany to import food—not out of concern for the ongoing death and suffering, but out of fear that desperate Germans would follow the Russians into Bolshevism. By the time it was lifted, the peacetime blockade had killed about a quarter of a million people, including many children who either starved or died from diseases associated with malnutrition. There were efforts meanwhile among the victors to blame the food crisis on the postwar chaos inside Germany itself. What Woodrow Wilson approvingly called "this economic, peaceful, silent deadly remedy" retained its place in the armory of nations powerful enough to use it, preserved in international law as a mechanism for dealing with recalcitrant foes.

During the Cold War, the United States deployed sanctions and embargoes on a routine basis to punish countries that had earned Washington's disfavor. The Cubans were embargoed for having a revolution and rejecting US supervision. The Vietnamese were embargoed for having the temerity to win the Vietnam War—and after the Vietnamese Army ejected the genocidal Khmer Rouge from Cambodia, US sanctions were brought to bear on that country too, down to school pencils. Sanctions also crushed the economy of Sandinista-ruled Nicaragua, where household goods such as toilet paper became virtually unobtainable.

Thanks to the Cold War standoff between the United States and the Soviet Union, countries subject to American sanctions, most notably Cuba, could survive on trade and aid from the communist bloc. The fall of the Berlin Wall altered this equation. The United States was suddenly free to enforce peacetime sanctions quite in the spirit of 1919. Today, as America's armies of occupation fly home, such sanctions have in fact become our principal tool for global enforcement.

This tool has turned into a "machine unto itself," claims Vali Nasr, who served in the State Department during Obama's first term and is now dean of the Johns Hopkins School of Advanced International Studies. "It becomes a rote habit," he says, "operated by a bureaucracy that is always looking to close that last loophole. Pressure becomes the end, not the means." The roster of the twenty-three separate US sanctions programs ongoing today—a living memorial to the national-security preoccupations of past decades—tends to support Nasr's contention, ranging alphabetically from the Balkans to Cuba (on the list since the Kennedy Administration) to Zimbabwe.

The Iraq Stabilization and Insurgency Sanctions Regulations are on the list, too, though sanctions on Iraq supposedly ended with the 2003 invasion. (There are still Americans in jail for violating them.) Iran has been targeted ever since the takeover of the US Embassy in 1979, when David Cohen, now the Treasury Department's undersecretary for terrorism and financial intelligence and the overall supervisor of American sanctions operations, was in high school. In consequence, Iran has lost 60 percent of its oil exports; it is not free to spend the money earned from remaining oil sales; it cannot insure its tankers; it has almost no access to the international banking system. Its economy is shrinking and inflation is gathering speed.

Though food and medicine are theoretically exempt from this blockade, Iranians face huge obstacles in importing them. Three thousand Iranian cargo ships are stranded. The dragnet is global. An American who inherits an Iranian business, for example, risks arrest for violating sanctions. Individuals face jail time for exporting medical equipment to Iran or investing in an Iranian certificate of deposit. Costco recently acknowledged that it had allowed six employees of targeted Iranian institutions in Japan and Britain to buy its deeply discounted goods—a clear violation of sanctions—and duly struck them from its membership rolls.

Elsewhere, Syrians shivered for much of last winter because sanctions had halted supplies of home heating oil. Lebanese banks, a traditional refuge for Syrian capital, have been threatened as well. Despite its recent elevation in US favor, Burma still finds itself facing sanctions, either active or threatened. The system is enforced with punitive rigor. In sharp contrast to the benign treatment meted out to Wall Street banks following the 2008 crash, fines for sanctions infractions have risen to the hundreds of millions for foreign banks caught transferring Iranian payments.

Just as air power has evolved from the area bombing of entire cities during World War II to "precision" drone strikes, so the theory and practice of sanctions has evolved from straightforward blockades into a more ambitious and intricate system known as "conduct-based targeting," aimed at the economic paralysis of thousands of designated "entities"—people, companies, organizations. Drone operations attract widespread comment, inquiry, denunciation. Our modern economic warfare, though it bends the global financial system to its ends and can blight entire societies, operates well below the radar, frequently justified as a benign alternative to military action.

"Sanctions are the soft edge of hard power," said Robert McBrien as he put aside the broad-brimmed hat and dark glasses he'd worn to our meeting at a downtown Washington hotel. "They make people suffer. They hurt. They can destroy."

McBrien may be considered an authority on the subject, given his twenty-four years directing Global Targeting at the Office of Foreign Assets Control, the obscure but immensely potent executor of US sanctions warfare. OFAC is headquartered in the Treasury Annex, a building across from the White House that bears no outward identification save a plaque attesting to its former role as the site of the Freedman's Bank, which served emancipated slaves. The 200 professionals in the well-guarded offices almost all carry SCI (Sensitive Compartmented Information) clearances, beyond Top Secret, authorizing them to read decrypted signals intelligence. Most of them are lawyers—increasingly, former federal prosecutors—and they tend to stay in the job.

Cohen has no qualms about acknowledging that his office does more than just enforce sanctions. "We very much see ourselves as involved in the policymaking process," he told me.

"First they make the policy," commented a Washington attorney with years of experience of the system. "Then they write the laws. Then they enforce the laws. Imagine if the police did all of that. It would be a scary world."

Should OFAC's targeteers ("I hired most of them," says McBrien) even suspect that you are in some way connected with a violation of a US sanctions program, you may suddenly discover you are an SDN (Specially Designated National). Roughly 5,500 people, organizations and businesses are listed as such on the OFAC website. SDNs are essentially economic pariahs. Not only are they cut off from any contact with the US financial system, but banks who deal with them are threatened with similar exclusion. Given that almost all international business is carried out in dollars or euros—and that the Europeans are willing partners in our sanctions enforcement—this is a persuasive threat. As a former Obama Administration official told me, "There are businessmen all over the world terrified that they might have had lunch with an SDN."

"I tend to like sanctions programs that come as a complete surprise," remarked McBrien, sipping an iced tea. "It's shock and awe." Thus, the first you may know of your newfound status is when a US bank declines your ATM card, followed shortly after by a listing on the website for all to see. Finding out precisely why you have been listed can be tough, since OFAC is under no obligation to give anything but a vague explanation to Americans, and none at all to foreigners, nor even to wait for airtight proof that you are engaged in a sanctioned activity.

"This is considered an administrative matter," explains Erich Ferrari, a Washington lawyer specializing in relief for SDNs. "So all they need is a 'reason to believe' you are up to something, which can be based on a press clipping or a blog entry. You start by listing your assets and business activities for them. They send you questions. You reply. And so it goes on," he said, laughing ruefully, "for a number of years."

Given a good lawyer and a lot of time, an SDN can get off the list, though with one's assets frozen there is obviously a problem paying legal bills. OFAC will release money for fees—but it caps them at a rate equivalent to $175 an hour, chump change for the D.C. bar. And while foreign SDNs may have liquid funds, their lawyers risk having their own names added to the roster.

"The same people who put you on the list are the ones who decide whether to take you off," says Ferrari. "It's up to them whether to review the case. Often the evidence is classified, and they won't show it to me." The classified information comes courtesy of OFAC's access to US intelligence, including the NSA's ubiquitous communications intercepts. ("When you've just talked to a European finance minister," one former Treasury official told me, "it's quite useful to read the transcript of the call he then makes to the head of his central bank.")

Death can bring relief from the list—but not automatically. Osama bin Laden is still there, the multiple spellings of his name meticulously noted. "Just because a party is dead does not mean that they cannot or will not be targeted for US sanctions," observes Ferrari. "Of course, it's hard to change their behavior. But without the targeted party alive to contest the designation, no one is going to be overly concerned with that aspect of it."

The system, according to the men who built it, has grown gradually but inexorably. The immediate predecessor to OFAC was created in 1950, when the Chinese entered the Korean War and President Truman decided to freeze all Chinese and North Korean assets. A Treasury official named Richard Newcomb took it over in 1987, when it had a staff of twenty, and ran it for the next seventeen years—one of those powerful Washington bureaucrats unknown to the wider world. He reminisced proudly to me about the invention of the SDN, which took place around the time the

Cold War ended. It "really was a [new] foreign policy tool in the state's quiver," Newcomb said.

He recalled a brief period in 1990 when it appeared that peace might break out all over and even the long-standing Cuban embargo was apparently winding down. "A major network was going to broadcast its morning show from Havana!"

Then, on August 2, 1990, came news that Saddam Hussein had invaded Kuwait. Summoned to an urgent meeting in the White House Situation Room, Newcomb was asked how quickly the US could freeze Saddam's assets. "I told them, 'You can implement it overnight,' and they woke up Bush to sign the order," he said. "It was very exciting." With the Soviets a spent force, the UN could easily be brought into line, and Iraq was soon under total blockade. As the merits of war with Iraq were hotly debated in Washington, sanctions drew hearty endorsements from the anti-war faction as a peaceful alternative: surely they could achieve the same objective if given "time to work."

It was the dawn of a golden age for sanctions. OFAC's portfolio steadily expanded, targeting opponents of the Israeli–Palestinian peace accords, zeroing in on the Serbian regime of Slobodan Milošević, shredding the business empires of Colombian cartel chiefs. And even before 9/11, OFAC had assumed a growing role in counterterrorism as Newcomb connected with Richard Clarke, a rising star in the security and intelligence apparatus.

Though Saddam was long gone from Kuwait, sanctions on Iraq were still a major operation. Meanwhile, the sanctions on Iran imposed back in 1979 had never been totally lifted. Along with enforcing a trade embargo, Carter had seized $12 billion of Iran's money held in American banks. Supposedly the money was to be released and the trade embargo lifted once the embassy hostages came home, but a large portion remained frozen pending claims by US corporations over contracts signed with the shah but never fulfilled. As McBrien puts it, "We grabbed much of Iran's wealth and kept it."

Formal sanctions were resurrected and gradually strengthened during the early 1990s, banning arms sales and spare parts for

Iran's American-built warplanes and airliners, as well as all imports of Iranian oil into the United States. By 1995, US investment in Iran's petroleum industry was forbidden, followed by a further bar on US trade with the country. But efforts to get other countries to support the campaign withered in the face of European resistance.

Indeed, up until this point, sanctions had suffered from a fundamental flaw: true effectiveness required international cooperation. The Cubans had survived decades of US embargo because the rest of the world had seen no reason to join in. But all that began to change when the United States learned to use its dominance of the international financial system as a weapon.

In 2004, George W. Bush appointed Stuart Levey, then an ambitious Justice Department lawyer, to oversee all sanctions operations. Levey realized that he could pressure foreign banks into cutting off relations with Iranian banks by threatening their access to US financial markets—a process that Cohen has demurely described as a "vigorous outreach and education effort." Since all international banks must be able to trade in dollars, this was a formidable threat. The point was driven home by an $80 million fine, huge for its time, imposed on a Dutch bank, ABN Amro, that had processed dollar transactions for Iranian and Libyan banks. The Amro settlement set a pattern, with fines climbing toward $1 billion within a few years.

The beauty of the "secondary sanctions" system lay in its self-enforcing nature. Repeatedly reminded of what could happen if they were caught dealing with a targeted Iranian, terrified foreign banks preferred to avoid contact with any Iranian of any description, whether they were on the target list or not. Meanwhile, the banks and other major corporations hurriedly expanded their "compliance" departments, a fruitful source of employment for OFAC veterans, to further ensure against unwitting contamination.

So for all the claims of precise, "conduct-based" targeting, Levey's revolution rendered sanctions far more blunt and indiscriminate than officially advertised. In theory, trade in humanitarian goods, food and medicine has always been exempt—but if payments for such goods cannot be processed, then the effect is the same. Meanwhile, European governments were now obediently adopting their own stringent sanctions against Iran. Paris was especially vigorous in leading this united front—as a former French diplomat told me, the foreign ministry "drank from the cup of neoconservatism."

If Iranians hoped that the election of Barack Obama would bring some relief, the new president's retention of Levey in his post was a clear indication that little would change. The same might be said of Levey's trip to Israel two weeks after the election. An instructive cable released by WikiLeaks detailed not only his reassurances to a slew of Israeli officials, but also the progress report he delivered on his success in curtailing most "major players" from doing business with Iran, as well as plans to hit Iran's oil-refining and insurance industries.

In contrast to Hillary Clinton, who threatened during her presidential campaign to "totally obliterate" Iran, candidate Obama had indicated an interest in a "dual track" approach to the Iranian nuclear issue—that is, pursuing diplomacy while maintaining "targeted" sanctions. In the end, though, it came to the same thing. Negotiations to swap Iranian stocks of low-enriched uranium for supplies of more highly enriched fuel (necessary for the production of medical isotopes to treat 850,000 Iranian cancer patients) ended up going nowhere. It was time, as David Cohen said later, to develop and implement "truly biting sanctions" against Iran.

So eager was the Obama Administration to proceed that other issues took second place. In return for Russian cooperation, for example, the United States abandoned its cherished goal of NATO expansion, discarded plans for a missile shield in Eastern Europe, stopped lecturing the Russians about human rights and lifted earlier restrictions on Russian arms exports. Just as bombing strategists had searched for the "critical nodes" that would cripple the German, Korean, Vietnamese and Iraqi war economies, so the sanctions planners successively targeted elements of the Iranian economy, including what Cohen called the "key node" for processing oil revenues: the Iranian central bank.

Since Iran refined little oil itself, gasoline imports were targeted in 2010 in the expectation that this would generate potentially destabilizing unrest. Fuel shortages did make it harder for ordinary Iranians to get around, thinning out Tehran's legendary traffic jams—but they also forced drivers to use low-quality, locally refined gasoline, increasing pollution to dangerous levels. A year later, sanctions were imposed on any foreign bank that processed oil deals with the Iranian central bank. In 2012, Obama signed the Iran Threat Reduction and Syria Human Rights Act, cutting off access to the US market for any foreign company doing business with Iran's energy sector and freezing any American assets they might have. A similar provision was inserted into Section 1245(d)(1) of the 2012 National Defense Authorization Act, which is meant to be about Pentagon funding, not sanctions.

Thanks to such "innovative tools," as Cohen has proudly called them, Iran's oil exports plummeted from 2.4 million barrels a day in 2011 to 1 million just a year later. "We have in place now," declared Cohen in September 2012, "an enormously powerful set of sanctions at home and around the world. It retains its essential conduct-based foundation as it broadens out to target an ever more comprehensive set of Iranian commercial and financial activities."

Once upon a time, such tactics had been the exclusive preserve of presidents. Kennedy had put Cuba under total embargo with a stroke of the pen (though not before securing a hoard of 1,200 Cuban cigars for himself). Carter had imposed sanctions on Iran in 1979 with a similar executive order, and Reagan had lifted them the same way—except, of course, for the frozen and effectively confiscated Iranian deposits in US banks. But in the 1990s Congress began passing its own sanctions laws. As Nasr pointed out to me, "It's a way for Congress to have a foreign policy." Having long since forfeited its ability to declare war, Congress can still impose sanctions—which it does with increasing avidity and no inhibitions about targeting ordinary citizens. ("Critics

[have] argued that these measures will hurt the Iranian people," wrote Brad Sherman, a Democratic congressman from California, in 2010. "Quite frankly, we need to do just that.")

In consequence, many of the "truly biting" measures cited by Cohen have come from Capitol Hill, passed with crushing bipartisan majorities, and can be repealed only from there. Certain members, such as Senators Mark Kirk of Illinois and Robert Menendez of New Jersey, as well as Ed Royce, chairman of the House Foreign Affairs Committee, have emerged as pacesetters on the issue. Behind these public figures stand an assortment of more shadowy aides, such as Kirk's deputy chief of staff Richard Goldberg or Royce's foreign policy adviser Matthew Zweig. They in turn work closely with powerful outside players in the world of sanctions, most notably a group called the Foundation for Defense of Democracies, chaired by former CIA director James Woolsey.

"A friend told me recently that we are the Special Forces of the Washington think-tank community," Woolsey said cheerfully when I called. "I liked that." Founded in the immediate aftermath of 9/11, the group has in the past secured its funding, currently around $8 million a year, from such traditional wellsprings as Edgar Bronfman and Michael Steinhardt. Fusing in one entity the parallel tracks of sanctions and drone warfare, the FDD also publishes *The Long War Journal*, a chronicle of American military conflict in the twenty-first century.

Woolsey quickly referred me to the foundation's executive director, Mark Dubowitz, who came to his $300,000-a-year job from the world of venture capital. Dubowitz was happy to endorse the Special Forces accolade when I reached him, though he insisted that "being a Canadian, [therefore] by upbringing modest," he couldn't take much credit for crafting the destruction of the Iranian economy. Others in the community are more generous, noting Dubowitz's handiwork in stipulations buried deep in congressional bills. Section 219 of the Iran Threat Reduction Act, for example, requires any company that files with the SEC to report any connection to trade with Iran—or any connection to *another* company that trades with Iran. This was the mechanism that unmasked the six Costco club members in Japan and Britain.

"The aim of sanctions," Dubowitz told me, "is to try and bring the Iranian economy to the brink of economic collapse and, in doing so, create fear on the part of the Supreme Leader and [his Revolutionary Guards] that economic collapse will lead to political collapse and the end of their regime . . . We're trying to break the nuclear will of a hardened ideologue."

Effortlessly reeling off statistics on hard-currency earnings and the technicalities of petroleum refining, Dubowitz lamented the resources still available to the enemy. He outlined a plan to cut off all remaining Iranian oil exports. "Countries would have to stop buying Iranian oil immediately, or their banks would be sanctioned," he explained. "Chinese, Japanese, South Korean, Indian, South African, Turkish, Taiwanese—everyone who's buying Iranian oil would be given a short period of time to go buy it somewhere else, or face sanctions against their financial institutions . . . We could take a million barrels of Iranian oil off the market tomorrow."

China? India? This seemed ambitious indeed. I asked Dubowitz whether the administration had the will to enact such measures. "Congress has the will to do this," he answered firmly, and predicted that I would see legislation along these lines within a few weeks.

Sure enough, on May 22, Ed Royce's Foreign Affairs Committee voted unanimously for the Nuclear Iran Prevention Act, aimed not only at eliminating practically all remaining Iranian oil exports but also at choking off Iran's access to its dwindling foreign-currency reserves. "We squeeze—and then squeeze some more," said Royce. Representative Tom Cotton, an Arkansas Republican, suggested a provision mandating punishment for relatives of sanctions violators, including uncles, nephews, great-grandparents, great-grandchildren and so forth. But this was too much even for his colleagues, who rejected the proposal.

Meanwhile, across Capitol Hill, in the Hart Building, Senator Kirk was germinating another bill, one that would dispense with the fiction that Iranian sanctions are aimed purely at the country's nuclear program. In theory, Iran's abandonment of its nuclear ambitions would lead to the end of sanctions. But the ayatollahs don't believe this. In their view, the United States has never accepted their revolution and is still bent on overthrowing them. According to two former State Department officials, Ayatollah Ali Khamenei, the Supreme Leader himself, made this very argument to the American diplomat Jeffrey Feltman (now UN undersecretary general for political affairs) when the latter visited Tehran with a high-level UN delegation in 2012. America's credibility with the Iranians is shot. Or as Trita Parsi, president of the National Iranian American Council, puts it: "We have sanctioned ourselves out of any influence on Tehran."

Khamenei will find no surprises in Kirk's upcoming bill, which will condition sanctions not on the cessation of the nuclear program but on OFAC's certifying that the Government of Iran has released all political prisoners, is transitioning to a free and democratically elected government and is protecting the rights and freedoms of all citizens of Iran, including women and minorities.

As Parsi notes, the Iranian leadership has responded to previous sanctions by redoubling work on its nuclear program—not exactly the intended effect. Nor is the election of Hassan Rohani as president of Iran, despite his reputation as a "moderate," likely to lead to any softening of sanctions. "My sense," Dubowitz assured me shortly after the vote, "is that it's full steam ahead."

Of course, we have been here before. For twelve years, we were asked to accept that the sanctions on Iraq were tied to Saddam's alleged weapons of mass destruction. UN inspectors dutifully combed the country year after year in an unrelenting search for the merest trace of a chemical, biological or nuclear weapon, but after initial nuclear discoveries, nothing was ever found. Even at the very end, as George W. Bush and Tony Blair pushed us into war, dovish commentators lamented that the inspectors "had not been given more time."

Once in a while, officials would casually concede the truth: WMDs had nothing to do with it. As George H. W. Bush noted immediately after the 1991 Gulf War, there would be no normal relations with Iraq until "Saddam Hussein is out of there," and we would meanwhile "continue the economic sanctions." In case anyone had missed the point, his deputy national security adviser, Robert Gates, spelled it out a few weeks later: "Saddam is discredited and cannot be redeemed. Iraqis will pay the price while he remains in power. All possible sanctions will be maintained until he is gone."

This sounded like an inducement to Iraqis to rise up and overthrow Saddam, and so relieve their misery. But I was assured at the time by CIA officials that an overthrow of the dictator by a desperate population was "the least likely alternative." There could be only one conclusion about the purpose of the sanctions program: the impoverishment of Iraq was not a means to an end, it *was* the end.

Visiting Iraq in that first summer of postwar sanctions, I found a population stupefied by the disaster that was reducing them to a lower-tier Third World standard of living. Baghdad auction houses were filled with the heirlooms and furniture of the middle classes, hawked in a desperate effort to stay ahead of rising inflation. Doctors, most of them trained in Britain, displayed their empty pharmacies. "No Iraqi babies invaded Kuwait, so why must they suffer?" cried one staffer in a hospital in Amara, as I toured a ward of sickly, wasted infants. Everywhere, people asked when sanctions would be lifted, assuming that it could only be a matter of months at the outside (a belief initially shared by Saddam). The notion that they might still be in force a decade later was unimaginable.

In theory, the doctors should not have had anything to worry about. Sanctions made a specific exception for "supplies intended strictly for medical purposes, and in humanitarian circumstances, foodstuffs." However, every single item that Iraq sought to import, including such clearly humanitarian commodities as food and medicine, had to be approved by the UN committee created for this purpose and staffed by diplomats from nations belonging to the Security Council, including OFAC officials. It met in secret and published few records of its proceedings.

Throughout the entire period of sanctions, the United States blocked attempts to import pumps desperately needed in water treatment plants along the Tigris. The river became an open sewer. Chlorine, vital for disinfecting such a tainted water supply, was excluded on the grounds that it could be used as a chemical weapon. The results were visible in hospitals' pediatric wards. Health specialists agreed that contaminated water was killing the children with gastroenteritis and cholera—diseases that overcame their victims with relative ease since the children were already weak from malnutrition.

Every so often a press report from Baghdad would highlight the immense, slow-motion disaster taking place in Iraq. For the most part, however, the conscience of the world, and especially that of the US public, was left untroubled. Administration officials reassured themselves that any hardship was purely the fault of Saddam, and that in any case reports of civilian suffering were deliberately exaggerated by the Iraqi regime. As one US official with a key role in the UN weapons inspections remarked to me with all sincerity at the time: "Those people who report all those dying babies are very carefully steered to certain hospitals by the government."

From time to time, this curtain of hypocrisy would slip, as when Madeleine Albright, then US ambassador to the United Nations, told *60 Minutes* that the price paid by the multitude of dead Iraqi children was "worth it." In 1997 the chief UN inspector, a Swedish diplomat named Rolf Ekéus, concluded that there were no WMDs in Iraq and informed the Clinton Administration that he would say so publicly, thereby alarming Clinton that Republicans might denounce him for letting Saddam off the hook. Accordingly, Albright quickly announced that sanctions would remain, WMDs or no. Saddam then ceased cooperating with inspectors—as the Clinton Administration fully expected he would—thus freezing both the bogus weapons issue and sanctions in place until superseded by war, occupation, IED's and suicide bombers.

Invading forces arriving in Baghdad found a society degenerated into criminality and corruption, its once vaunted education and health systems in tatters, its populace seeking solace in fundamentalist Islam. With the slender threads of state authority finally broken, the capital dissolved into anarchy. "We destroyed the middle class," observes Vali Nasr, "so when we arrived, we got Sadr City"—the impoverished slum from which rioters emerged to pillage Baghdad.

It should be noted in passing that although sanctions are frequently promoted as, in Cohen's words, "a heck of a lot better than war," Iraqi sanctions are conservatively estimated to have killed at least half a million children, while estimates of the total death toll from subsequent violence—a still horrific 174,000—are lower.

No one in Washington these days likes to talk about Iraqi sanctions, or to reflect on whether they might have had anything to do with Iraq's inability to recover as a functioning state. "First of all, I don't believe half a million died," a former sanctions official told me. "And secondly, there were supplies of food and medicine, but Saddam controlled them. He was a brutal dictator." I asked Cohen if he saw any parallels between that era and his present activities. "Not really," he replied. "I think the sanctions that we have in place today are far different from those that we constructed at that time . . . The differences far outweigh whatever similarities there may be."

Yet there are ominous echoes of the Iraqi disaster in recent reports from Iran. The most obvious similarity is the collapsing currency, dropping from 16,000 rials to the dollar in early 2012 to 36,000 a year later—very much according to the sanctions plan. (As Cohen noted with satisfaction in Senate testimony in mid-May, "There's a tremendous demand for gold among private Iranian citizens, which in some respects is an indication of the success of our sanctions.") The price of a kilo of low-quality minced meat, for example, recently doubled in a week, to the equivalent of a day's pay for a construction worker.

The echoes recur in less statistically obvious ways. Aircraft are crashing in greater numbers, largely because of an ongoing shortage of long-embargoed spare parts. Crime and drug addiction are growing exponentially, there being absolutely no shortage of narcotics, especially heroin from nearby Afghanistan, but also cocaine, the perquisite of the rich. Just as sanctioned Iraqis found a class of "new billionaires" flaunting their wealth in the midst of want, so sanctions are enriching a similar class of Iranians, not only drug dealers but smugglers, refinery operators and other profiteers.

The clearest echo of all is to be found in the sanctions on medicine. As in the case of Iraq, where "humanitarian" goods and services were supposedly exempt, this embargo does not officially exist. Even Congress, despite calls to "hurt" the Iranian people, makes an exception for such goods in its otherwise draconian legislation. OFAC will grant licenses for shipments, though not always expeditiously. (As a former OFAC staffer told me, "Licenses get done when they get done.") Cohen, too, insisted that his organization would not bar such aid: "The reality is that our sanctions do not forbid the export to Iran of food, medicines, [or] medical devices, whether it's some US company or some foreign company that wants to export those humanitarian goods. There's nothing that forbids that."

Reality gives the lie to these assertions. Simply put, licenses and waivers are irrelevant, because the excision of Iranian banks from the global financial system makes it practically impossible for anyone exporting medical supplies to Iran to get paid. The US campaign to scare banks out of dealing with Iran under any circumstances has seen to that. And while Levey, like Cohen, insists that "US sanctions carve out transactions for medicine and agricultural products," Siamak Namazi, a Dubai-based researcher who has made the deepest study of this issue, argues otherwise. He quotes a senior Iranian pharmaceutical executive who flew to Paris to present a French bank with documents showing a trade was fully legal, only to be told, "Even if you bring a letter from the French president himself saying it is OK to do so, we will not risk this."

So, years pass. We "squeeze, and then squeeze some more" with no end in sight. I am told that there were high-level intelligence briefings in Washington late last year predicting popular unrest in Iran due to hardships inflicted by the sanctions. I myself saw evidence of this misapprehension in a chance dinner conversation with a very senior State Department official and a wealthy Iranian-American businessman.

"The Iranians will respond to pressure," said the official confidently.

I repeated this remark to the Iranian sitting beside him, whose eyes promptly widened in astonishment. "Oh no, not at all," he replied. "You should meet my aunts in Tehran. They are from the old regime, nothing to do with the government, and yet they are so angry about the sanctions, they demonstrate for a nuclear Iran."

The official looked astonished in turn. The notion that sanctions might be counterproductive was clearly new to him. But then, that was never the point of the "perfect instrument." As for those "skinny and bloated children" who so disgusted the British troops in Germany a century ago, a later survey of 600 young Nazis on their motivations for supporting Hitler suggested that a major influence was their vivid memories of childhood hunger and privation.

Bipartisan thirst for this especially cruel form of collective punishment continued unabated through the Trump regime and beyond, and with it the power of the OFAC sanctioneers. Without serious debate or calculation of the consequences, Syria, already destroyed by years of war, was subjected to the 2019 Caesar Act, which effectively destroyed its economy and reduced much of its population, whether supporters of the government or opposition, to grinding poverty and worse.

PART IV

Simple Billion-Dollar Money-Grubbing

15

Saving the Whale, Again

April 2015

As we have seen, "policy" in war and diplomacy invariably turns out to be a polite way of referring to the pursuit of money and/or domestic political advantage. When the policy is explicitly greed and fraud, the sums get bigger, and the fallout more catastrophic for everyone else.

In the late fall of 1970, a forty-five-foot sperm whale beached itself on the Oregon coast and expired. Local authorities, puzzling over how best to dispose of the huge rotting carcass, decided to blow it up, trusting that seabirds and other scavengers would consume any remains not carried out to sea. A half-ton of dynamite was accordingly packed around the whale and detonated, but things did not go as planned. Instead of the intended tidy dissolution, huge chunks of decaying blubber rained down far and wide, destroying property and inflicting a noxious stench throughout the landscape.

That fiasco, a financial-industry lobbyist suggested to me recently, was the perfect metaphor for Citigroup, the megabank described by one leading Wall Street analyst as "the Zelig of financial recklessness," involved in every speculative catastrophe of the past few decades. Here, after all, was another beached leviathan perpetually threatening to die, leaving a nondisposable corpse, unless the rest of us keep it alive by pouring water over it.

Back in 2008, this potent threat elicited hurried bailouts in the trillions of dollars to save Citigroup from its latest debacle. The bank had placed enormous bets on risky derivatives that had gone very, very wrong—a prime cause, many argued, of the overall crash. In hopes of warding off a repeat disaster, Congress passed the Dodd–Frank Act, in 2010, which, among other corrective measures, banned taxpayer-insured banks from trading the more toxic varieties of derivatives, notably credit-default swaps. The law stipulated that such trades should be "pushed out" to uninsured affiliates, thereby forcing the firms to assume the risk themselves.

All the major banks chafed at this restriction, but Citigroup took the lead in overturning it. Its eagerness is best explained by the fact that while the other Wall Street behemoths are currently tapering their derivatives trading, Citi has been expanding its own. As of September 2014, its portfolio of potentially lethal financial instruments had a notional value of $70 trillion.* So as Congress rushed to vote on a "must pass" spending bill a few months ago, Citigroup lobbyists enlisted a pliable legislator to insert a provision eliminating the push-out rule.

Dennis Kelleher, of the financial-reform group Better Markets, pithily summarized the issue for me. "The push-out rule said you can do all the derivatives trading you want," he noted. "You just can't shift your losses to the American people." By inserting its stealth provision, the banking giant ensured that "taxpayers are now on the hook for high-risk derivatives trading. That's why Citigroup drafted it. That's why Citigroup spent a fortune on lawyers and lobbyists and campaign contributions to make it happen."

Congressional leaders in both parties made sure that Citigroup got its way. Republicans, with the exception of a dwindling band

---

* Notional value is the "face amount" of the contract. For example, ABC Company might purchase a credit-default swap that will pay $100 million if XYZ Company defaults on its debt. The notional value of the swap is $100 million, even if the instrument itself is trading at a fraction of that amount.

of Tea Party stalwarts, were enthusiastic in their support. Democrats were more sheepish, with the president himself publicly decrying the measure even as he lobbied Congress to pass the spending bill itself. Even so, the megabank's maneuvers generated widespread outrage, and Elizabeth Warren seized the moment.

"Enough is enough!" she declared in an impassioned speech on the Senate floor, denouncing Citigroup's coup. Comparing the bank's power to that of the Democratic and Republican parties, she highlighted Citigroup's "unprecedented" grip on the Obama Administration, citing seven current or recent high-level policy-makers with close ties to the firm. Her roll call included Jacob Lew, a former chairman of the Office of Management and Budget— "also a Citi alum," said Warren, "but I'm double-counting here, because now he's the Secretary of the Treasury."

Sheila Bair, who was chair of the Federal Deposit Insurance Corporation (FDIC) from 2006 to 2011, confirms Warren's assessment, citing her own experiences on the inside. "They intimidate you," she told me recently, referring to the big financial institutions. "I think this has been a big problem with this administration. You see all these former Citi people influencing government, and you're afraid to voice opinions that are critical of them or different from their views."

Multitrillion-dollar derivatives trades may have little direct impact on ordinary Americans, unless and until they bring down the economy, as they did in 2008. But other recent Citigroup initiatives will have more immediate effects. According to the Federal Reserve, 52 percent of Americans are unable to lay their hands on as little as $400 in an emergency. Instead, millions of people in urgent need turn to consumer-loan companies, which charge high interest rates. Among the leaders in this field is OneMain Financial, a Citigroup subsidiary, whose website declares its dedication to the penniless consumer: "Your needs. Your goals. Your dreams.™"

Intent on shedding consumer-related subsidiaries in order to concentrate on trading, Citi has for some time been planning to sell OneMain. To hit its target price of $4 billion, however, Citi needed to boost the company's already substantial profit margin, which was up 31 percent in 2013—and the way to do *that* was to persuade state legislatures to loosen restrictions on interest rates. This usurer-relief campaign has been increasingly successful, with lawmakers in Arizona, Florida, Indiana, Kentucky, Missouri and North Carolina buying the argument that lenders such as OneMain actually "work with their customer," as demonstrated by low default rates.

OneMain "definitely led the lobbying effort in North Carolina," Chris Kukla, senior vice president at the Center for Responsible Lending, told me. He said the loan company was "pretty aggressive" in collecting its money. When a borrower does default, companies like OneMain "back up a truck to the house and take the furniture and the TV set." However, the company much prefers to keep customers on the hook by repeatedly and expensively refinancing their loans—which helps to explain the low default rates.

Citi's efforts paid off in June 2013, when the North Carolina legislature raised the ceiling on interest rates. By Kukla's calculation, the revised law has made the situation for borrowers much worse. The interest on an average loan of about $3,000 has risen from slightly more than 20 percent to 30 percent; borrowing that money costs the company itself just 3 percent, at most.

OneMain is part of Citigroup thanks to a Wall Street dealmaker named Sandy Weill, who realized the stunning possibilities of this kind of business back in 1986. At the time, Weill had recently been eased out from Shearson Lehman/American Express, a financial conglomerate he had helped to build. Eager to get back in the game, he bought a Baltimore firm called Commercial Credit. In the view of Weill and his protégé, Jamie Dimon, their new acquisition was in the beneficent business of supplying "consumer finance" to "Main Street America." Their office receptionist, Alison Falls, thought otherwise. Overhearing their conversation at work one day, she called out: "Hey, guys, this is the loan-sharking business. 'Consumer finance' is just a nice way to describe it."

Falls had it right. Commercial Credit made loans to poor people at predatory interest rates. Strapped to pay off their loans, borrowers were encouraged to refinance, with added fees each time. Gail Kubiniec, who was then an assistant sales manager at the company's branch office in Tonawanda, New York, remembers that the basic aim was to lend money to "people uneducated about credit. You could take a $500 loan and pack it with extra items like life insurance—that was very lucrative. Then you could roll it over with more extra items, then reroll the new loan, and the borrower would go on paying and paying and paying."

Weill considered these practices a "platform" on which his company could grow—and indeed, Commercial Credit stock rose 40 percent in his first year. Not only did this boost his already considerable personal fortune, it enriched his loyal team, the members of which would one day reach commanding heights on Wall Street. Dimon is now the head of JPMorgan Chase. Charles Prince served first as CEO and then as chairman of Citigroup. Robert Willumstad became president of Citigroup and later headed American International Group, where he oversaw the insurer's spectacular crash in 2008.

By 1988, Commercial Credit was generating enough profit for Weill to take over Primerica, a much bigger company involved in insurance, stockbroking and other financial services. Three years later, however, a *Forbes* article reported that "the insurance operations are a can of worms," and that Weill's ambitions were still being underwritten by his Baltimore-based cash cow. "Primerica does have one crown jewel," the article noted, "the company Sandy Weill started with: Commercial Credit."

Weill bought the venerable Travelers Insurance in 1993, at which point his empire had assets of $100 billion. That same year, he acquired the Shearson Lehman brokerage house (the latest iteration of the company that had ejected him back in 1986). As deal followed deal, Weill fixed his eye on Citicorp, a huge commercial bank with billions of dollars in customer deposits. The fact that such a merger would be against the law was of no consequence. This was, after all, the Clinton–Greenspan era, when a rising tide of corruption was lifting anything on Wall Street that could float, however rotten.

The law that would have blocked the merger was the Glass–Steagall Act, passed in the depths of the Great Depression and prompted by the catastrophic speculations of none other than Citi (i.e., the National City Bank, as it was known at the time). Under the leadership of Charles "Sunshine Charley" Mitchell, the bank had vigorously embraced "cross-selling": lending money to investors to buy shares of companies in which the bank itself held stakes. Those funds vaporized in the 1929 meltdown. "Mitchell more than any fifty men is responsible for this stock crash," said Senator Carter Glass of Virginia soon after the market plummeted.

Glass, along with Representative Henry B. Steagall of Alabama, sponsored the eponymous law that decreed a rigid separation between commercial banks, which manage deposit accounts for individuals and businesses, and investment banks, which facilitate the buying and selling of stocks, bonds and other financial instruments. Glass–Steagall should have barred Weill from getting his hands on Citicorp. Instead, he got provisional clearance for the merger from Alan Greenspan at the Federal Reserve. Once the deal was consummated, in 1998, Weill moved to secure a repeal of the irksome legislation—an easy task, given the enthusiastic support he received from President Bill Clinton and Treasury Secretary Robert Rubin, a former co-chair of Goldman Sachs. Glass–Steagall was duly struck down a year later. A beaming Clinton, extolling the repeal of "antiquated laws," signed the bill with Weill at his side. By then Rubin had already become co-chairman of Citigroup, as the merged entity was called, garnering a total of $126 million in compensation over the following nine years.

"These guys are excellent at politics," Arthur Wilmarth, a professor specializing in banking law at the George Washington University Law School, told me. "Look at how they persuaded Clinton, Greenspan and Rubin to do their bidding. But they're lousy at running their own business."

Bair agrees, insisting that Citigroup was "really a cobbled-together series of acquisitions. I think they relied too much on their government connections, as opposed to managing the bank well."

Even before the merger, Citicorp had a historic record of bad bets stretching all the way back to the War of 1812: one of the bank's founding directors made an investment in a licensed privateer, only to see the ship sail out of New York Harbor and disappear without a trace. Since then, the firm has repeatedly brought itself to the brink of ruin, making a slew of foolhardy loans to corporations during the 1970s and to developing countries during the 1980s.

Under Weill, however, the merged firm set new records for reckless gambles and fraud. It was Citigroup that helped to cook Enron's books, disguising $4 billion worth of loans on the balance sheet as operating cash flow. Citigroup's executives apparently understood what they were doing but carried on regardless—the payoff being the $200 million in fees earned from the energy-trading firm before it collapsed amid bankruptcy and criminal charges. (As it turned out, crime did not pay, at least not for Citigroup's stockholders, since the firm ended up shelling out $100 million in civil penalties to the SEC and $3.7 billion to settle claims by Enron investors.)

Equally favored as a client was the WorldCom communications conglomerate. Jack Grubman, Citi's star telecom analyst, served as an adviser to Bernard Ebbers, WorldCom's CEO, while relentlessly touting the company's stock to unwitting investors. For his services, Grubman received more than $67.5 million between 1999 and 2002—hardly excessive compensation, considering that he had helped Citigroup to generate almost $1.2 billion in fees from WorldCom and other communications firms. Subsequent events followed their normal course. WorldCom declared bankruptcy, Ebbers went to jail, Grubman paid a $15 million fine and was banned from the securities industry for life, and Citigroup settled a WorldCom investors' suit for $2.6 billion and paid a $300 million fine to the SEC. None of Citigroup's senior executives suffered any penalty.*

---

* In a striking example of the law of unintended consequences, Grubman's promotion of telecom led to huge overcapacity in the industry—which became a boon to the US military after 9/11 for use in drone operations, among other things.

As Weill and his associates scaled the heights of New York society, contributing to such worthy causes as the refurbishment of Carnegie Hall, they retained their loan-shark business, which they renamed CitiFinancial in the wake of the big merger. For Gail Kubiniec, who continued to work for the firm as an assistant sales manager, little else changed. As the great housing bubble of the new millennium got under way, however, she noticed increased demands from management to push high-interest home mortgages.

"I felt those house values were inflated," Kubiniec told me recently. In addition, the fact that "people didn't always understand about making timely payments" worked to the company's advantage. A late payment was an opportunity. "The hammer would come down," she recalled. "You'd call them and call them to get them to come in and refinance"—at which point more fees could be tacked on to the loan. Finally, disgusted with the high-pressure tactics inflicted on poor clients, Kubiniec decided to "hang up," as she put it.

In a devastating affidavit filed with the Federal Trade Commission in 2001, Kubiniec laid bare the sleazy practices at the heart of CitiFinancial's business model, such as "Rocopoly Money"—quarterly bonuses for employees based on the number of existing borrowers they could lure into new loans:

> I and other employees would often determine how much insurance could be sold to a borrower based on the borrower's occupation, race, age and education level. If someone appeared uneducated, inarticulate, was a minority or was particularly old or young, I would try to include all the coverages CitiFinancial offered. The more gullible the consumer appeared, the more coverages I would try to include in the loan.

Such revelations may have been embarrassing, and moderately expensive: Citi ended up paying $240 million in penalties and legal settlements. They made little difference, however, to the company's operations. As Kubiniec pointed out to me, these fines amounted to "pennies" compared with the firm's consumer-loan profits—more than $4 billion between 2002 and 2003, a nice percentage of the $33 billion in overall profits hauled in by Citigroup during those years. As part of the settlement, CitiFinancial pledged to reform its abusive lending practices, but there was little change in the way the sales force marketed its loans.

Still, the fitful attention from regulatory agencies began to irritate Weill, making his life "extraordinarily difficult," as he later recalled. In 2003, he resigned as CEO of Citigroup, bequeathing control to Prince, the lawyer he had found at the loan-shark firm in Baltimore. (Weill retained the office of chairman until 2006.)

Prince certainly had the merit of knowing a great deal about Citigroup's checkered past. He also had a powerful supervisor in Rubin, the affable, media-friendly operator who had not only greased the wheels for the repeal of Glass–Steagall but also helped to fend off regulatory curbs on risky speculation. Now, as chairman of the Citigroup executive committee, with a $15 million annual paycheck, the former treasury secretary was ready to provide guidance on boosting earnings, profits and, of course, executive bonuses. One colleague described Rubin as "the Wizard of Oz behind Citigroup . . . He certainly was the guy deferred to on key strategic decisions and certain key business decisions vis-à-vis risk."

Despite Citi's recent troubles with Enron and WorldCom, Rubin urged Prince to dive into even riskier waters by amping up proprietary trading—using the firm's own money to bet on market movements, often with complex financial instruments. Thanks to the 1998 merger, these bets could now be made using Citibank depositors' funds, which were helpfully insured by the FDIC. Furthermore, in the wake of the Commodities Futures Modernization Act, a toxic piece of legislation signed by Clinton in his final days in office, riskier forms of speculation—notably credit-default swaps—were now exempt from regulation and oversight.

As the housing bubble continued to inflate, opportunities for "prop trading" were becoming more lucrative by the day, powered by subprime mortgages that CitiFinancial and other bottom-grazing lenders were selling to poor people, especially African Americans. In particular, Citi's sales force pushed adjustable-rate mortgages, which offered borrowers a low interest rate that later adjusted upward. In the blunt words of Bair, such loans "were purposefully designed to be unaffordable, to force borrowers into a series of refinancings and the fat fees that went along with them."

This, of course, was the Commercial Credit business model. The idea was to maneuver poor borrowers into debt bondage, now rendered even more attractive because Wall Street had devised ways to securitize the designed-to-fail subprime loans. The loans were packaged into bundles of mortgage-backed securities, which were then repackaged into collateralized debt obligations (CDOs), which were sliced into interest-bearing tranches according to their presumed credit-worthiness. These CDOs could then be chopped into ever more abstruse instruments that were increasingly divorced from reality. Asked who constituted the market for such exotic stuff, an anonymous trader in the 2009 documentary *American Casino* gave the only possible answer: "Idiots."

As other banks started to see big returns from the CDO bonanza, Rubin felt increased pressure to join the party. Accordingly, in early 2005, the Wizard helped Prince persuade the Citigroup board to take on much more risk. The firm's CDO production soared, doubling to $35 billion between 2005 and 2007. This river of cash had a suitably tonic effect on senior-executive bonuses. In 2006 alone, Tom Maheras, the chairman of Citigroup's investment bank, was awarded $34 million in salary and bonuses, and his colleagues and subordinates received similarly lavish amounts.

But the pyramid of profit rested on a narrow point: the borrowers cajoled into loans they couldn't afford by the aggressive sales teams at CitiFinancial and other subprime lenders. Well before Maheras and his associates received their bonus checks, the market had turned. Home sales peaked in the summer of 2005 before starting a steady, then steepening, slide. By spring 2007, subprime borrowers were defaulting on their loans and losing their homes to foreclosure at an accelerating rate. The bubble was bursting, but Citi's management was in denial. "I think our performance is going to last much longer than the market turbulence does," a defiant Prince declared in August of that year.

Eager to ensure adequate supplies of subprime debt for the CDO machine, Citi took over the notoriously abusive lender Ameriquest in September 2007. As CDOs became harder to sell, the firm's traders joined the idiots and began hoarding their own bogus creations, while relentlessly pumping out more for a market that no longer wanted them.

Others on Wall Street were waking up to what was happening. Goldman Sachs, "a ruthless shop," in Wilmarth's words, had reaped billions from marketing CDOs, and it continued to do so. But as early as 2006, it began to short (that is, bet against) CDOs it sold to credulous customers. Citi, meanwhile, held on blindly to its deteriorating portfolio.

Prince was forced out at the end of 2007, after the bank admitted to $10 billion in losses on subprime loans and CDOs—a figure that would balloon to $40 billion by the end of 2008. He had taken home $158 million in cash and stock during the previous four years. His replacement, a hedge-fund manager named Vikram Pandit, collected $165 million when Citi obligingly bought his fund, which went belly up a few months after the purchase.

The executive shake-up made no difference to the firm's cratering fortunes. By November 2008, Citigroup was insolvent. But it knew where to turn for help. Bair laughed as she recalled how Rubin was lauded at the time for arranging Citi's latest round of bailouts—"like that was his job as titular head of the organization, to make sure the government took care of them."

Given the outcome, that might not have been such a bad business plan. Three successive bailouts at the height of the crisis pumped a total of $45 billion in taxpayer money into the firm, along with $306 billion in loan guarantees, not to mention more than $2.5 *trillion* in low-cost loans from the Federal Reserve. Regulators also turned a blind eye to such little matters as Citigroup's lies to investors and the SEC, in late 2007, about the bank's $39 billion exposure to subprime losses. "While financial fraud of this magnitude would typically be worthy of jail time,

the SEC delivered minor slaps on the wrist to just two individuals," Pam Martens, a Wall Street money manager for twenty-one
years and subsequently an acerbic commentator on the industry,
later wrote. "Citigroup paid the pittance of $75 million."

The multitrillion-dollar bailouts generated public revulsion
against all the major banks and were an important factor in the
rise of the Tea Party. But in the view of key decision-makers,
including Bair, the bailouts were largely about Citigroup. "The
over-the-top generosity," she told me, "was driven in part by
the desire to help Citi and cover up its outlier status." In other
words, everyone was showered with money to distract attention
from the one bankrupt institution that was seriously in need of it.

As the world of finance had grappled with the deepening
crisis in the summer of 2008, the country at large remained oblivious to the drama, focusing instead on the presidential race, in
which Barack Obama and John McCain were running neck and
neck. On September 15, the day Lehman Brothers filed for bankruptcy, McCain was almost two points ahead in the polls. But the
collapse of the nation's fourth-largest investment bank woke
voters to the reality of the crash. They swung over to the "change
candidate," handing Obama an overwhelming victory in
November. Three days after the vote, the president-elect appeared
onstage in Chicago to discuss his economic policy. At his side
was Rubin.

Unsurprisingly, the new administration was soon well stocked
with Citigroup alumni such as Jacob Lew, who was appointed chief
operating officer of the State Department. He had most recently
been the chief financial officer of Citi's Alternative Investments
unit, a prop-trading group that lost $509 million in the first quarter
of 2008 alone. Lew's 2006 Citi employment contract provides
useful insight into at least one of the ways in which big business
infiltrates government. The contract stipulated that if Lew left the
company, he would lose his "guaranteed incentive and retention
award," amounting to about $1.5 million in 2008—*unless* he
departed in order to accept a "full-time high-level position with the
United States government or regulatory body." In other words,

Citigroup was effectively paying Lew to take a government job in which he would either direct policy or regulate Citigroup.

Joining Lew in Washington as deputy national security adviser for international economic affairs was Michael Froman, a Harvard acquaintance of Obama's who had introduced the president to Rubin in 2004. Froman had more recently headed the Emerging Markets Strategy division at Citigroup, pocketing more than $7.4 million in 2008, even as taxpayers were pouring billions into the failing firm.

Yet another friend of Citi's was moving into an even more potent position. As head of the immensely powerful New York Federal Reserve Bank, Timothy Geithner had stood resolutely in Citi's corner, his loyalty perhaps enhanced by a call he had received from Weill in November 2007, as the crisis was gathering speed. Prince had just been fired. "What would you think of running Citi?" Weill reportedly asked him. Geithner eventually demurred, after considering the offer, which may have been less than straightforward, since Rubin had already decided on Pandit, a move he would certainly have discussed with Weill. In any event, it seems fair to say that Geithner gave the firm little cause for complaint in the following months—deriding, for example, Bair's suggestion that bankruptcy proceedings be started for its insolvent commercial bank. "Tim seemed to view his job as protecting Citigroup from me," Bair later wrote in her memoir, "when he should have been worried about protecting the taxpayers from Citi."

Once installed at Treasury, Geithner had the more important task of protecting Citigroup from the president of the United States, since Obama had sensibly concluded that the whale should be broken up and disposed of. "Okay, so we do Citigroup and we do it thoroughly and well," the president told his advisers in March 2009. But only Treasury had the bureaucratic resources to dismantle such an enormous financial carcass, and Geithner showed no interest in handling the job. According to the journalist Ron Suskind, he simply ignored the president's directive, and Obama let the matter drop.

Freed from the threat of termination, Citigroup returned to business as usual. Subprime foreclosures were still ripping through communities across the country, peaking in 2010. Cara Stretch, a foreclosure-prevention specialist at St. Ambrose, a Baltimore housing-aid center just two miles from CitiFinancial head-quarters, was working overtime, helping desperate homeowners to hang on to their houses. CitiFinancial, she recalls, was "imposs-ible to deal with," totally resistant to loan modifications and eager only to collect or foreclose. Stretch's clients were at least luckier than Irzen Octa, a Citibank credit-card customer in Jakarta, Indonesia. Octa was beaten to death in 2011 by collec-tion agents on contract to Citi when he visited a bank branch to discuss his account.

By this time most firms had abandoned the bubble-era practice of handing out shady housing loans, then securitizing and resell-ing them. But not CitiMortgage, the company's other, supposedly upmarket mortgage arm. CitiMortgage carried right on selling mortgages it had every reason to believe were unlikely to be repaid—and it did so all the way through 2011. Since the private market had dried up, the firm's most frequent customer was the Federal Housing Agency, which meant that the American taxpayer was getting it in the neck once again.

CitiMortgage had every reason to know it was moving fraud-ulent paper, at least as of March 2011. That was when Sherry Hunt, a quality-control officer at the company's headquarters in O'Fallon, Missouri, explained to the HR department that CitiMortgage was processing and selling thousands of such loans, and had even set up a "quality rebuttal group" to ensure that as few loans as possible got rejected, however questionable. Nothing came of her complaint, so Hunt forwarded her copious documen-tation to the US Attorney in Manhattan, who promptly brought suit against Citi. So damning was the evidence that the bank not only caved, paying $158.3 million to settle the charges, it even admitted that it had done something wrong, a rarity in such cases.

Such unseemly revelations about Citigroup, along with those of its fellow banks, evoked a vehement reaction from Wilmarth.

"You had systematic fraud at the origination stage," he told me, "then you had systematic fraud at the securitization stage, then you had systematic fraud at the foreclosure stage. At what point do we consider these institutions to have become effectively criminal enterprises?"

Naturally, no such charges were ever brought against Citigroup or its peers. Critics complained that the banks were considered "too big to jail." Or, as Attorney General Eric Holder ponderously phrased it in March 2013, "I am concerned that the size of some of these institutions becomes so large that it does become difficult for us to prosecute them when we are hit with indications that if you do prosecute, if you do bring a criminal charge, it will have a negative impact on the national economy, perhaps world economy."

Nevertheless, there was general agreement in Washington that *something* had to be done to prevent another such fiasco. An initiative by Senators Sherrod Brown and Ted Kaufman to break up the big banks was speedily crushed, confirming a reflective comment from Senator Richard Durbin of Illinois: "The banks own this place." Instead, after extensive labors, Congress assembled the 2,300-page Dodd–Frank Wall Street Reform and Consumer Protection Act—a huge revenue-spinner for the battalions of lobbyists and lawyers deployed to whittle down anything deemed hurtful to Wall Street.

They failed, however, to stop the push-out rule, which was inserted by Senator Blanche Lincoln of Arkansas. Lincoln had previously been deemed "reliable" by Wall Street, but in 2010 she was facing a tough primary battle against a union-backed opponent—hence her opportunistic swing to the left. Thereafter, attempts to delete Lincoln's rule became an almost annual event in the congressional calendar, indicating just how important a cause this was for the banks in general, and for Citi in particular.

Pandit, having overseen an 89 percent decline in Citi's stock price during his tenure, was shown the door in October 2012. His send-off: a paltry $6.7 million, which showed just how far things had declined for failed executives since the financial crash. His successor, Michael Corbat, had spent almost his entire career at Citigroup. Soon after his appointment as CEO, he announced that one of his goals was to "stop destroying our shareholders' capital." He hoped Citigroup "served a social purpose" and later added that he wanted banking to be thought of as "boring."

The past few years, however, suggest that Citi culture has not changed much. Corbat has moved to shrink the firm's consumer business, closing bank branches—even in important markets such as Dallas and Houston—in favor of stepping up speculative trading operations. The effort to unload OneMain, with its associated crusade on behalf of extortionate interest rates, is part of that same initiative.

So eager is Citigroup to be seen as a dynamic trading concern that it has been offering Citibank depositors the opportunity to trade in the riskiest arena of all: foreign-currency exchange. Citi FX solicits customers who have a minimum balance of $10,000 to wade into FOREX trading. It also offers them thirty-three-to-one leverage, meaning amateur traders can wager with just 3 percent down—a $330,000 bet on a $10,000 deposit. Clicking on the Citi FX "Risk Disclosure" link reveals that this is a purely in-house operation, and reminds visitors that "when you lose money trading, your national bank is making money on such trades." In other words, the customer is betting against the house, exactly as in a casino. Pam Martens, who unearthed this shabby initiative, wonders whether a "US-subsidized bank that is attempting to restore its reputation after a decade of outrageous missteps" should be enticing retail clients into currency trading, which she describes as a "surefire way to lose their money."

While introducing customers to the wonders of FOREX may not be risky for the bank, ratcheting up derivative trades, especially when other megabanks such as JPMorgan Chase are backing off, is, as Bair expressed to me, "quite alarming." Yet it does help to explain Citi's determination to quash the push-out rule in spite of the terrible PR. (Representative Kevin Yoder, the obscure Kansas Republican delegated by the lobbyists to insert

Citigroup's provision, found his Facebook page erupting with abusive comments, one of the more printable of them calling him a "pathetic waste of a slime mold.")

Within days of killing the push-out rule, Citigroup bought the commodity- and energy-trading arm of Credit Suisse, an adventurous move in view of the ongoing collapse in global oil prices. Even more troubling is the heavy investment Citigroup, along with JPMorgan and Wells Fargo, has made in collateralized loan obligations—this decade's CDOs, which consist of high-yield, high-risk junk bonds sliced into tranches. A high proportion of such junk was issued by energy firms and snapped up in massive quantities by Wall Street largely on the back of the shale-oil boom, now deflating at a precipitous rate. "I think those bonds are already on the edge of the cliff," says Martens.

Watch out for falling blubber.

In 2020, Citigroup once again needed a federal handout, being the one and only major Wall Street bank to request funds—$3 billion—under the pandemic-related Paycheck Protection Program. Later that year the Federal Reserve fined the bank $400 million for an offense so serious that the Fed declined to reveal details.

16

Swap Meet

January 2018

"When you're in the Street's casino, you gotta play by their rules," said the late, great, financial reporter Mark Pittman. Even when other people, such as the US Congress, tries to make the rules, Wall Street gets what it wants in the end.

For 173 years, the Stoneman House stood peacefully in the Tuscarawas Valley, close to Leesville, Ohio. The elegant two-story brick structure was owned and occupied by just three families over successive generations, and when the last of them died, in 2015, it was bought by Energy Transfer Partners, a Texas pipeline company, which promised there would be "no adverse effects" on the historic site. But that turned out to be untrue, since ETP razed the house to the ground the following year. In a further adverse effect, the demolition cost Goldman Sachs $100 million.

The doomed mansion was located close to the projected path of the Rover Pipeline, which was being built to carry natural gas from the Marcellus Shale in Ohio, Pennsylvania and West Virginia to Canada. Once the $4 billion project was completed, Goldman traders had calculated, the price of Marcellus gas would rise. They placed their bet accordingly. Their wager depended on the pipeline proceeding according to schedule. But the brazen destruction of the beloved mansion, which had been eligible for inclusion in the National Register of Historic Places, enraged national and state regulators, who were further dismayed by toxic spills in protected wetlands and other environmental depredations. Rover was temporarily stopped in its tracks in May 2017. Instead of rising, Marcellus gas prices plummeted—and Goldman lost its bet.

Such wagers were meant to be a thing of the past. A decade ago, Wall Street was a roaring casino and a trader could toss away $9 billion on a single bet. The financial crisis that followed in 2008 generated a forest of new regulations, most of them incomprehensible to the average observer, not to mention the legislators who voted for them. But there was one reform that seemed simple to understand. It was named for the man who conceived it: Paul Volcker, the venerated former chairman of the Federal Reserve.

In the early days of the crisis, as the collapsing industry ran to the federal government for bailouts, Volcker proposed that commercial banks should be forever barred from proprietary trading (referred to on Wall Street as prop trading)—meaning speculative bets with their own capital. Nor should such institutions be permitted to bankroll hedge funds or other inherently risky ventures. His aim, Volcker told me recently in a phone call from his office in Midtown Manhattan, was to change the "whole psychology" of the banking system. Is the primary function of banks to "make loans and serve the banking needs of their clients," he asked, or are they "preoccupied with going off and making money with proprietary trades, which will often conflict with their customers' interests? That's the issue involved here. They all talk about how the client comes first. They'll say, 'All our remuneration, all our everything, is directed toward the client.' That can't be true when you're doing proprietary trading."

Once he touched on the subject of prop trading, I brought up Goldman Sachs. "They want to trade everything, for God's sake!" cried the sharp-tongued nonagenarian, cutting me off. "They'll trade the office rug that I'm looking at."

As we spoke, Goldman, its second-quarter trading profits down (in part because of the losing Marcellus bet), was leading an industry charge to make the Volcker Rule go away—not by getting it repealed in Congress but by adjusting the rules and regulations through which it has been enforced.*

They were certainly assured of a sympathetic hearing from the Trump appointees now ensconced in the regulatory agencies, notably Keith Noreika, a corporate lawyer and frequent advocate for the banking industry who currently serves as acting comptroller of the currency, the chief regulator of the banks. Meanwhile, the US Treasury, headed by the former foreclosure profiteer Steven Mnuchin, announced plans in June for "improving" the Volcker Rule, which the department chided for having "far overshot the mark." Duly encouraged, banking groups and their lobbyists argued that the rule's complexity imposed unbearable burdens on bankers and had dried up liquidity, meaning that banks lacked sufficient funds to lend to deserving businesses.

I cited some of the lobbyists' complaints to Volcker. "They're paid to do that," he replied scornfully. "All I know is that people stop me on the street. Some of them are bankers, who say: 'Thank God for the Volcker Rule. It has changed the psychology of the trading operation in the bank.' I don't know how many of these people are just being nice to me, but I don't get many coming up to me and saying, 'It's a terrible rule.'"

The Volcker Rule was born of political expediency. Despite his towering prestige as the man who stamped out the rampant inflation of the early 1980s, Volcker and his plan were studiously ignored by President Obama and his advisers until early in 2010. At that point, it dawned on the administration that the American people were outraged at the way the banks had crashed the economy and then been bailed out. Furthermore, popular anger was

---

* Goldman spokesman Michael DuVally informed me that "Goldman Sachs takes all of its regulatory obligations seriously, including those imposed by the Volcker Rule," adding the general observation that "market makers facilitate trades for clients looking to buy or sell, thus providing liquidity when there is an imbalance between clients looking to add to their exposures and clients looking to reduce or hedge their exposures." DuVally avoided addressing why the bank, rather than a client, took the loss on the Marcellus gas trade.

taking a dangerous turn, signaled by the election of Scott Brown, a former Cosmo nude model running on an antiestablishment platform, as a Republican senator in Massachusetts, presaging the rise of the Tea Party. Two days after Brown's victory, Obama summoned Volcker to the White House and announced his support for the Volcker Rule as a key component of financial reform.

Sponsoring enactment of the rule in the Senate were Carl Levin of Michigan and Jeff Merkley of Oregon, both of them Democrats. Levin, a veteran lawmaker, had a clear-eyed understanding of the way the banks operated. Merkley was a freshman senator, spurred, as he told me recently, by having "seen firsthand the impact of predatory mortgages" on his constituents back in Portland. Now he had the chance to do something about the system that was generating those loans: prop trading. There was no logic, he told me, in having a bank "that is designed to take deposits and make loans be placing high-risk bets in a Wall Street casino."

By 2010, the crash in the housing market was tearing communities apart across the country, as millions of people faced foreclosure and eviction. Yet these hapless borrowers had already generated vast profits for others. Unbeknownst to most of them, their mortgages had been "securitized"—that is, welded together by financial engineers into investment "products," which were, in turn, sold to other buyers. It was rarely possible to track an individual subprime mortgage through the financial Cuisinart in which Wall Street transformed such loans into profitable instruments. Thus the eventual buyers had no idea whether the underlying mortgages were being paid or not.

I was, however, able to follow one such mortgage: a loan to Denzel Mitchell, a young African-American high school teacher, which passed through successive hands until Goldman Sachs blended it, along with 3,061 others, into a $629 million bond called GSAMP 2006 HE–2 (Goldman Sachs Alternative Mortgage Product Home Equity–2). In those years before the crash, Goldman was doing a roaring trade in GSAMPs, selling them to credulous institutions, many of them foreign, that were either oblivious or indifferent to the fact that the underlying loans were almost certain to default. Such prop trades brought in a river of cash for Goldman—more than $25 billion in net revenue in 2006—with commensurate payoffs for the traders who generated them. That year alone, Gary Cohn, who oversaw Goldman's trading division, garnered $53 million in total pay. The following year, he took home $70 million. Today, he is Donald Trump's chief economic adviser.

But there was more to it than that. Back in 2005, at the peak of the subprime boom, Wall Street traders had dreamed up the ABX index. By tracking a selected sample of mortgage-backed housing bonds, the index would reflect the mortgage-backed securities market as a whole, and by extension, the American housing market. Launched in January 2006, the ABX also offered the attractive option of buying and selling index futures. That is, traders could now place bets on the movement of the entire housing market.

Goldman was quicker than most to place negative bets, predicting that the housing market would tumble as more and more homeowners defaulted. So, as Denzel Mitchell struggled to keep a roof over his family, the bank that owned his loan was betting that he and others would fail. That turned out to be a very good bet, generating nearly $4 billion in profits in 2007 alone.

Goldman was by no means the only establishment to use the ABX. Among the others were a small number of traders in the London branch of JPMorgan Chase's Chief Investment Office, a division of the bank charged with investing customers' deposits. These particular London traders oversaw what the bank management termed the synthetic credit portfolio, largely composed of exotic derivatives.

The activities of the group, which included a Frenchman named Bruno Iksil, were kept secret from the bank's government regulator. According to a subsequent explanation by Jamie Dimon, JPMorgan's CEO, the purpose of the SCP was to make "a little money" when the overall market was doing well—and to make a lot more in the event of a crash.

Such transactions were cascading through the global financial system in those years, powered by the bank-promoted boom in subprime loans. Vastly magnifying the scale of operations was another recently invented instrument: the credit default swap. These enabled traders to take out insurance, or "protection," as they preferred to call it (labeling it "insurance" would subject the deals to insurance regulations), on bonds they didn't own—just like insuring someone else's house against fire. There was no limit on the number of bets riding on a particular bond; a post-crash inquiry found one that had nine separate CDS bets against it. Thus, if a $600 million GSAMP collapsed because its loans were worthless, those on the wrong side of the bets stood to lose *multiples* of that sum: the single most important reason why the subprime crash almost dragged the entire economy down with it.

By 2007, the bets were going bad at an ever-accelerating rate. In October, Howie Hubler, a senior trader at Morgan Stanley, managed to lose more than $9 billion on a credit default swap bet—the single largest trading loss in Wall Street history. Huge financial institutions began to crumble. Bear Stearns collapsed in March 2008. On September 15 came the cataclysm of the Lehman Brothers bankruptcy. An internal Federal Reserve email sent five days later, and published here for the first time, tersely conveys the prevailing mood of official panic as Morgan Stanley, Timothy Geithner and Goldman Sachs attempted to circle the wagons:

> FYI, MS called TFG late last nite and indicated they can not open Monday. MS advised GS of that and GS is now panicked b/c feel that if MS does not open then GS is toast.

Washington rushed to shore up the collapsing financial system. AIG, the giant insurance company that had thoughtlessly taken the other side on a huge proportion of the banks' CDS bets, was bailed out with $185 billion of taxpayer money. By March 2009, the Treasury and the Federal Reserve had committed $12.8 *trillion*—almost as much as the entire US gross national product—to save the economy. Fearful of public outrage over such generosity to those who had fomented the disaster in the first place, the Fed and the banks struggled to keep the numbers a secret.

Fortunately for the bankers, they had protection from the top. In March 2009, President Obama reportedly assured a roomful of bank CEOs that his administration was "the only thing" standing between them "and the pitchforks." He would neither allow them to fail nor send any of their top administrators to jail for fraud (although the banks would subsequently disgorge billions in civil fines for their fraudulent behavior).

Despite such welcome news, the banks did face the unwelcome prospect of new rules and regulations likely to impinge on cherished modes of operation. They prepared their defenses. By November 13, 2008, just a month after being raised from the dead by the government's largesse, the biggest derivatives dealers—including JPMorgan, Goldman Sachs, Citigroup and Bank of America—were already investing $25 million in setting up the CDS Dealers Consortium, a lobbying group aimed at preserving their freedom to trade credit default swaps without irksome restrictions.

Volcker's rule represented a partial resurrection of the Glass–Steagall Act, the Depression-era law that had separated commercial banks from investment banks, effectively banning prop trading. (It was repealed by a stroke of Bill Clinton's pen back in 1999.) As noted, the former Fed chairman's idea found little support in an administration predisposed, as Treasury Secretary Geithner infamously put it, to "foam the runway" for the banks.

The Volcker Rule was even more anathema to the banks themselves, which, flush with bailout cash, were once again generating profitable trades and executive bonuses. At the end of 2009, Goldman handed employees nearly $17 billion in pay and bonuses. In London, the traders in JPMorgan's SCP unit generated $1 billion in revenue, thanks largely to a shrewd bet that General Motors would go bankrupt. Bankers and their representatives argued vehemently that their prop trading had absolutely nothing to do with the crash, despite the trillions in bailout money needed to keep them afloat.

The Volcker Rule meanwhile had to undergo a long and tortuous gestation, beginning with its passage through Congress as part of the financial reform legislation introduced by Senator Chris Dodd and Representative Barney Frank. On hand to observe the progress of the legislation was Jeff Connaughton, formerly a high-powered lobbyist, who had recently signed on as chief of staff to the reform-minded senator Ted Kaufman, a Democrat from Delaware. In his instructive memoir *The Payoff*, Connaughton describes how the banking committee functioned:

> Staffers gave lobbyists information about bills being drafted or what one senator had said to another . . . The lobbyists passed the information on to their clients in the banking or insurance or accounting industry . . . Sometimes within an hour, the news would be emailed to the entire financial-services industry and all of its lobbyists. With multiple leakers from the banking committee keeping K Street well informed, the banking world had complete transparency into bill drafting.

Among the lobbyists' prime sources, according to Connaughton, was Dodd himself, who spent hours hashing out the bill with them behind closed doors. ("I remember when I told Jeff that I'd just spent forty-five minutes discussing the bill with Dodd," one lobbyist told me recently, laughing at the memory. "Jeff was so upset!")

As veterans of the committees they now monitored, many of these financial lobbyists had inside knowledge. Michael Paese, for example, was the deputy staff director of the House Financial Services Committee for seven years until moving to the Securities Industry and Financial Markets Association, a trade group, in September 2008. He left with committee chairman Barney Frank's blessing, so Frank told me, after assuring him that he was joining SIFMA in hopes of converting the group to the benefits of regulation. When Paese then joined Goldman Sachs in April 2009 as its chief lobbyist, Frank, furious that his former aide would now be working "for the people who were likely to try to undermine the bill," banned him from contacting the committee for two years.

The lobbyists saw little point in exercising their skills on Carl Levin, a seasoned politician whose views on the banks were well known. "They knew my boss was probably not going to be taking advice from Goldman about the Volcker Rule," Tyler Gellasch, Levin's staffer on the issue at the time, told me. "He was busy investigating them for fraud, and they were smart enough to realize that."

But the industry emissaries could always find more pliable senators to convey the message. Ironically, Scott Brown, whose election had prompted the White House to endorse Volcker's initiative in the first place, became "a bit of a poster child" for such horse trading, Gellasch recalled. "He was perceived to be one of the swing votes. The staffers basically used that as leverage: 'We're a swing vote on Dodd–Frank. You're going to give as many things as we can ask for.'" Some Senate staffers joked about setting up an ATM machine for campaign contributions out in Senator Brown's lobby. Among other concessions extracted by the Massachusetts senator was a loophole in the Volcker Rule allowing banks to own a small stake in hedge funds after all. (Coincidentally or not, the securities and investment industry was Brown's most generous contributor during his single Senate term, donating more than $4.6 million, while his legislative director, Nat Hoopes, went on to run the Financial Services Forum, another well-endowed lobbying group.)

Thanks to such negotiations, the rule acquired significant concessions before Dodd–Frank was passed on July 21, 2010. Connaughton, whose boss's proposal to break up the big banks had gotten short shrift from the administration and Congress, thought little of the final result. "Dodd and the Treasury wanted a squishy bill, and the Republicans were willing to work with him to weaken it," he told me disgustedly. "Dodd–Frank wasn't really a law but a series of instructions to regulators to write rules." To start with the basics: What did "proprietary trading" actually mean? If you kept a supply of, for example, foreign-currency swaps in stock, just in case a customer ordered some, were you engaging in prop trading? Such issues could keep many lawyers well remunerated for a long time.

The banks pressed to be allowed to carry a much bigger inventory of any given product—which Dennis Kelleher of Better Markets, a financial watchdog group, described as "just a disguised form of prop trading." They also saw a potential loophole in even the most straightforward language. "Normal people in the real world would understand those things quite easily," Kelleher told me. "But when you get together all the lawyers, lobbyists, traders, and bonus-salivating bankers, it's as if those words were being spoken in a foreign language, given the amount of questions and ambiguities that they can see in them."

The regulators overseeing implementation of the Volcker Rule were from five separate agencies. These included the Office of the Comptroller of the Currency (OCC) and the Commodity Futures Trading Commission (CFTC), obscure to the public but potent acronyms in the financial world. Though immediately touted as a signal achievement by Obama and the Democrats, the Volcker Rule would be toothless unless and until these agencies spelled out what it actually meant.

Unsurprisingly, the banks and similarly interested parties launched human waves of lawyers and lobbyists at the agencies to ensure that rules were crafted to their liking. A painstaking academic study of the public record by Kimberly Krawiec of Duke University revealed that the agencies were subjected to almost 1,400 meetings with those seeking to influence their deliberations, the vast majority with representatives of the financial industry.

Though the rule sprouted increasingly dense thickets of complexities, the true objects of the lobbyists' labors were often invisible to the untrained eye. An ambiguous word here, an obscure footnote there, could be worth billions down the road. "What's interesting," Gellasch told me, "is that the complexities were added as a result of lobbying by the firms that were going to be affected, as a way to mitigate the impacts." Now, he said, those complexities are being viewed as regulatory millstones by those same firms, whose reactions he summarized as "Oh, my God, this is so burdensome."

The tactics were subtle, even ingenious. For example, although the original act applied only to American institutions, major banks, including JPMorgan and Morgan Stanley, lobbied the Federal Reserve to extend the rule to any financial firm with any kind of stake, even a single branch, anywhere in the United States—the rationale being that American firms would otherwise face a "competitive disadvantage" from their overseas counterparts. They then called on foreign embassies in Washington to say that their banks back home, now limited by the rule to buying only US Treasuries, would consequently be barred from buying bonds issued by their own governments. Predictably, this generated a torrent of high-level complaints to the US government from foreign capitals demanding that the rule be changed. (It was, at least partially.) "The criticism of foreign governments on behalf of their banks is helping US banks fight the rule," the Stanford finance professor Anat Admati told Bloomberg News at the time. "It also muddies the water, shifting the debate away from the main issue, which is reducing the risks banks impose on the real economy."

Was it in the interest of the banks to make the regulations more complex? "Of course!" Volcker assured me. "It's endemic in the United States between the lawyers and bankers. 'You've got a regulation? Let's find a way around it.' Then the regulator has to respond. 'All right, we'll make a rule against that.' If that's the environment, you're going to get detailed regulations. It's maximized in this case, where you've got five different agencies, all with a proprietary interest in their own authority."

The Volcker Rule was hardly the only component of Dodd–Frank to be undermined by semi-covert means. Over the past two years, the law professor and former regulator Michael Greenberger has been investigating another such maneuver, and an especially artful one. This was in connection with an effort to regulate swaps contracts, including credit default swaps—"the killer that caused the meltdown," in Greenberger's words—by requiring that the bulk of them be traded on public exchanges, with deals recorded in a database available to regulators. In the run-up to the crisis, for example, no one had understood that AIG was on the hook for bets it could not possibly pay. Had such information been public, the witless insurer's rush to catastrophe might have been stopped.

The CFTC duly published a "guidance" in July 2013 stating that any foreign affiliate of an American bank "guaranteed" by its corporate parent (generally taken as a matter of course, since no one would otherwise do business with a subsidiary) was subject to the new regulations on swaps trading. The agency's chair, Gary Gensler, was a former Goldman banker whose enthusiasm for cleaning up Wall Street had attracted the rancor of his erstwhile peers. AIG, Gensler pointed out, had "nearly brought down the US economy" by running its trades through a British subsidiary. With his enthusiastic endorsement, the rule was approved by a majority vote of the commissioners. There was just one dissent, from Scott O'Malia, a former aide to Senator Mitch McConnell.

Given its relevance to the $700 trillion derivatives market, the rule attracted intense scrutiny from interested parties, especially the International Swaps and Derivatives Association, the industry overseer that issues the standard contract for swap transactions. Searching the CFTC guideline's 84 pages of text and 660 footnotes for crevices that could be expanded into loopholes, ISDA found just what they needed buried, whether deliberately or not, in footnote 563. Referring to the "guaranteed affiliate" requirements of the guidance, the footnote stated:

> Requirements should not apply if a non-US swap dealer or non-US MSP [the counterparty, or person on the other side of the trade] relies on a written representation by a non-US counterpart that its obligations under the swap are not guaranteed with recourse by a US person.

There it was, cloaked in bureaucratese. All that was required to dodge the regulation was to state that the foreign subsidiary was "not guaranteed." Just one month after the CFTC issued its edict, ISDA quietly rewrote its boilerplate swaps contract. According to Greenberger, the organization simply put "amended contract language into the swaps agreement, where you checked the box and said the subsidiary was now de-guaranteed." On the basis of a single sentence in a single footnote, a major component of the promised reform of the Wall Street casino was "shredded," Greenberger said, "in a way no one understands." It was not until the spring of 2014 that anyone at the CFTC realized that a large fraction of all swaps trades were now being run through London or other overseas trading centers.

In August, around the same time that ISDA was amending its contract, Commissioner O'Malia, who had resisted the reform, resigned from the agency to become the head of ISDA, with a salary of at least $1.8 million a year. Meanwhile, very slowly, the CFTC (no longer led by Gensler) creaked into action. Eventually, the agency published a proposal for a rule that would close the loophole. That was in October 2016, one month before Donald Trump was elected president. The proposed reform has not been heard of since.

In April 2012, as regulators and Wall Street haggled over the swaps trading regulations, news broke of a massive prop-trading scandal. As initially reported by the *Wall Street Journal* and Bloomberg, JPMorgan was facing enormous losses thanks to a series of trades in the synthetic credit portfolio. The group had earlier done well dealing in ABX futures and other derivatives. It had won recent favor at headquarters because of a correct bet the previous year that American Airlines would go bankrupt, netting a $400 million profit. The parent corporation had also funneled much of a recent $100 billion inflow, entrusted by crash-panicked depositors to the "safe" JPMorgan, to SCP for further investment.

But in the early months of 2012, SCP trader Bruno Iksil's CDS bets cratered. So huge were his losses that traders at other firms dubbed him the London Whale. It appeared to be a clear case of an irresponsible trader gambling away enormous sums—the projected loss ultimately amounted to $6.2 billion of taxpayer-insured deposits—and exactly the kind of action the Volcker Rule was designed to prevent.

Dimon did not help matters by telling analysts that a multi-billion-dollar loss was a "tempest in a teacup." In any event, the bank claimed, this was by no means a case of speculative prop trading, which would be forbidden by the Volcker Rule; it was simply a hedge, offsetting an investment risk with an equivalent bet on the other side. However, when pressed, bank executives appeared at a loss to explain what they were hedging against.

To appease the critics, Iksil and his colleagues in London were offered up in sacrifice, fired on the grounds that they had fraudulently concealed losses. US and British authorities prepared criminal indictments against some of them on the same grounds. (The charges were eventually dropped.)

Sensing that there was a lot more to the story, Carl Levin asked the Senate's Permanent Subcommittee on Investigations to conduct a proper probe. Equipped with subpoena power to elicit the bank's cooperation, the investigators grilled executives and pored over thousands of documents. Their eventual report was damning. It flatly asserted that the bank's Chief Investment Office had

> used bank deposits, including some that were federally insured, to construct a $157 billion portfolio of synthetic credit derivatives, engaged in high risk, complex, short term trading strategies, and disclosed the extent and high risk nature of the portfolio to its regulators only after it attracted media attention.

Despite this, noted the report, the bank's management had insisted they were obeying the regulations. The entire debacle, in Michael Greenberger's words, was the "number one story showing the danger of naked credit default swaps" and the vital necessity of the Volcker Rule. (Asked to comment, JPMorgan referred me to its in-house report on the affair, which states that the "direct and principal responsibility for the losses lies with the traders who designed and implemented the flawed strategy.")

Though generally perceived as a case of a rogue trader risking gigantic sums of customers' money, the JPMorgan meltdown of 2012 was no such thing. Senate investigators concluded that the entire strategy had been directed from a high level, and that the traders, though ejected from their jobs and facing jail time, were not to blame. As a former Senate investigator, who asked not to be identified, confirmed to me recently, "Evidence shows the London traders advised selling the derivatives at a loss, but were overruled and directed to keep trading."

The investigators arrived at this conclusion without having actually talked to the traders, who had stayed in Europe, well out of reach of US authorities. Iksil, the so-called Whale (he hates the title), remained secluded in his house in the French countryside about sixty miles from Paris—he declines to say exactly where. He seldom talks to the press. Recently, however, Iksil discussed his story with me over a long phone call, during which he politely corrected, in excellent English and despite a heavy cold, my layman's misapprehensions about the technicalities of the credit markets.

Unsurprisingly, he agreed with the Senate investigators' conclusion that he and his colleagues were not to blame for the fiasco. "All the decisions," he told me, "were made miles away and far above my head." In his view, the bank was circulating "complete crap about my role."

He had, he said, been pondering the events over the past five years. He concluded that the whole mess could be traced to the fact that the bank's Chief Investment Office was required to keep its funds in readily available liquid investments. Instead, the CIO parked its investments in highly *illiquid* swaps. In 2010, according to Iksil, Dimon and other senior executives had discussed this problem with the OCC regulator, at a time when public anger that not a single bank executive had been charged in connection with the crisis was cresting. As Iksil put it to me, "People were saying: 'No prop trading. No illiquid stuff.'"

It would certainly have been possible, Iksil told me, to set aside a reserve against potential losses on these CDS investments, the latter amounting to $40 billion or $50 billion. But that would have wiped out two years' worth of earnings. Instead, the bank simply plunged deeper into esoteric credit trades in the expectation that such hedges would lessen the risks associated with the portfolio. However, the market moved stubbornly against JPMorgan's bets, bringing huge projected losses and a PR disaster when the story broke in the press. Under cover of the furor, Dimon, who Iksil insisted must have personally overseen the entire strategy, was able to get rid of the remaining embarrassingly illiquid assets on the CIO balance sheet by folding them into the company's investment bank.

Given the outpouring of falsehoods from the banking lobby concerning the Volcker Rule, Iksil's story seemed plausible enough. SIFMA, for example, had stated that the rule was a "solution in search of a problem," since prop trading had had nothing to do with the crisis. I quoted this to Volcker. "Didn't AIG have something to do with the crash?" he responded mildly. "They did a little proprietary trading, as I recall." (He could have added that the banks were on the other side of AIG's fatal prop trades.)

No matter. Tim Keehan, a senior official at the American Bankers Association, unblushingly lamented to me that the Volcker Rule had brought about a "reduction in the level of service that customers were formerly used to receiving." He insisted that the Volcker Rule "has substantially impacted venture capital fund-raising." He went on to echo a common industry concern and decry the bewildering complexity of the Volcker regulations, ignoring or forgetting that many of the ambiguities had been inserted at the behest of his colleagues. Finally, he bemoaned the lack of liquidity unleashed by Volcker's rule. To buttress his argument that the Volcker Rule has reduced liquidity, Keehan pointed to an academic paper issued under the auspices of the Fed's Finance and Economics Discussion Series, "The Volcker Rule and Market-Making in Times of Stress." The paper has been much touted by the anti-Volcker community. Yet the evidence cited by the authors appears to be confined to a narrow subset of the corporate junk-bond market, and not representative of the bond market as a whole.

Dennis Kelleher had no patience with such lines of argument when I spoke to him. After pointing to a recent SEC study confirming that there was no lack of necessary market liquidity, he continued heatedly: "There was certainly massive liquidity before 2008—of worthless securities that crashed the global financial system and almost caused the second Great Depression. It is true that the trading today is way below that, because we're no longer allowing them to trade in worthless securities. That's true!"

Among those protesting the Trump Administration's obvious eagerness to oblige Wall Street has been Senator Merkley of Oregon. Yet when I asked him whether he thought the industry offensive would succeed, his reply was despondent. "I'm afraid it will," he said.

Acting comptroller Noreika has promised to issue suggested amendments to the Volcker Rule by the spring, but there are grounds for suspecting that it is already becoming a dead letter. Bank analyst Chris Whalen, formerly of the Federal Reserve, told me that a resurgence in credit trading by the banks indicates to him that they're already "cheating more on Volcker." He also asked why Goldman was placing bets on the Marcellus Shale with its own funds to begin with, given the restrictions laid down by the rule. "That's a good question," he said. "But you can be pretty sure that no regulator is going to ask it as long as the administration is filled with Goldman Sachs executives and Gary Cohn works at the White House."

The bank lobby finally succeeded in securing a significant weakening of the Volcker rule in August 2020. In September 2019 (six months before the Covid crisis disrupted markets), the Federal Reserve began pumping enormous sums of money into major Wall Street banks and trading houses. By the end of 2020, the total amounted to more than $9 trillion. The Fed resolutely refused to reveal which firms were in enough trouble to need the money.

17

The Malaysian Job

May 2020

And so to straightforward crime. How the world's financial and legal establishment worked smoothly to cooperate in the largest robbery in history, a profitable exercise all round.

This past January, Goldman Sachs CEO and chairman David Solomon strode onto a stage at the bank's Lower Manhattan headquarters to launch the first "Investor Day" in the famously secretive institution's 150-year history. The celebration was promoted as an inspiring review of Goldman's "strategic road map and goals," and the presentations were replete with pledges of "transparency" and "sustainability," though the overall performance was unkindly summarized by bank analyst Christopher Whalen as "investment bankster BS." Early in his opening address, Solomon expounded the "core values" of the firm he had headed since October 2018. After "Partnership" and "Client Service" came "Integrity." Solomon stressed that he was "laser-focused" on this last term, emphasizing that the company "must always have an unrelenting commitment to doing the right thing, always." There followed, however, a glancing reference to a singular black cloud hovering over the proceedings. "In the wake of our experience with Malaysia," he said, "I am keenly aware of how the actions of a few can harm our reputation, our brand and our performance as a firm." With that brief mention, he moved on to a fourth core Goldman value: "Excellence."

Everyone in the room had recognized the allusion. "Malaysia" was shorthand for a gigantic fraud—possibly the largest in financial history—in which, beginning in 2009, billions of dollars were diverted from a Malaysian sovereign-wealth fund called 1Malaysia Development Berhad (1MDB) into covert campaign-finance accounts, US political campaigns, Hollywood movies and the pockets of innumerable other recipients. The "few" Solomon referred to were those Goldman executives whose active participation in the scam's bribery and money laundering had since become undeniable.

Despite efforts by Solomon and other senior employees to plead innocence by reason of ignorance, Goldman's pivotal role in the heist has exposed another obvious, if unspoken, core value: greed. But years of diligent investigation into 1MDB by courageous journalists and law-enforcement officials have revealed a network that extends far beyond Wall Street. Like the veins and arteries of a patient highlighted by an angiogram, the money's crooked pathways illuminated the bloodstream of a corrupt world and the lengths to which its beneficiaries were prepared to go to protect themselves and their gains. A Swiss whistleblower who leaked damning evidence of the scheme to the media was arrested in 2015 by Thai police on trumped-up charges. He signed a forced confession and spent eighteen months in jail. At least one Malaysian official investigating the crime was murdered, his body stuffed into an oil barrel and encased in concrete. Well-remunerated international legal and PR firms worked to suppress public knowledge of their clients' misdeeds by lying to the media and threatening litigation. Coursing across the globe, the money reached many distant corners, including both the Obama and Trump campaigns. Former British prime minister Tony Blair was on the payroll of one of the conspirators for $65,000 a month. Jamal Khashoggi, the late, murdered *Washington Post* columnist, was paid $100,000 to conduct a friendly interview for a Saudi newspaper with the scam's most prominent protagonist.

The scheme laid bare the dark underbelly of globalization. A racket concocted in far-off Malaysia came to involve people and institutions all across the world, owing to a system of elite networks seemingly fine-tuned for criminal enterprise. "Using prestigious, brand-name gatekeepers is often the key to pulling off complex financial crimes," Dennis Kelleher, CEO of the financial watchdog group Better Markets, told me. "They effectively sell their credibility and imprimatur, which criminals use to overcome their victims' skepticism. When they get caught, the enriched gatekeepers that made it all possible claim no knowledge or liability for the billions of dollars in damage done. The corruption of the enablers and their lack of accountability is what makes people so angry."

In broad outline, the Malaysia scheme worked in the following way: In 2009, Najib Razak, the country's prime minister, oversaw the creation of 1MDB, a state-owned and -controlled fund supposedly dedicated to domestic investment and development. Scion of a powerful family that had ruled Malaysia for much of its post-independence history, Najib was no stranger to corruption. In 2002, as defense minister, he had, according to French prosecutors in an ongoing case, taken a 114 million–euro bribe to buy French submarines. Altantuya Shaariibuu, a Mongolian translator and aspiring model who threatened to make that arrangement public, was murdered by two of Najib's bodyguards, who then destroyed her body with plastic explosives. One of them, who was scheduled to be hanged, confessed that the minister himself had ordered the killing. (His allegation is being investigated and may yet result in Najib's arrest.)

To operate 1MDB, Najib recruited a twenty-eight-year-old hustler named Low Taek Jho, commonly known as Jho Low. Born to a wealthy Malaysian-Chinese family, Low, who would become notorious for his efforts to buy himself friends with costly presents (Leonardo DiCaprio got a Picasso) and extravagant parties financed with stolen money, has often been credited as 1MDB's mastermind. True power, however, seems to have remained with the prime minister. As a former senior employee of the fund would later testify, Low and Najib had a "symbiotic relationship," in which "Jho executes what . . . Najib wants."

The first major payoff, like subsequent depredations, was both complex—involving a thicket of shell corporations and offshore money-laundering entrepôts—and crude, in view of the fraud's effrontery. The fund's initial stake was raised through the sale of $1.4 billion worth of bonds; $126 million was immediately siphoned off by Low. The Malaysians then teamed up with a pair of Saudis—one of whom was a son of then-king Abdullah—to form a joint venture with a company they pretended was backed by the Saudi government. Having paid a former US State Department official to certify an inflated value for that company's purported energy concessions (of which it actually had none), they then sent $1 billion raised from the earlier bond sale to the joint venture. Seven hundred million of that sum, disguised as the repayment of a loan—which didn't actually exist—was then wired to a private Swiss bank account controlled by Low through a corporation in the Seychelles.

As documented in correspondence between the conspirators, all of this was enabled by aboveboard institutions. The London branch of the New York law firm White & Case crafted the legal paperwork. Respectable banks, such as the Swiss branch of JPMorgan and Coutts (where Queen Elizabeth II keeps her money), handled massive transactions without asking too many questions, or, in some cases, any questions at all. Over the next few years, maneuvers similar to this initial grift netted as much as $4.5 billion for the plotters. Najib helped himself to $1 billion, including $681 million wired into his personal bank account in March 2013 for the urgent purpose of financing his 2013 presidential campaign. Thanks to the money, he eked out a narrow victory, reportedly by showering voters with cash at the doors of polling sites, stuffing ballot boxes, and recruiting illegal voters.

Outside Malaysia, bankers, politicians, lawyers, accountants and public-relations specialists all ultimately shared in the loot. Even a humanitarian news agency funded by the United Nations got a cut. Through the patronage of Low, Najib and his family, huge sums flowed to Hollywood studios, Las Vegas casinos, jewel merchants, art auctioneers and other vendors catering to the super-rich. The exuberant excesses of Low's circle inevitably attracted publicity, notably his bankrolling of *The Wolf of Wall Street*, in partnership with Najib's stepson, Riza Aziz. Low's efforts to ingratiate himself with some of the tackier elements of celebrity culture also garnered attention. According to *Billion Dollar Whale*, a book by a team of *Wall Street Journal* writers who covered the 1MDB scandal, he paid Paris Hilton to attend his parties at $100,000 per bash. Other high-dollar outlays included private jets, $100 million properties and a $250 million yacht called *Equanimity*.

All the while, money also surged into more mainstream channels such as Goldman Sachs. According to federal indictments, Goldman was drawn into the plot early in 2009, when two senior employees—Tim Leissner, head of investment banking for Southeast Asia, and Roger Ng, a managing director—first met Low. As Leissner would testify to a US court in 2018, at that point he "entered into a conspiracy . . . to pay bribes and kickbacks to obtain and then retain business from 1MDB for Goldman Sachs." Following an initial deal with Low, in which Leissner, for a small fee, advised on the formation of the provincial Malaysian fund that would grow into 1MDB, the relationship burgeoned.

It was not the best of times for Goldman, which had survived the 2008 crash thanks only to multibillion-dollar bailouts from the US Treasury and Federal Reserve. Revelations of the firm's unseemly behavior in the lead-up to the crisis, such as marketing securities to its own clients that it knew were worthless, were battering its reputation. As part of an institutional reform effort, senior management had set up a "business standards committee," a report from which concluded that Goldman should maintain a "constant focus on the reputational consequences of every action."

Rather than clean up its act, however, the bank began seeking profits in sunnier climes, well away from public scrutiny and irksome regulations imposed in the wake of the crash. Shortly before the onset of the recession, the firm's executives in London had discerned the rich pickings to be had in Muammar Qaddafi's Libya, whose vast sovereign-wealth fund lay in the hands of managers whom Goldman coolly assessed as displaying "zero-level" financial sophistication. Following a series of bewilderingly complex derivatives deals in 2008, the Libyans, courted with lavish hospitality (allegedly including prostitutes), were out $1.2 billion, while Goldman took home fees totaling as much as $350 million. Chafing at the loss, the Libyans sued on grounds that they had been misled, but an indulgent British judge let the bank off the hook, ruling that the Libyans had only themselves to blame. One of the key players in Goldman's Libya operation, Andrea Vella, was promoted and moved from London to Hong Kong. Soon after, Vella was hard at work with Leissner on Malaysia.

In September 2009, when Leissner recommended Low for an account with Goldman's private-wealth bank in Switzerland, the internal compliance office summarily rejected the proposal on account of the mysterious provenance of Low's wealth. Not-withstanding this emphatic red flag, according to the *Wall Street Journal*, Lloyd Blankfein met personally with Najib, Low and Leissner just two months later at the Four Seasons Hotel in New York City to discuss future deals. This was the first of no fewer than three meetings that the CEO reportedly had with Low. In 2012, seemingly oblivious to any possible "reputational consequences," the bank embarked on a series of three major deals with the Malaysian conspirators, even as Kuala Lumpur was rocked by mass demonstrations against government corruption.

First, through an operation code-named Project Magnolia, in May 2012 Goldman sold $1.75 billion in 1MDB bonds, mostly to unwitting mutual funds in Asia, creaming off $192 million for itself. As 1MDB lacked a credit rating and was heavily in debt at the time, the conspirators secured a guarantee for the bonds from yet another sovereign-wealth fund, in the United Arab Emirates, a paper transaction that netted handsome bribes for the relevant Emirati officials. (According to Leissner, all those involved were fully briefed on the bribery.) Goldman's enormous cut, 11 percent, was as much as 200 times the customary rate. A few months later, the bank sold another $1.75 billion worth of bonds, with a similar whopping rake-off for Goldman. Then, in March 2013, only ten months after the first bond sale, Goldman launched Project Catalyze, the third and largest deal, a $3 billion bond issue, purportedly for "energy" and "strategic real estate." According to US prosecutors, nearly $300 million went to Goldman, while $681 million sped to Najib for his aforementioned election fund.

Over the course of a year, Goldman had earned $600 million from its deals with Low, a man whom its own internal watchdogs had warned was highly suspect. David Ryan, president of Goldman Sachs Asia, excluding Japan, protested without avail and eventually resigned. Another Goldman executive in Asia, Alex Turnbull, son of former Australian prime minister Malcolm Turnbull, later claimed that he, too, had raised questions about the bond sales, telling an Australian paper: "When the 1MDB deal was done with Goldman I sent an email to some of my colleagues saying: 'What the fuck is going on with this? The pricing is nuts, what is the use of the funds?'" In reference to the murder of Altantuya, he added, "How many Mongolian models did we have to bury in the jungle for this pricing?" Turnbull claimed that the only reaction on behalf of Goldman was a "talking to" on keeping his mouth shut. Sidelined, he, too, quit.

Leissner and Vella, meanwhile, were hailed by their bosses as exemplary employees and rewarded with bonuses and promotions. "Look at what Tim and Andrea did in Malaysia," Blankfein told employees in a 2014 meeting, around the time federal prosecutors launched a criminal investigation of Vella's dealings in Libya. "We have to do more of that."

Though the con remained largely unnoticed by the outside world, observers in Malaysia began to raise questions about the fund's operations as early as 2010. As one of the few Malaysian news outlets not controlled by Najib cautiously hinted, regarding Low's initial deal, "Some critics have suggested that certain intermediaries had pocketed a hefty profit from the [pre-Goldman] bond issue." But the story did not take on an international life until several years later, when an attentive British journalist received a tip.

Clare Rewcastle Brown, sister-in-law of former British prime minister Gordon Brown, spent her early childhood in Sarawak, a Malaysian state on the island of Borneo that was then a British colony. In 2009, working as a journalist in London, she revisited Sarawak and learned of corrupt government lumber deals that were stripping the land of its forests and replacing them with destructive palm-oil plantations that impoverished the local population. As she investigated further, she received the first of many death threats and was banned from Sarawak. Undeterred, she launched a blog, *Sarawak Report*, and began detailing governmental corruption in a way that the generally muzzled Malaysian press could not. In July 2013, a source slipped her inside details of the Goldman bond deals, and she posted a series of articles questioning the outrageous fees and interest on the loans. Later that year, she followed up with a report detailing the curious involvement of Najib's stepson, Riza Aziz, in the financing of *The Wolf of Wall Street*. "If the money is Najib's," asked Rewcastle Brown, "how did the PM get to be so rich?" Subsequent posts highlighted Low's partnership with Aziz in film financing and the latter's high-priced property acquisitions, including a $35 million Manhattan condominium.

These revelations spurred a growing outcry within Malaysia and in the international business press. Less so, it seemed, in Washington, where for years Najib's underlings had made efforts to garner high-level goodwill. Frank White is a case in point. White was the national vice chair of President Obama's reelection campaign, raising at least $500,000 for the race, and he went on to serve as a co-chair of Obama's Inaugural Committee. In 2012, he received a $10 million "consulting" payment from a firm owned by one of Low's business partners, one who had played an integral role in the Goldman-brokered bond deals. Additional millions were channeled from the fund into DuSable Capital, an "energy and infrastructure firm" co-owned by White and Pras Michel, a former member of the hip-hop group Fugees whom Low had met on the party circuit. (According to a 2019 federal indictment, Low sent Michel $21 million, much of it to be laundered into a number of Democratic campaigns. Among Michel's initiatives was Black Men Vote, a super PAC funded with illegal, foreign money.)

Shortly after DuSable was founded, and despite the absence of any track record, the company announced it had raised an impressive $505 million from a private equity firm, some of which came from the chief executive of the same United Arab Emirates fund that had been so helpful in the Goldman deals. In short order, DuSable partnered with 1MDB to build a $300 million solar plant in Malaysia, for which White received a fee of $506,000. By October 2014, there was little sign of construction on the solar plant, but 1MDB nonetheless paid DuSable a handsome $69 million for its 49 percent share in the project.

Najib and Low must have thought their money well spent. On December 18, 2013, White escorted Riza Aziz and other members of the Najib family, along with Leonardo DiCaprio, to a private Oval Office visit with Obama, at which they gave the president a *Wolf of Wall Street* DVD. Four months later, Obama made the first visit to Malaysia by an American president in fifty years. Eight months after that, on Christmas Eve, he hosted Najib for a round of golf in Hawaii. As reported in *Billion Dollar Whale*, the administration cherished Malaysia as a key component in its projected "pivot" to Asia and as an impediment to Chinese expansionism. In a September 2014 address to the United Nations General Assembly, Obama hailed Malaysia's culture of "vibrant entrepreneurship," which was "propelling a former colony into the ranks of advanced economies."

It seems that the conspirators found such high-level lobbying to be both worthwhile and increasingly important as more and more of the grimy truth regarding 1MDB's operations leaked out. In February 2015, Rewcastle Brown published a plethora of compromising emails between the Malaysians and the Saudis, revealing for the first time how the original scam had worked. Major American newspapers began covering the story, drawing heavily on Rewcastle Brown's reporting, often without credit. That summer, Malaysian anticorruption investigators discovered evidence of the $681 million wired into Najib's personal bank account ahead of the 2013 election. Federal investigators in Washington, including the FBI, were also on the case. Starting in July 2016, the DOJ moved to seize $1 billion worth of assets (including the $250 million yacht), artworks (including a Picasso and a Basquiat), profit rights (including those to *The Wolf of Wall Street* and *Dumb and Dumber To*), and other investments owned by Low and his fellow collaborators.

As the investigations continued into 2017 and Donald Trump moved into the White House, Low mounted a determined effort to retrieve the $1 billion worth of laundered plunder that had been targeted by the DOJ. Again the conspirators chose the tried and trusted route of political "contributions." This time their conduit was Elliott Broidy, a Los Angeles–based defense contractor who had been convicted of bribing New York State pension officials in 2009. (His charge was reduced to a misdemeanor after he informed on others involved in the scheme.) Since then, Broidy had secured Trump's affections by helping to raise $108 million for his campaign, eventually becoming vice chairman within that organization, and later serving in a senior role on Trump's Inaugural Committee. (The two even shared the same fixer in matters of the heart: Michael Cohen, the go-between for Trump's settlement with Stormy Daniels, who performed a similar service in negotiating a $1.6 million payoff to a Playboy Playmate whom Broidy had impregnated.)

As with the efforts to buy influence with the Obama Administration, Low funneled tens of millions of dollars to Michel, who was then to get it to Broidy, thus, according to another participant's plea agreement, resolving Low's "issues surrounding the 1MDB forfeiture matters and the DOJ's investigations thereof." The parties drew up a draft agreement to regularize the arrangement: Low would pay $8 million up front. Success in "settling the Matter"—the DOJ investigation—within a year would earn Broidy a $50 million fee. If he worked fast and got things sorted in less than 180 days, there would be a handsome $25 million bonus.

On September 12, 2017, three months *after* DOJ prosecutors filed a formal 251-page complaint detailing the progress and scope of the entire fraud, Najib returned to the Oval Office. In preparation for the visit, Broidy had sent a colleague an email with the subject line "Malaysia talking points *Final*," recommending that Najib emphasize to Trump that "Malaysia fully backed US efforts to isolate North Korea." Before the two leaders sat down for their private meeting, Trump remarked publicly that Najib "does not do business with North Korea any longer. We find that to be very important." Trump also praised his visitor's commitment to fighting terrorism—a point that surely gratified the 1MDB chief, given that Najib was claiming this as the very reason he had received a cool $681 million as a present from the Saudis. One month later, Michel sent Broidy at least $6 million from an account controlled by Low, using George Higginbotham, a DOJ attorney moonlighting as a money launderer, as the conduit.

In May 2018, the cascade of corruption reports regarding 1MDB finally caught up with Najib, and Malaysians voted him out of power. Arrested two months later, he has been fighting charges of money laundering and abuse of power ever since. In February, in the first of what will likely be several trials, he finally dropped his long-held pretense that the fund was legitimate, instead opting to blame everything on Low. "He must have thought that if he didn't continue to make sure donations flow into my account, it would have affected his relationship with me," testified Najib, "and this would lead me to uncover the scams." Should he be found guilty, appeals will likely keep the disgraced former prime minister out of prison for years, unless the murder of Altantuya puts him behind bars first.

The Malaysian people, meanwhile, will be paying for Najib's crimes for decades to come. The government will be spending almost half a billion dollars a year in interest and principal on 1MDB's debt—which includes the bonds sold by Goldman—until 2039. "Worst of all," Tony Pua, an opposition politician, told me, because most of the money was stolen, "there is nothing to show for the large debt burden." As for the bankers, lawyers and other professionals who enabled the scam, Pua said, "Many of them knew it was wrong, or at the very least knew it was suspicious, yet they turned a blind eye and went through with it anyway."

So far, few of these parties have paid much of a price, let alone seen the inside of a jail cell. Two Emirati officials in Abu Dhabi were jailed for their role in the fraud, as were two non-Goldman bankers in Singapore, and both Roger Ng and Pras Michel are awaiting trial in the United States. Andrea Vella was placed on administrative leave by Goldman and later resigned, while Leissner and Higginbotham remain free on bail until their sentencing.

Jho Low is reportedly somewhere in China, where authorities apparently feel little obligation to surrender him to Malaysia. The country's inspector general of police recently claimed that he had been informed that Low had surgically altered his appearance and now "looked like a bear." Whether that's true or not, Low maintains a tastefully designed website promoting the message that he was merely a pawn in the scheme. Having apparently anticipated the possibility of eventual attention from law enforcement, he acquired Cypriot citizenship in 2015. According to an investigation done by a Cypriot newspaper, this was managed courtesy of Henley & Partners, a British firm that advertises itself as "a global leader in citizenship and residence planning" for clients with a lot of money and a desire to sink below the radar—one more service on offer in the world of 1MDB. (Henley denies that Low was ever a client.)

Although Low is still wanted in the United States for making illegal contributions to the 2012 Obama campaign, as well as on bribery and money-laundering charges, he has held his own on other fronts. He fought a legal battle to recover his share of the $1 billion in loot seized by US authorities in 2016, an effort that seemed to take a turn in his favor when he added former New Jersey governor Chris Christie and Kasowitz Benson Torres—a New York law firm with close ties to Donald Trump—to his legal team. In November, this high-powered defense negotiated a settlement with the DOJ in which Low agreed to abandon claims to the seized property. Low himself, who was not required to admit guilt, certainly seemed happy with the deal. In an amiable interview conducted online with a Singaporean newspaper, he called it a "historic agreement," and "the result of a multiyear, collaborative effort between the US government and my team of advisers and lawyers. I am appreciative to all parties for their hard work." Indeed, it was undeniably historic that the government allowed Low to use $15 million of the money he had stolen to pay his lawyers and publicists. Today, Low is represented by Schillings, a British firm of lawyers and intelligence professionals who specialize in deterring publicity unwelcome to wealthy clients. "We understand your world," proclaims Schillings's website. "We will be your best advocate." Legal threats from this same firm had earlier dissuaded Rewcastle Brown's publisher from releasing her book on the scandal, whereupon she founded her own press and published it herself.

As for Goldman Sachs, when revelations regarding 1MDB began to sap its reputation—not to mention its stock price—top executives in New York sought to pin all responsibility on Leissner and other colleagues in Asia, a charge that many analysts find unconvincing. In the derisive words of Kelleher, the Better Markets CEO, "Goldman's position is that a 'rogue' banker lied and fooled all of the smartest, highest-paid bankers in the world; all of Goldman's risk, compliance, legal and audit systems and controls; and all of Goldman's management." So far as Kelleher is concerned, "the thirty senior Goldman executives who were witting of what went on should forfeit every penny they took home during the time they were assisting in this crime."

Nevertheless, Goldman has stoutly maintained its institutional innocence. Just this January, the company filed a motion to dismiss a class-action lawsuit brought by stockholders seeking damages inflicted on the plaintiffs' holdings as a result of the revelations surrounding 1MDB. Goldman's motion asserts that

Blankfein and company were kept ignorant of criminal goings-on by their subordinates, and disputes any direct correlation between the scandal and the bank's stock price, which has performed poorly of late relative to Wall Street competitors. Meanwhile, the Malaysian government has charged the bank and seventeen current and former directors with criminal activities, and is aggressively seeking as much as $7.5 billion in punitive damages, a potent threat to the bank's already battered reputation, not to mention its bottom line.

More immediately, the Justice Department is mulling a deal with Goldman in which the company would issue a guilty plea and pay a fine for its behavior. Initially, the projected penalty was reported to reach as much as $6 billion, but more recent accounts suggest that the figure may be far lower—under $2 billion. (The bank has already set aside $1.1 billion for "litigation expenses.") Such comparative leniency might be due to the presence of friendly faces around the bargaining table, where Goldman is represented by the powerful firm of Kirkland & Ellis and the government side is headed by Attorney General William Barr, himself a former Kirkland partner, who is said to be "directly immersed" in the negotiations. Barr obtained an ethical waiver permitting him to proceed with his involvement, as did Brian Benczkowski, head of the DOJ's Criminal Division, another Kirkland alum and a close friend of his former boss at the DOJ, Mark Filip, who also joined the Goldman team.

"Everyone has always told me," Rewcastle Brown remarked when we spoke, "that there'll never be any action taken against Goldman Sachs. I would find that sickening, because it proves the corruption in America is every bit as bad as what I was sneering at in covering Najib." The 1MDB criminals who poured so many millions into totemic American institutions, from Hollywood to Wall Street to the White House, evidently came to the same conclusion. It's a big swamp.

Goldman did in the end plead guilty to one count of bribery in October 2020, and paid fines totaling over $5 billion. In the same *month, the bank reported net earnings of $5.2 billion for the first nine months of the year. David Solomon remained CEO. Trump pardoned Elliott Broidy. Jho Low, as of late 2020, was reportedly living in well-protected seclusion in Macau.*

Acknowledgments

Many thanks to Leo Hollis, who selected the pieces out of many possible candidates. I am additionally grateful to everyone at *Harper's Magazine*, a citadel of quality, where the bulk of these chapters originally appeared. Most especially I thank publisher Rick MacArthur for his confidence and enduring support, editors Ellen Rosenbush, James Marcus, and Christopher Beha; Matthew Sherill for his enduringly patient wrangling of untidy texts, as well as Stephanie McFeeters and Joseph Frischmuth, whose unflagging attention to detail so often saved me from error. It has also been a pleasure and privilege to write for the *London Review of Books*; much thanks here to the effusively encouraging Daniel Soar and Adam Shatz.

Most of all, and always, I thank my wife Leslie for everything, not least for her own fearless reporting that informed so much material in this book, and for urging me to undertake this book in the first place.

Index